Principles of Marketing

Second Edition

Neeru Kapoor
Associate Professor
Department of Commerce
Delhi College of Arts and Commerce
University of Delhi

PHI Learning Private Limited
Delhi-110092
2024

In fond memory of ***Shri Asoke K. Ghosh*** *(October 1942 – February 2024), Founder Chairman and Managing Director of PHI Learning, whose vision endlessly inspires.*

The Legacy Continues....

Published by Pushpita Ghosh, PHI Learning Private Limited, Rimjhim House, 111, Patparganj Industrial Estate, Delhi-110092 and Printed by Syndicate Binders, A-20, Hosiery Complex, Noida, Phase-II Extension, Noida-201305 (N.C.R. Delhi).

₹695.00

PRINCIPLES OF MARKETING, Second Edition
Neeru Kapoor

ISBN-978-93-91818-12-8 (Print Book)
ISBN-978-93-91818-13-5 (e-Book)

Contents

Preface

After the immense success of the Ist Edition of our Marketing book, we proudly introduce the revised IInd Edition. We have tried to incorporate all the changes and developments which have taken place in the field of marketing in the last few years. As we all understand that marketing is an indispensible activity for the success of every business in today's competitive world, they won't be able to succeed if they are not able to handle their marketing activities efficiently. Thus, the knowledge of various marketing principles and fundamentals has become a necessity for all those students who want to make a career in this field.

This book has been written with the intention of providing its readers with the most comprehensive and current text regarding marketing in a simplified manner with the help of real-life examples from the current business scenario. Use of diagrams have been made to present facts in an illustrative manner. Case studies are also incorporated in all the chapters to provide a practical orientation to the text. Every chapter begins with the learning outcomes, which the student will be able to understand after going that particular chapter. Important definitions and terms are highlighted in boxes throughout the text. At the end of each chapter 'Things to Remember' section is given, which serves as a quick review of important topics that are covered in the chapter. Both, short and long answer questions are given at the end of each chapter to give students an opportunity to test their understanding of the concepts and their applications. These questions can also serve as a basis for class discussions and assignments.

The book is divided into 16 chapters. Each chapter describes meanings, characteristics, scope, importance, process, and relevant fundamental aspects of various marketing issues. First chapter deals with the introduction of marketing where fundamental concepts of marketing have been explained clearly. The second chapter explains the various environmental factors and their interaction with marketing precisely. The third chapter gives knowledge of the information systems and the concept of market research in detail. Consumer buying behaviour has been dealt with care in the fourth chapter, whereas the concept of market segmentation has been defined in chapter 5. Chapter 6 to 9 discusses about the 4Ps of the marketing-mix, i.e product, price, place and promotion. The concept of retailing in India has been defined in chapter 10. The growing power of rural marketing and how to arrive at the marketing-mix for rural India has been explained in chapter 11, whereas chapter 12 and 13 deal with green marketing and marketing of services.

Maintaining relationship with the customer is the call of the hour, so chapter 14 discusses customer relationship management. None of the marketing book is complete without having a chapter on digital marketing, so chapter 15 has been dedicated to this concept. In the end chapter 16 talks about consumerism in India and the legal structure available to consumers for protecting their consumer rights.

Though I have made a sincere effort to cover each and every aspect of marketing from the student's perspective in the book, it will be my pleasure to receive feedback and constructive suggestions from the students and faculties of various colleges.

NEERU KAPOOR
drneerukapoor@yahoo.co.in

Acknowledgements

I have been teaching marketing at the undergraduate and post graduate levels in Delhi University for more than 30 years. My teaching experience has helped me a lot in writing this book from the student's perspective. I have also been benefitted by the exchange of views with my colleagues, students and experts in the area while writing this book. I would like to extend my sincere thanks to all of them. Their valuable critiques and thoughtful recommendations have helped me in improving the quality of this book. I even referred to various reference books, journals and periodicals to enrich the contents of this book. I am deeply indebted to various authors and scholars whose contributions have been referred to in this book. I am also grateful to the various Internet sources from where we picked up some real life examples of the corporate world to enrich the text. I would also like to put on record my appreciation for the constant encouragement and support received from my family.

A manuscript does not become a book without a great deal of effort on the part of the publisher. So, I would like to acknowledge with grateful appreciation, the creative efforts of the people at PHI Learning. I hope the book will be able to meet the expectations of the academic circle.

Reader's views, comments and criticism relating to the present work, are most welcome. Please feel free to give me your suggestions through mail at drneerukapoor@yahoo.co.in.

NEERU KAPOOR

CHAPTER 1

Marketing
An Introduction

Learning Outcomes

After studying this chapter, you will be able to:

- ❖ Understand about the different perspectives in marketing
- ❖ Explain the various core concepts of marketing
- ❖ Describe the evolution of marketing
- ❖ Differentiate between marketing and selling
- ❖ Identify the importance of marketing
- ❖ Define the social, economic and ethical effects of marketing
- ❖ Elaborate the concept of marketing-mix
- ❖ Discuss some new concepts in marketing

Marketing is an indispensable activity in today's scenario as marketplaces are enormously more complex. Domestic markets, at one time, safe from foreign invaders, are now the happy hunting grounds of giant global corporations. Major developments in technology have considerably shortened time and distance. New products are launched at an astonishing pace and are available worldwide in a short time. A variety of communication media is available to marketers making it possible for them to spread messages across to their customers at great speed and efficiency. New distribution channels and formats keep appearing. Competition is increasing tremendously.

Marketers are confronted with endless opportunities mainly because of the three developments—globalisation, technological advances and deregulation.

Due to the deregulation and globalisation policies of the government, our markets are flooded with products from various domestic as well as multinational organisations. The increasing expenditure on research and development is resulting in technological advancements due to which the marketers are trying to provide the consumers with technically sophisticated products. In the midst of these changes, busy consumers are changing their ways. These days consumers are highly informed, they are able to have access to information regarding the product—its features, quality, price, and various discounts and schemes offered through various sources. They are even able to compare the products with the competitor's products and decide which one to buy. All this is resulting in a shift of power from the hands of marketers to the hands of consumers. Earlier, they used to be the passive recipients of the goods but now they are the active and demanding forces in the market. Due to these reasons, there is a lot of pressure on marketers and they are constantly trying to come up with new and improved ways of handling their marketing policies and strategies. Some of the changes observed in the recent past are—

- A shift in the production department's designing the products alone, keeping their production capacities into account, to involving marketing experts as well as customer's response in the product development.
- A shift in the pricing strategy followed by organisations from simply cost driven to value driven, as earlier, the focus used to be on recovering the cost as early as possible, but now the marketers want to set prices at a level where they can deliver value to the consumer.
- A shift in the promotional strategy from simply relying on advertising and personal selling for using a combination of promotional tools for promoting the goods in the market.
- A shift in the distributional strategy from relying exclusively on the traditional middlemen or a single channel of distribution to opting for a combination of various modern distribution channels.
- A shift in treating marketing and selling as independent activities to integrating them with various other departments and ensuring an integration and coordination in the marketing efforts.

The list is long but we are simply quoting some of the important changes taking place in the marketing scene in our country. The reason for all these changes is that marketing is emerging as one of the most important activity as it is required for marketing everything—products, services, ideas, places, organisations, events and personalities. It involves carrying out plans, evaluating results, and making further improvements. Therefore, the focus in the current text is to highlight the growth and development which has taken place in the field of various marketing principles and strategies. Starting with the traditional concepts, we are trying to take you through the various changes which are taking place in the emergence of the new marketing concepts in India.

1.1 DEFINITION OF MARKETING

In simple terms, *marketing* is defined as identifying and meeting human needs profitably. It adds form utility, possession utility, time utility, place utility and information utility to the products. In simple words, we can say that marketing is getting the right goods and services to the right person, at the right place, at the right time, at the right price and with the right communication and promotion.

In general terms, any interpersonal or inter-organisational relationship involving an exchange is called *marketing*. Marketing has been defined differently by different authors. The very first definition of the concept was given by The American Marketing Association (1960)—

> *It defines marketing as the performance of business activities that direct the flow of goods and services from producer to consumer or user.*

But this definition is a very narrow perspective of looking at marketing because it is being defined just as a distributional activity which starts when the goods have already been produced and ends simply at the delivery of goods to the consumers. But these days marketing starts long before that with the identification of the needs and wants of the consumers, conceptualises the product accordingly and ends with ensuring satisfaction to the consumers by providing them with a whole lot of after sales services. Hence, this definition needs to be extended at both ends.

There was another definition given by The American Marketing Association (1995) which states that—

> *Marketing is the process of planning and executing the conception, pricing, promotion, and distribution of ideas, goods, services to create exchanges that satisfy individual and organisational goals.*

This definition gives a broader perspective of marketing, where it comes into picture at the product planning stage and ends with delivering after sale services and ensuring customer satisfaction.

Philip Kotler (1999) defined marketing as—

> *Marketing is a social process by which individuals and groups obtain what they need and want through creating and exchanging products and values with others.*

According to William J Stanton (1994)—

> *Marketing is a system of business activities designed to plan, price, promote, and distribute something of value-want satisfying goods and services to the benefit of the market-present and potential household consumers or industrial users.*

From all these definitions, it has clearly emerged that marketing is an ongoing social process with the help of which individuals and groups obtain the various goods and services to satisfy their needs and wants. A good marketer tries to satisfy the current consumers while an excellent marketer looks for potential consumers and tries to convert them into their users. Effective marketer tries to design the goods as per consumer's requirements, price them appropriately, promote them effectively and with the help of effective distribution channels make them available to the users' right next door. An effective after sales service network is maintained by marketers to ensure utmost satisfaction to the consumers and to retain them for long term. Marketing can be further understood by defining several of its core concepts.

1.2 CORE CONCEPTS IN MARKETING

1.2.1 The Concept of Need, Want and Demand

The starting point for the discipline of marketing lies in understanding human needs and wants. But it is very important for us to understand the difference which exists between the three terms—needs, wants, and demands—which are used most of the time interchangeably by marketers'. According to Philip Kotler (1999)—

> *A human need is a state of felt deprivation of some basic satisfaction.*

It is something which is the basic requirement of an individual. It cannot be created by society or marketers'; it exists in the very texture of human biology and the human conditions. The moment an individual is born, he/she has a set of needs and it is essential for them to satisfy their needs to ensure their survival. Some of the examples of need are the need for food, air, water, clothing, and shelter. These needs become wants only when they are directed to specific objects that might satisfy the need. According to Philip Kotler (1999)—

Wants are desires for specific satisfiers of these deeper needs.

For example, when an American needs food, he looks for a burger, french-fries and soft drink, a Chinese looks for noodles, choupsey, etc., while an average Indian satisfies his hunger by pulses, roti, rice, vegetables, etc. Thus, we observe that the needs are basic and common to all but wants can be different. Wants are shaped and reshaped by our society and in the due course of time, in the life of an individual. While people's needs are few, their wants are many. Not all wants get converted into demand. According to Philip Kotler (1999)—

Demands are wants for specific products that are backed up by an ability and willingness to pay for them—purchasing power.

It is only those wants which are backed by purchasing power and a willingness to purchase that get converted into demand. Therefore, when people criticise marketing by saying that *marketers create needs*, we need to be correcting them because needs can never be created–they pre-exist, marketers simply create wants by showing the various options to the consumers and only few of those wants get finally converted into demand.

1.2.2 The Concept of Product

In order to satisfy their needs and wants, people require products. According to Philip Kotler (1999)—

A product is a set of tangible and intangible attributes that can be offered to someone to satisfy a need or want.

It includes everything the product is capable of offering to the consumers—its features, functions, price, packaging, prestige and brand image.

1.2.3 Value and Satisfaction

It can be defined as a ratio between what the customer gets and what he gives or in other words, the benefits divided by cost. Benefits include functional benefits as well as emotional benefits and cost includes monetary costs, time cost, energy cost, and psychological cost. Thus value is given by—

Value = benefits/costs = functional benefits + emotional benefits/monetary costs + time costs + energy costs + psychological costs

The marketer can increase the value of the product for the customer simply by either raising the benefits or reducing the cost.

1.2.4 Exchange and Transaction

According to Philip Kotler (1999)—

Exchange or transaction is the act of obtaining a desired product from someone by offering something in return.

But not every transaction can be called an exchange. There are certain basic conditions which are to be fulfilled only then a transaction can be called an exchange, which is:

1. The presence of at least two parties is a must;
2. Each party must have something of value and utility to offer to the other party;
3. Both the parties should be free to communicate with each other and receive as much of information as they want;
4. They should be able to exercise their free will to accept or reject the offer; and
5. They should be interested to deal with each other and enter into an exchange.

Any transaction which takes place at gunpoint or using some other threat or pressure tactics can never be called an *exchange*.

1.2.5 The Concept of a Market

The concept of exchange leads to a market. According to Philip Kotler (1999)—

> *A market consists of all the potential customers sharing a particular need or want who might be willing and able to engage in exchange to satisfy that need or want.*

Originally, markets stood for a place where buyers and sellers gathered to engage in an exchange. But in today's context, markets are seen as a collection of buyers and sellers—sellers as constituting the industry and the buyers as constituting the market. Figure 1.1 clearly highlights the concept of a market.

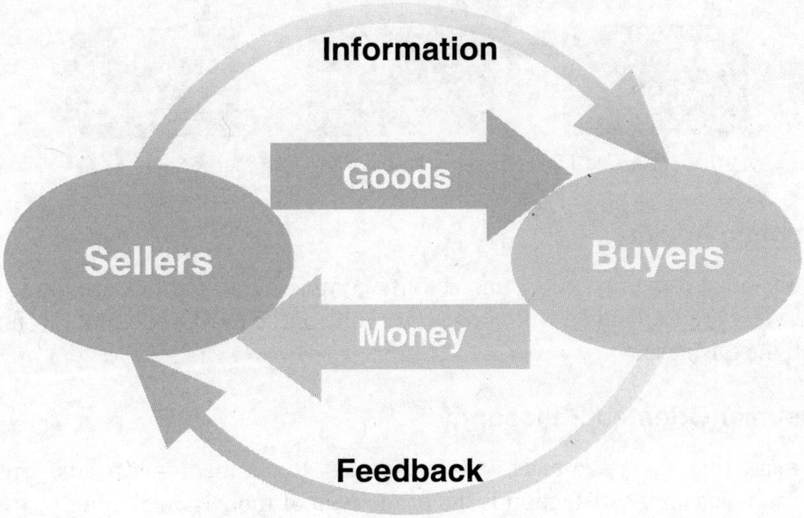

Figure 1.1 The concept of market.

The inner loop shows an exchange of money for goods and the outer loop shows an exchange of information about the product from the industry with the feedback from the buyer. Wherever these two exchanges take place, that place is called a *market*. Market can also be defined as a *need market* (such as diet-seeking market), *product market* (shoe market), *demographic market* (youth) and *geographic market* (such as Delhi, Mumbai, Chennai).

1.2.6 The Concept of a Marketer

A marketer is someone seeking a resource from someone else and willing to offer something of value in exchange.

1.3 CHARACTERISTICS OF MARKETING

From all the definitions and the discussions which have taken place in the proceeding paragraphs, certain characteristics of modern marketing have evolved. Some of the important ones are listed as under in Figure 1.2.

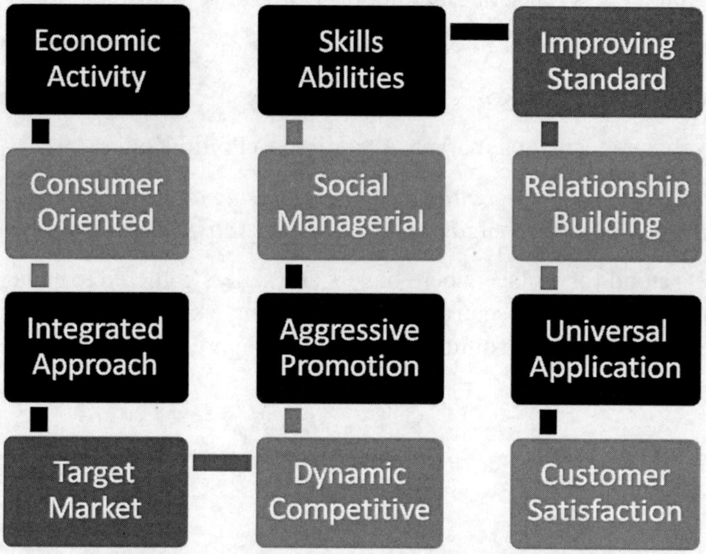

Figure 1.2 Characteristics of modern marketing.

1.3.1 Economic Activity

Marketing is the most important economic activity comprising of various economic transactions. Goods and services are exchanged with money. It is one of the most important revenue generating activity for all the businesses.

1.3.2 Consumer Oriented Philosophy

The modern marketing starts and ends with consumers. It is a medium of satisfying consumers' needs at a profit. Consumer satisfaction is the prime goal of modern marketing.

1.3.3 Integrated Approach

Modern marketing lays emphasis on coordinated efforts of all the departments in an organisation to satisfy customer's needs and wants. Thus, it shows an integration and coordination amongst all the departments to conduct the business.

1.3.4 Focuses on Target Market

These days most of the companies, instead of targeting the goods to masses, are trying to provide utmost satisfaction to the needs and wants of a well-defined group of target customers known as *target market.*

1.3.5 Dynamic and Competitive

Today's marketing activities are performed under highly competitive situations. It changes as per the change in consumer attitude and interest. Its focus is on serving consumers' needs and wants better than that of the competitors.

1.3.6 Aggressive Promotional Efforts

In order to face the competition and convince the consumers to purchase their products, modern marketing involves aggressive promotional efforts.

1.3.7 Social and Managerial Process

It operates within the society and directly or indirectly affects social welfare. Therefore, in order to ensure the optimum satisfaction of consumers and the general public at large, efficient management practices are applied in marketing.

1.3.8 Involves Special Skills and Abilities

Marketers these days need special skills and abilities to identify the needs of the customers, design products and convince the target customers to buy the products at profit.

1.3.9 Improving Standard of Living of Society

Modern marketing, along with ensuring adequate profits, has helped in raising the standard of living of people as well as the society at large by producing and distributing qualitative products at reasonable prices.

1.3.10 Relationship Building

These days, marketing stresses on the need of building long-term relationships with their customers and other stakeholders by being fair and just in their activities.

1.3.11 Universally Applicable Activity

Marketing activities can be applied in every sphere of human life-economic, social, political, religious and business.

1.3.12 Ensuring Profit with Customer Satisfaction

Marketers are applying innovative and creative techniques for providing maximum consumer satisfaction along with ensuring adequate profits. Satisfying customers with profit is the principle of modern day marketing.

As discussed in the above paragraphs, marketing in India is different than what it is in Western countries.

We would like to support our argument by a quote from Harminder Sahni, Founder and Managing Director, Wazir Advisors (2013), a management consulting firm, who says that, "The Great Indian Marketing story is different because it is a volume-driven—not margin-driven. Thus, most companies, especially those in the FMCG business, sell their products in low-unit packs, which allow the maximum number of consumers to connect with the brand and experience it too". According to FICCI estimates, as on February 2013, as much as 40 per cent of the total FMCG market sales of ₹ 28,700 crore in India are driven by low unit packs. In the West, it's not more than 20 per cent. Therefore marketers in India have to make lots of adjustments in their marketing strategies to win the customers.

Source: An article by Abhilasha Ojha, "Things that make market in India different", Brand Equity, The Economic Times, dated February 24th, 2013.

Question for Discussion

1. Can you explain the reason as to why marketing in India is volume driven than margin driven?
2. Give few examples of FMCG companies which are selling their products in low unit packs.

1.4 MARKETING CONCEPTS OR EVOLUTION STAGES OF MARKETING

Marketing has evolved through various stages over the period of time as represented in Figure 1.3.

Figure 1.3 Evolution of marketing.

The various stages through which the concept of marketing has evolved have been listed as under—

1.4.1 Stage I: The Production Concept/the Production Stage/or the Production Orientation

According to Philip Kotler (1999)—

> *The production concept holds that consumers will favour those products that are widely available and low in cost.*

It is one of the oldest concepts in business. Management in production oriented organisations has been concentrating on achieving high production efficiency, wide distribution coverage, and making the goods available to consumers at low prices. This concept prevailed for a long time because initially demand was far greater than the supply of the goods and consumers were more than keen to purchase whatever was being offered to them. The only criterion was—low price and easy availability. The three basic fundamentals of this approach are depicted in Figure 1.4.

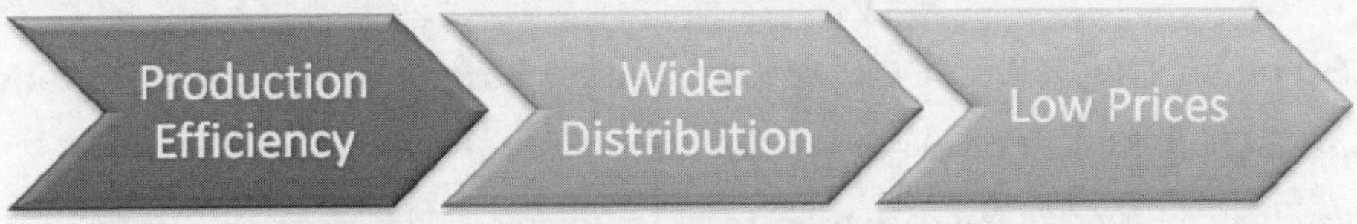

Figure 1.4 Fundamentals of production concept.

1.4.2 Stage II: The Product Concept/the Product Stage/the Product Orientation

According to Philip Kotler (1999)—

> *The product concept holds that consumers will favour those products that offer the most quality, performance and features. Management in these product-oriented organisations focus their energy on making good products and improving them over time.*

The product concept is an improvement over the production concept, as the management in organisations following this concept realise the importance of improving upon the quality of the product by adding certain unique features and making it more useful for the consumer. They are of the view that if they will make qualitative products, the consumers will like the product more and will purchase them more, but the improvements in the quality of the product is done by the management according to their own perceptions. They add certain new features in the product keeping their production capabilities into account. While adding these new features the consumer's point of view is never taken into consideration. This concept reflects the philosophy quite similar to the one given by Emerson when he said, *if a man makes a better mousetrap-the world will beat a path to his door*. But this later resulted in the problem of *better mousetrap fallacy* because even if the marketer's made a better mousetrap according to their own views, nobody turned out to their doors. It is important for them to realise that taking the customer's perspective into account is essential. But these organisations are ignoring this major aspect and making improvements in product according to their own conveniences. Another renowned author Theodore Levitt (1960) commented on this situation, as *where an undue concentration is being levied on the product rather than the consumers.*

Product oriented companies often design their products with little or no customer input. This concept can also lead to the problem of *marketing myopia*, where marketers are looking into the mirror when they should be rather looking out of the window. Because of all these reasons even this concept does not remain profitable in the long run and marketers have no choice but to move to the next concept. The three basic fundamentals of this approach are being presented in Figure 1.5.

Figure 1.5 Fundamentals of product concept.

1.4.3 Stage III: The Selling Concept/the Selling Stage/the Selling Orientation

According to Philip Kotler (1999)—

> *The selling concept holds that consumers and businesses, if left alone, will automatically not buy enough of the organisation's products. The organisation must, therefore, undertake an aggressive selling and promotion effort.*

As discussed in the previous stage, despite making improvements in the quality of the product, when marketers are not able to sell the product, they generally arrive at one conclusion that the consumer is not willing to purchase and will not purchase unless and until they are forced to purchase. The companies following this concept believe in coaxing the consumer into buying more in order to overcome their buying inertia or resistance. They employ salesmen who use their charm and are given the task of using various selling and promotional incentives and make consumers buy the product by hook or by crook. This concept is built on three basic fundamental concepts—that is making a product, selling and promoting it aggressively to the consumers and earning profit by increasing sales volume.

Figure 1.6 Fundamentals of sales concept.

This concept, as shown in Figure 1.6, is generally followed by companies suffering from overcapacity. Their aim is to sell whatever they have produced rather than producing what they can sell. A lot of emphasis is laid down on advertising the product aggressively and using various sales promotion incentives to increase the sale of the product. Most of the people even, till date, confuse selling with marketing. This concept is generally practised by those companies who are selling unsought goods or goods which are not usually in great demand, such as, insurance policies, vacuum cleaners, encyclopaedias, fire extinguishers and home safety alarms, etc.

1.4.4 Stage IV: The Marketing Concept/the Marketing Stage/the Marketing Orientation

According to Philip Kotler (1999)—

> *The marketing concept holds that the key to achieving its organisational goals consists of the company being more effective than competitors in creating, delivering and communicating customer value to its chosen target markets.*

The marketing concept has been expressed in various colourful ways:

Colourful Ways of Explaining Marketing Concept

- Meeting needs profitably
- Find wants and fill them
- Love the customer and not the product
- Putting people first (British Airways)
- Have it your way (Burger King)
- Make what you can sell instead of trying to sell what you can make
- We have to stop marketing makeable products and learn to make marketable products

Thus, we can say that marketing concept is built on three foundation stones—customer needs being fulfilled through integrated marketing and generating profit through customer satisfaction, as shown in Figure 1.7.

Figure 1.7 Fundamental of marketing concepts.

In essence, companies following this marketing concept hold the consumer at the centre and their focus remains on fulfilling customer's needs and wants backed by integrated marketing efforts aimed at generating customer satisfaction as the key to satisfying organisational goals.

According to Peter F Drucker (1990), a leading management scholar—

> *There will always, one can assume, be need for some selling. But the aim of marketing is to make selling superfluous. The aim of marketing is to know and understand the customer so well that the product or service fits him and sells itself. Ideally, marketing should result in a customer who is ready to buy. All that should be needed is to make the product or service available.*

Therefore, selling is defined as only the tip of the marketing iceberg. It is something which is quite visible to the outside world but a whole lot of efforts which goes underneath this basic activity are not to be seen by many people. The marketing concept requires that the executives must start thinking in terms of what benefits they market and what needs of consumers are they satisfying. Some of the examples of the companies following the marketing approach are as shown in Table 1.1.

Table 1.1 Companies Following the Marketing Approach

Company	Product-oriented answer	Market-oriented answer
Universal Studios	We make movies	We make entertainment
LG	We make air-conditioners	We provide a comfortable climate in the home
Revlon	We make cosmetics	We provide a hope to look good

The marketing concept expresses the company's commitment to the concept of *consumers sovereignty.* Mahatama Gandhi, the father of the nation, was such a great visionary that he could long way back in the 1940s understand the importance of the marketing concept and gave a statement—

> *A customer is the most important visitor on our premises. He is not dependent on us, we are dependent on him. He is not an interruption on our work he is the purpose of it. He is not an outsider on our business he is a part of it. We are not doing him a favour by serving him he is doing us a favour by giving us an opportunity to do so.*

1.4.5 Stage V: The Societal Marketing Concept/the Societal Marketing Stage/ the Societal Marketing Orientation

According to Philip Kotler (1999)—

> *The Societal marketing concept holds that the organisation's task is to determine the needs, wants, and interests of target markets and to deliver the desired satisfactions more effectively and efficiently than competitors in a way that preserves or enhances the consumers and society's well-being.*

The societal marketing concept calls upon the marketers to fulfil their social responsibilities towards the society. While designing the product they do have to keep the interest of the consumer into mind but at the same time they should ensure that while serving the consumer better than the competitor's they have to keep the interest of the society at large also into account. Most of the times, in order to make the goods available to the consumers in fresh condition, marketers make use of polythene bags which cannot be recycled and create a lot of pollution in the environment. Maggi noodles, when introduced initially in the market, had to face stiff criticism mainly because they were being considered unhealthy for the children. It is only due to this reason that the company has introduced Maggi Atta noodles and various other healthy options of the product. These days marketers are trying to balance out all the things. The focus is on serving the consumer better than the competitor but at the same time they are trying to protect the interest of the society at large. Various green marketing initiatives are being taken by the companies in order to fulfil their societal orientation.

This concept rests on three basic fundamental factors—generating profits for company, by fulfilling the consumers' wants satisfactorily, and keeping the society's interest into account. The concept is shown in Figure 1.8.

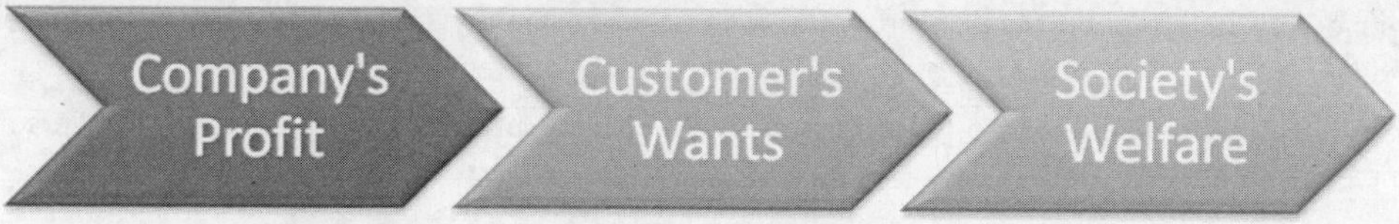

Figure 1.8 Fundamentals of societal marketing concept.

In this context we would like to give the example of the Girl Child's Education Campaign being initiated by Procter & Gamble where they have Anupam Kher, a cinema personality making a claim in their television advertising that on any purchase of the P&G products made by the consumers, the company is going to contribute ₹1.00 towards sponsoring the girl child's education in rural areas. Another very interesting initiative undertaken by Surf Excel towards fulfilling their societal marketing orientation is being explained as under. Lots of such small efforts are being carried out by marketers these days.

Lifebuoy's Help a Child Reach 5

One of the important examples of societal marketing orientation is Lifebuoy's help a child reach 5 campaign. Through this campaign they tried to create awareness amongst the rural people regarding hand hygiene and washing their hands with soap. As we all know that, preventable infections like diarrhea as well as pneumonia kills over 1.3 million children every year in our country before they reach the age of five. Most of these infants and children are from rural as well as semi-rural regions and low-income families. Their mothers who are, often their primary babysitters have less awareness about how the simplest little act of cleaning hands with soap can help to stop the infections in their children. Lifebuoy trained 130 million parents of children who were at risk for better hand hygiene with help a child reach 5 program. It resulted in healthy children as well as their healthy parents.

Source: https://vishalbheeroo.wordpress.com/2013/09/22/make-lifebuoys-help-a-child-reach-5-campaign-a-reality/

Questions for Discussion

1. Can you explain as to why should companies follow societal marketing orientation?
2. Give examples of few companies who have initiated such social incentives as discussed in the case above.

1.5 DIFFERENCE BETWEEN SELLING, MARKETING AND SOCIETAL MARKETING

According to Theodore Levitt (1960)—

> *Selling focuses on the needs of the seller, marketing on the needs of the buyer. Selling is preoccupied with the sellers need to convert his product into cash, marketers with the idea of satisfying the needs of the customers by means of the product and the whole cluster of things associated with creating, delivering, and finally consuming it.*

Broadly speaking the differences which exists between the concept of selling, marketing and societal marketing are depicted in Table 1.2.

Table 1.2 Difference between Selling, Marketing, and Societal Marketing Concepts

Key Points	Selling Concept	Marketing Concept	Societal Marketing Concept
Basic objective	To maximise sales volume	To maximise consumer satisfaction	To maximise long-term interests and welfare of consumers and society
Basic emphasis	Emphasis is on the product	Emphasis is on customer's needs and wants satisfaction	Emphasis is on society's welfare
Basic philosophy	Believes in the philosophy of coveat emptor—the let the buyer beware	Believes in the philosophy of coveat vendor—let the seller beware	believes in the philosophy of consumer satisfaction and social welfare
Management's orientation	Management is sales-volume oriented	Management is consumer-oriented	Management is social welfare-oriented

Key Points	Selling Concept	Marketing Concept	Societal Marketing Concept
Assumption	Consumer will not buy if they are left alone	They will buy only if they are satisfied	They will buy if they are satisfied with the protection of the long-term interests of the society
Main theme	Sell what you can produce	Produce what you can sell	Produce what you can sell but with protecting long-term interests of consumers and society
Basic nature	It is the traditional concept	It is the modern concept	It is the latest concept
Scope	Scope is narrow	Scope is wide	Scope is wider or comprehensive
Company's philosophy	Company first makes the product then sells it	Company first determines the consumers' needs and wants and then designs the product to satisfy those wants	Company first finds out needs and wants of target market and satisfies them in a way that consumers' and society's interest and welfare are protected
Profitability	Results in short-term profits	Results in long-term profitability, future growth and increased markets	Results in long-term profitability with protection of consumers' interest and social welfare
Benefits	Mostly one-way, towards seller only	Probably two-way, towards sellers and buyers	Three-way benefits– towards consumers, sellers and society
Planning	Planning is short-term oriented, in terms of today's products and markets	Planning is long-term oriented, in terms of new products, tomorrow's markets, and future growth	Planning is long-term oriented in terms of loyal clientele and satisfied public
Approach followed	Fragmented approach to selling	Integrated approach to marketing	It follows an integrated and relationship approach

Key Points	Selling Concept	Marketing Concept	Societal Marketing Concept
Market focus	The entire market	The target market	The target market and the entire market
Moral justice	No scope for moral justice	Somewhat, but no guarantee	There is guarantee for moral justice

1.6 PRESENT DAY IMPORTANCE OF MARKETING

Marketing is an indispensable activity. Companies are spending crores of rupees on marketing activities in order to face the stiff competition prevailing in the markets. Here we would like to see the reasons as to why marketing is becoming important to the manufacturer, consumer and the society at large.

1.6.1 From the Point of View of a Business Enterprise/Manufacturer

1. Source of revenue: Marketing is the only revenue generating activity for the business and revenue is considered as the lifeblood or the heartbeat of the business.

2. Foundation of business activities: Marketing serves as a foundation to all other business activities. It helps the production department decide as to what to produce; purchase department decide about the quality of the raw material and machinery to be purchased; finance department decide about the amount of funds to be raised; and the research and development department decide about the new inventions or innovations in the product. It tries to co-relate and ensure coordination between the activities of various departments.

3. Information function: Marketing activities perform a two-way information function. Firstly, they inform the consumer about the various products or services being provided by the manufacturer and secondly, whatever is the consumers' response about the product is informed by the marketers to the company.

4. Loyal clientele: Marketing activities help the organisation to generate loyal clientele for their product by serving the consumer well and designing the goods as per their needs and wants.

5. Ready and smooth demand in the market: It helps in ensuring a ready and smooth demand for the product in the market throughout the year, thus minimising the demand fluctuations.

6. Demand forecasting: With effective market forecasting techniques it is possible for the marketers to project the likely demand in advance, facilitating the manufacturers to produce accordingly.

7. Faster turnover of goods: Because there is a ready and smooth demand existing, it ensures the faster turnover of goods resulting in the low inventory cost.

8. Large-scale production and economies of scale: Because marketing activities are able to generate a huge demand for the product, it enables the organisation to enter into large-scale production which results in better utilisation of the production capacity and bulk buying of raw material ensuring economies of scale benefits.

9. Price stability: Stable demand ensures stable prices in the market. Marketing has been successful in reducing the price fluctuations to a large extent.

10. Better image and goodwill of the organisation: Effective marketing strategies result in a healthy competition in the market, as a result of which both the consumers as well as the competitors remain happy, satisfied, and contended. All these result in earning a better image and goodwill for the organisation in the long run.

11. Satisfied and committed employees: An organisation which enjoys a good image or repute in the market is always considered a better place to work from the employee's perspective, as a result of which the rate of employee turnover goes down, which is considered very healthy for the organisation.

1.6.2 From the Customer's Point of View

1. Information function: Marketing is an important activity which informs the consumers about the availability of various products and brands in the market. It gives them information regarding the distinctive features of various brands and helps them decide which one to buy.

2. Satisfaction of their needs and wants: Marketers help consumers in getting their desired products by giving the feed back to the manufacturers about their needs and wants and getting the goods designed accordingly.

3. Wider variety to choose: It facilitates the consumer to choose from various brands available according to their likes and dislikes.

4. Time and place utility: Marketers try to make the goods easily available to the consumers at all the times at convenient locations ensuring time and place utility.

5. Better products: Marketing results in increased competition in the marketplace, where every company tries to give more value to the consumer. In the process it benefits the consumer as they are able to get better quality products at lower rates.

6. Better services: In order to attract consumers towards their product, companies are trying to provide better and innovative services to them.

7. Improvement in the standard of living: Because of marketing activities consumers know about the availability of various goods and services which can add comfort and luxury in their lives. This has resulted in an increase in the marginal propensity to consume as people are trying to procure more and more goods, resulting in an overall improvement in their standard of living.

1.6.3 From Society's Point of View

1. Bridges gap between production and consumption: Marketing has bridged the gap between the production and consumption activities in our economy.

2. Mobilises unknown and untapped money: This is achieved by increasing the marginal propensity to consume in comparison to the marginal propensity to save. As people are now buying all types of products and brands, this brings more money into circulation which is highly beneficial for the economy.

3. Creation of gainful employment opportunities: In an economy like ours, which is suffering from the problem of large scale unemployment, marketing has turned out to be a blessing as it has created lots of gainful employment opportunities for people.

4. Fullest utilisation of existing resources: As there is a ready and smooth demand for all types of products in the economy, various industries are running at nearly full capacity and all the resources of the economy have been put to the best possible usage ensuring their better utilisation.

5. Improvement in the national income: The overall national income of the country has gone up because of various marketing activities. Increased production in various sectors has resulted in an increase in the GDP rate. The foreign exchange reserves have also improved over the years because of the reduced import bill and increased export bill. As all the brands are available in the country itself, people have stopped importing goods from abroad.

6. Stability in the price level: Marketing activities have brought stability in the price level leading to a more stable economy. Indian economy had suffered from price volatilities for long, because of which the multinational organisations were not keen to enter Indian markets. But now as there are stable markets, we have all the multinationals lined up to enter into our economy.

7. Improvement in the overall image of the Indian economy: As the standard of living of people has gone up and there is a ready demand for all types of products ranging from necessities to luxuries, it has given a boast to our economy. Earlier it was used to be treated as an underdeveloped economy but now India is considered as a rapidly developing economy with huge potential of demand. Marketing has played a very important role in improving the overall image of our economy.

8. Handle economic cycles effectively: Whether the economy is going through inflation or recession, marketing as an instrument comes to the rescue of the government to help the economy come out of it.

From the points discussed above it is quite evident that marketing is becoming a very important activity for all—manufacturer, consumers and society at large.

1.7 LIMITATIONS OF MARKETING

Marketing has been viewed as an activity of the firm that seeks to interpret buyer's needs and creatively respond with good products. But not all marketing firms conform to this theory. Some individuals and companies, in their attempts to maximise their returns, indulge in questionable marketing practices that harm consumer welfare. All the criticism against marketing can be categorised as:

- Marketing practices that affect the society or its social effects
- Marketing's impact on business competition or its economic effects
- Marketing's impact on the consumer ethics or its ethical effects

Each category of criticism, as depicted in Figure 1.9, has spawned a major reaction in the society. Dysfunctional and illegal consequences of marketing seek to destroy society. As a result of all this there has been an emergence of a counterculture on consumer welfare, i.e. consumer protection or in other words, an initiation of a movement known as *consumerism*.

1.7.1 Social Effects of Marketing

Marketing, a tool which originated with the intentions of helping the society and promoting good has, in the longer run, resulted in various negative social effects. Some of the important ones are listed as under:

1. Excessive materialism: Increasing marketing activities lay too much emphasis on material possessions. People tend to judge others by what they own rather than by what they are like. Emphasis on material accumulation initiates a race amongst people and leaves those who lag behind unhappy. Marketing makes people less important than things. It reduces human beings to the status of things. This depersonalisation is against our ethical attitude, 'lesser the needs better it is'.

2. Neglect of social goods and costs: Marketing stimulates demand for private goods at the expense of public goods. Private consumption activities generally create social costs in some form such as creating pollution, excessive materialism, divisions in societies, etc. Thus, it becomes very important to find some ways to increase the output of public goods to restore a social balance with private goods.

3. Cultural pollution: Human senses and intelligence are constantly attacked by cultural noise created by marketing that strongly affects their values and cultural beliefs. The projection of men and women in a highly vulgar and obscene manner in some of the advertisements is one such example which creates cultural pollution.

4. Control over media: In order to promote their own interests, large business houses try to control media decisions by investing heavily in advertising, thereby curbing its freedom to report independently.

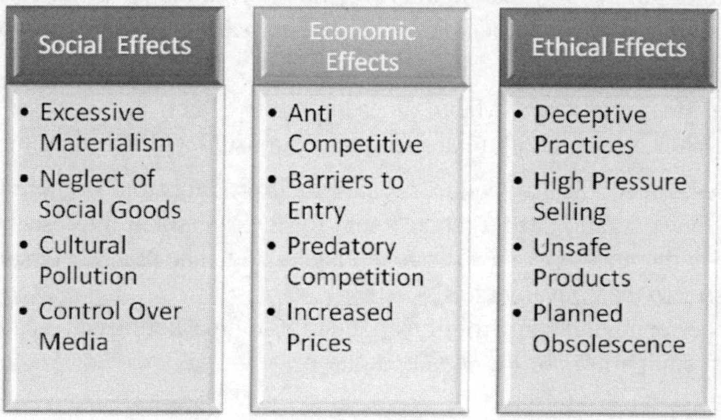

Figure 1.9 Limitations of marketing.

1.7.2 Economic Effects of Marketing

Marketing increases competition amongst business firms. Therefore, many a times the marketing practices are resulting in excessive, unhealthy or in other words cut-throat competition.

1. Anti competitive acquisition: Many firms choose to acquire or merge with other firms in order to unnecessarily reduce competition which can be unethical at times.

2. Barriers to entry: Heavy advertising done by large companies create artificial barriers to entry for small firms in certain industries. Other barriers may be in the form of patents, substantial promotion and tie-ups with suppliers or dealers.

3. Predatory competition: Firms attack their competitors by offering unusually lower prices to drive them out and reduce competition which is not in the interest of the consumers.

4. Increased prices: Marketing causes prices to be higher than they otherwise would be because of the high cost of promotion and distribution. Lots of middlemen are employed by marketers to distribute goods to the consumers. Each and every middleman adds a mark-up to the cost of product and finally the increased cost is passed on to the consumer in the form of increased price. Same is the case with promotional expenditure. Huge amount of money is spent on advertising, personal selling and various sales promotion activities. These expenses are then passed on to the consumer in the form of increased prices.

1.7.3 Ethical Effects of Marketing

It is commonly held that marketing has raised the standard of living of the people. Despite this, marketing system leads to many socially undesirable consequences. Some of the commonly quoted ethical criticisms are:

1. Deceptive practices: Some manufacturers engage in deceptive practices that mislead consumers into believing that he or she will get more value than he actually does. Giving them false guarantees, exaggerated advertising claims, not filling the package to the top or exaggerating contents of a package through large design, etc., are examples of deceptive practices.

2. High pressure selling: At times, salespeople pressurise consumers and persuade them to purchase poor quality products by making false appeals or creating an artificial fear amongst them. Salesmen are encouraged to do so because there is competitive selling and companies give big rewards to the best salesman.

3. Shoddy or unsafe products: Many times products which are not designed properly or products which are hazardous in nature are sold to the consumers for petty gains.

4. Planned obsolescence: Many producers cause their products to obsolescence functionally or materially before they actually need a replacement for their personal interests by bringing in new improved models in the market or new improved packaging. The planned obsolescence results in huge financial losses to the consumers.

Thus, it can be concluded that wrongful applications of marketing can create certain problems for the consumers, competitors or the society at large.

1.8 THE CONCEPT OF MARKETING MIX

The concept of marketing mix for products talks about the inter-relationship that exists between the 4P's—product, price, place, and promotion as highlighted in Figure 1.10. E.J. McCarthy (1996) was the first person to popularise the four factor classification of these variables. All these 4P's are interrelated. Decision in any one area usually affects actions in the others. Marketing mix concentrates on the satisfaction of the needs of the customers by ensuring an integration and coordination amongst all the 4P's. If the needs of the customers change, the marketing mix will also change. If we consider marketing mix for services, there are seven P's instead of the four, as the basic nature of a physical product is different from that of a service. In marketing mix of services three more P's such as people, physical evidence and process are added to the list which are discussed later in the book.

According to William J Stanton (1994)—

> *Marketing mix is the term that is used to describe the combination of the four inputs that constitute the core of an organisation's marketing system. These four elements are the product offering, the price structure, the promotional activities and the distribution system.*

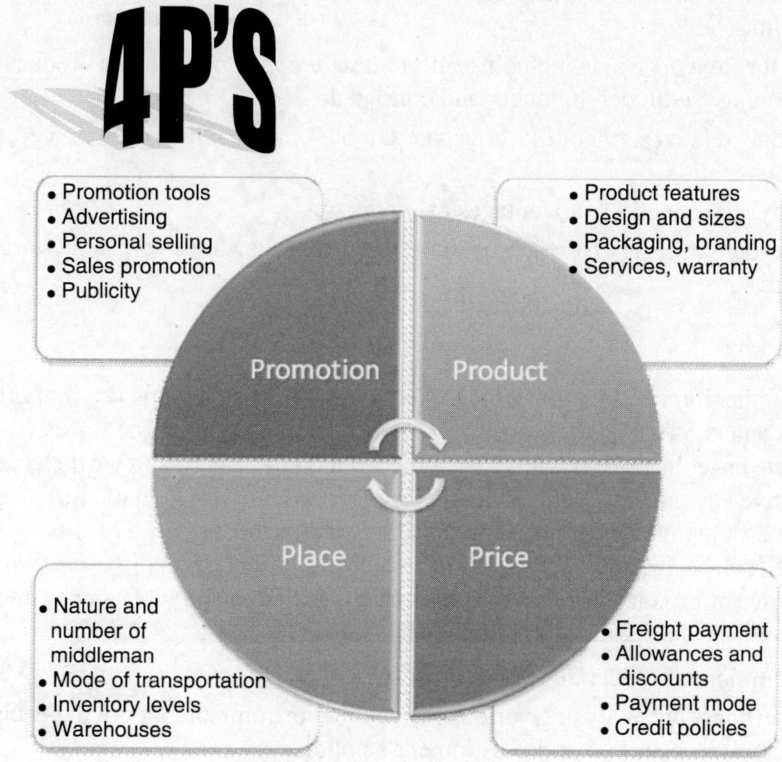

Figure 1.10 Marketing mix.

A company may market one item or several related or unrelated items. They may be distributed through wholesalers, retailers or directly. Ultimately from the multitude of variables, management must select a combination that will best adapt to the environment. In other terms, management is seeking the mix that will lead to the optimal synergistic results. The four P's which constitute the concept of marketing mix are described as under—

1.8.1 Product Mix

Managing the product ingredient includes planning and developing the right product or services to be marketed by company. Product is the basic element of marketing mix because all other elements are required only when there is a product. It is the centre of all the marketing activities. Marketers can satisfy needs and wants of consumers only by designing excellent products for them. Important and long term marketing decisions on product may be termed as product strategies. Some of the important product mix strategies are listed as under:

1. Development and introduction of new products and services to meet customer's needs and wants.
2. Modifications (in terms of qualities, features and performance) on existing products to deliver better value and satisfaction to the consumers.
3. Product related strategies including branding, packaging, labelling, colour, weight, grading, seals, etc.
4. Product line decisions including different varieties or models and product mix decisions including width, depth, length and consistency.
5. Product related services like after sale services, home delivery, guarantee, warrantee and demonstration.
6. Study of competitive advantages of products.
7. Relevant strategies for each of the stage of product life-cycle and consumer adoption process.

1.8.2 Price Mix

Price mix is another important element of marketing mix. This element is very important especially in the Indian context as the Indian consumer is considered a highly price sensitive consumer. On the one hand we have the price sensitive customers but on the other hand we do have the emerging prestige sensitive customers. Thus, pricing decisions become vital in marketing. Determining the right base price and strategies concerning discounts, allowances, etc., has to be worked out very carefully. *Price* can be defined as the economic value of product normally expressed in the form of money. The price of product should be set in such a way that the buyers can pay and the company can earn adequate profits. Normally, pricing decisions involve:

1. Determining product development costs
2. Identifying and analysing various relevant factors influencing pricing decisions, such as, demand, competition and government's policies
3. Determining manufacturing (variable and fixed) costs of the product
4. Study of pricing policies and strategies of the close competitors
5. Deciding on the level or margin of profits
6. Formulating appropriate base pricing policies for the products
7. Decisions on price discrimination, discounts, allowances, and seasoned effects
8. Pricing policies/strategies in different stages of the product life-cycle

9. Decisions on price setting methods
10. Price decisions for direct and indirect distribution of products
11. Decisions regarding inclusion of freight charges in prices
12. Decisions regarding credit terms and other payment policies

1.8.3 Promotion Mix

It is the ingredient used to inform and persuade the market regarding a company's product. It is also known as *market communication.* In today's marketing practices, market promotion has a vital role to play. Promotion mix involves all those efforts directed to increase sales of products on a continuous basis. It includes providing information to customers, inspiring them to buy and offering incentives. Promotion is not only required for increasing the sales volume for the organisation but it also plays a very important role in increasing the goodwill, image and prestige of the organisation and maintaining long-term sustained relations with the customers and other stakeholders of the company. Promotion mix consists of the four basic tools—advertising, personal selling, sales promotion and publicity. It includes the following aspects:

1. Deciding about the advertising objectives, message, copy, media, schedule, agency and budget
2. Evaluating social and ethical aspects of advertising
3. Measuring advertising effectiveness
4. Setting personal selling objectives
5. Deciding about the size, and nature and quality of sales force required
6. Recruitment, selection, training and motivational activities
7. Supervision, regulation, and controlling salesperson
8. Remunerating and motivating salesmen
9. Introducing various sales promotion incentives
10. Deciding about sales-promotion methods—consumer level, salesmen level and dealer level
11. Assessing cost and effectiveness of sales promotion measures
12. Regulating publicity in the interest of the organisation
13. Deciding about the types of efforts to get publicity
14. Assessing impact of publicity on sales and reputation of the company
15. Ensuring overall coordination and integration amongst various promotional tools

1.8.4 Distribution Mix

Management's responsibility is to select and manage the trade channels through which the products will reach the right market at the right time. They develop a distribution system for physically handling and transporting the products through these channels. It is the last element of marketing mix but is very important as marketing goals can be achieved only if the product reaches the hands of consumers conveniently and in time. This element ensures that the right product can be made available to the right consumer, in the right way, at the right time, at the right place and in the right form. Therefore, decisions regarding the channel length, coverage, locations, transport and inventory become very important. Some of the important place decisions include:

1. Deciding about the geographic concentration of the market
2. Finalising the type of distribution channels and channel members to be used
3. Deciding about the channel length and the number of middleman to be used
4. Taking physical distribution decisions which include transportation, communication, warehousing, inventory control, insurance, banking, etc.
5. Balancing distribution costs and selling price
6. Designing a suitable distribution network, and long-term distribution strategies
7. Developing and adopting logistics management for effective distribution of products

Thus, the purpose of determining the marketing mix is to ensure that the needs of the customers are satisfied in the most efficient manner by ensuring proper coordination between all the 4P's. Since the needs of the customers keep on changing the marketing mix also keeps on changing.

According to Philip Kotler (2011)—

> *Marketing mix is the mixture of controllable marketing variables that the firm uses to pursue the desired level of sales in the target market at a particular point of time.*

The company's marketing mix at time, *t*, for a particular product can be represented by the vector—

$$MM = (P1, P2, P3, P4)t$$

where P1 = product quality

P2 = price

P3 = place

P4 = promotion

For example, if a company produces a product with quality standard of 1.5, price ₹10,000, distributional expenditure ₹40,000 a month and promotional expenditure ₹15,000 a month, the marketing mix will be—

$$MM = (1.5, ₹10{,}000, ₹40{,}000, ₹15{,}000)t$$

As these components can take different values, a firm's current marketing mix is selected from a great number of possibilities. Market research, farsightedness and judgement are used in determining the marketing mix as they are used in locating target customers and discovering their needs. But one thing must be noted that the 4P's represent the seller's view of the marketing tools available for influencing buyers. From a buyer's perspective, each marketing tool is designed to deliver a customer benefit. Robert Lauterborn (1984) suggested that the sellers' 4P's correspond to the customer's 4C's, such as given in Figure 1.11 and Figure 1.12.

Winning companies will be those who can meet customer needs economically and conveniently and with effective communication.

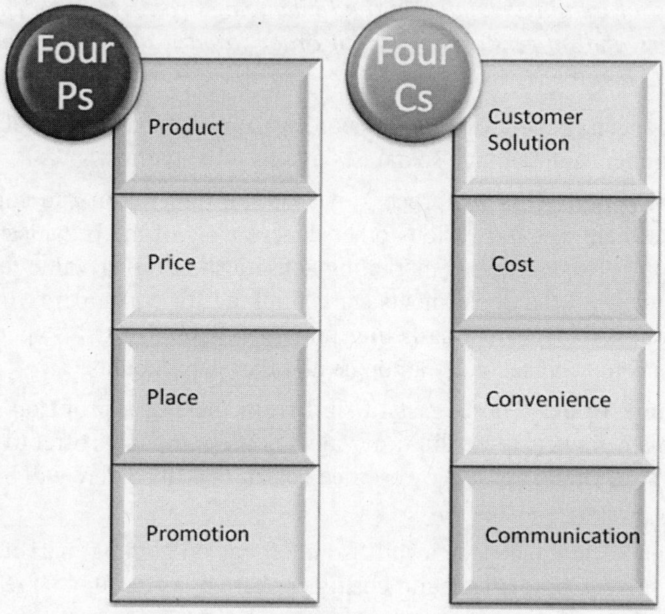

Figure 1.11 Sellers 4 P's correspond to buyers 4C's.

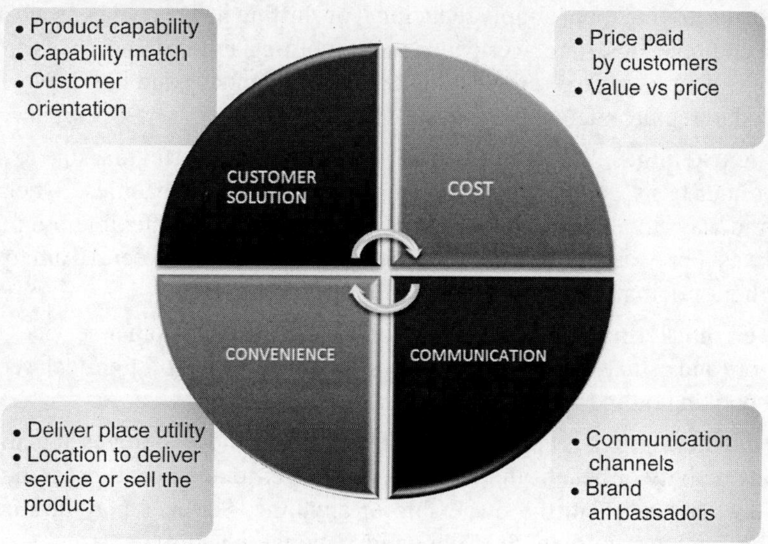

Figure 1.12 Four 4C's.

1.9 NEW CONCEPTS IN MARKETING

1. Relationship marketing: Believes in maintaining long-term relationship with the customers because it is always in the interest of the organisation to retain their customers in comparison to creating new customers. According to Philip Kotler (1999)—

It is the process of creating, maintaining and enhancing strong value-laden relationships with customers and other stakeholders in order to earn and retain their long-term preference and loyalty.

Companies provide special benefits to select customers to strengthen bonds. Relationship marketing builds strong economic, technical and social ties amongst the parties.

2. Integrated marketing: It is the process of ensuring integration and coordination amongst the marketing department and the various other departments of the organisation. It is important to ensure integration between various marketing activities to deliver value to the customers and it is possible only when all the departments start 'thinking for consumers'. Integration has to be ensured firstly amongst the various marketing functions like advertising, personal selling, sales promotion activities, etc., and secondly amongst all other departments.

3. Customer lifetime value: It suggests a shift from making a profit on each transaction to making profits by managing customer lifetime value. Some companies offer to deliver a constantly needed product on a regular basis at a lower price per unit because they will enjoy the customer's loyalty for a longer period.

4. Customer share: There has been a shift from a focus on gaining market share to a focus on building customer share. Companies build customer share by offering a large variety of goods to their existing customers.

5. De-marketing: It is a marketing strategy to reduce demand temporarily or permanently with the aim of not destroying it but simply reducing it or shifting it. This happens when there is overfull demand. For example, buses are overloaded in the morning and evening, roads are busy for most of times, zoological parks are overcrowded on Saturdays, Sundays and holidays. Here de-marketing can be applied to regulate demand.

6. Synchro-marketing: When the demand for the product is irregular due to season, some part of the day or hour-basis, causing ideal capacity or overworked capacities, Synchro-marketing can be used to find ways to alter the same pattern of demand through flexible pricing, promotion and other incentives. For example, in order to attract the customers between 10 am to 6 pm, restaurants offer happy hour pricing.

7. Augmented marketing: It is the provision of additional customer services and benefits built around the core and actual products that relate to the introduction of high-tech services like movies on demand, booking online, online banking transactions, etc.

8. Services marketing: It is applying the concepts, tools and techniques of marketing to services. Service is any activity or benefit that one party can offer to another. It is essentially intangible in nature and does not result in the ownership of anything. Services may be financial, insurance, transportation, banking, tourism, retailing or educational in nature.

9. Direct and online marketing: Information technology and communication revolution promises to change the nature of buying and selling. People anywhere in the world can access the Internet and the company's home pages to scan offers and order goods. Via online services, they can give and get advice on products and services, determine the best values, place orders and get next day delivery. As a result of advances in database technology, companies can do more direct marketing and rely less on wholesale and retail intermediaries. All these trends portend greater buying and selling efficiency in the years to come.

LET US SUM UP

- Today's marketplace is enormously more complex. Marketers are confronted with endless opportunities mainly because of the three developments—globalisation, technological advances, and deregulation.
- In simple words, we can say it that marketing is taking care of 6R's—ensuring that right goods and services are made available to the right person, at the right place, at the right time, at the right price, and with the right communication and promotion.
- A human need is a state of felt deprivation of some basic satisfaction.
- Wants are desires for specific satisfiers of these deeper needs
- Demands are wants for specific products that are backed up by an ability and willingness to pay for them—purchasing power.
- Value is the customer's estimate of the products capacity to satisfy a set of goals.
- Markets are seen as a collection of buyers and sellers, where sellers as constituting the industry and the buyers as constituting the market.
- Marketing has evolved through various stages over the period of time, such as, production, product, sales, marketing and societal marketing stage.
- The production concept holds that consumers will favour those products that are widely available and low in cost.
- The product concept holds that consumers will favour those products that offer the most quality, performance and features.
- The selling concept holds that consumers and businesses, if left alone, will automatically not buy enough of the organisation's products. The organisation must, therefore, undertake an aggressive selling and promotion effort.
- The marketing concept holds that the key to achieving its organisational goals consists of the company being more effective than competitors in creating, delivering and communicating customer value to its chosen target markets.
- The societal marketing concept holds that the organisation's task is to determine the needs, wants and interests of target markets and to deliver the desired satisfactions more effectively and efficiently than competitors in a way that preserves or enhances the consumers and society's well-being.
- Marketing is becoming important to the manufacturer, consumer and the society at large because of various reasons.
- Marketing has been criticised by people mainly because of its negative effects of the society, competition and consumer welfare.
- The concept of marketing mix talks about the inter relationship that exists between the 4P's—product, price, place, promotion.
- Marketing mix is the mixture of controllable marketing variables that the firm uses to pursue the desired level of sales in the target market at a particular point of time.
- Winning companies will be those who can meet customer needs economically and conveniently and with effective communication.

QUESTIONS TO CHECK YOUR PROGRESS

Short Answer Questions

1. Define marketing as given by William J Stanton.
2. Differentiate between the concept of need, want and demand.
3. Explain the relationship between the customer value and satisfaction.
4. Taking care of social and ethical considerations while formulating the marketing plan is a part of which marketing concept?
5. Who gave the old adage, "build a better mousetrap and the world will beat a path to your door?"
6. Defining the concept of marketing myopia.
7. What makes an exchange to be called a marketing transaction?
8. What is a market?
9. Who are marketers?
10. Who gave the concept of marketing mix?
11. Explain the concept of marketing mix given by Philip Kotler.
12. Explain the concept of relationship marketing.
13. What is de-marketing and why is it required?
14. Explain the concept of integrated marketing.

Long Answer Questions

1. A committee of The American Marketing Association defined marketing as, "the process of planning and executing the conception, pricing, promotion and distribution of ideas, goods and services to create exchanges that satisfy individual and organisational objectives". Does this definition explain the concept of modern day marketing clearly?
2. Give the customer oriented definition of marketing. How can marketing help a firm build its goodwill in the market?
3. What is the essence of modern marketing concept? How does it differ from the traditional concept?
4. How does marketing affect the lives of people? Explain with reference to various utilities created by marketing.
5. "We are to produce what people want and not what we can sell". Explain the statement elaborating the various stages of evolution of marketing.
6. Explain the concept of marketing. Also discuss the factors that a marketing manager must take into account while developing the marketing mix for his products.
7. "The present day marketing is consumer-oriented". Explain the statement with examples.
8. Discuss the impact of consumer orientation on the marketing mix of a company producing dishwashers.
9. "Marketing begins and ends with the consumer". Discuss the statement in the light of the difference between the concept of marketing and selling.
10. "Marketing begins before production and ends after production". Explain the statement in the light of the modern marketing concept.
11. How would you use different marketing mix elements to formulate a marketing strategy?
12. "Marketing mix is a mix of mixes". In the light of this statement explain the components of marketing mix.

13. "The marketing concept replaces and reverses the logic of the selling concept". Do you agree? Explain with examples.
14. Distinguish between product orientation and marketing orientation with the help of suitable examples.
15. Differentiate between the concepts of need, want and demand with the help of suitable examples.
16. Explain the impact of societal marketing orientation on marketers, consumers and society at large.
17. "Marketing is a multiplier of economic development". Comment upon the statement explaining the role of marketing as an instrument of economic growth in a developing country like India.
18. "Marketing is the creation and delivery of a standard of living". Do you agree with the statement? Explain it in the light of the importance of marketing from the consumer's perspective.
19. "The adoption of the marketing concept in India seems to be on the increase". Elucidate the statement highlighting the importance of marketing from the manufacturer and middleman's perspective.
20. "India consists of rural and urban markets". Briefly explain as to how be they different from each other from marketing point of view.
21. "Marketers create superfluous needs". Do you agree with the statement? Explain in the light of the negative effect of marketing on consumers and society at large.
22. Write a short note on augmented marketing.
23. Analyse the major challenges for future marketers.
24. Which of the marketing concept ensures the short term profitability and which ones ensure profitability in the long run? Why?
25. How can a company dealing in products that run contrary to society's interests, such as tobacco, liquor or environmentally harmful products, can handle their marketing activities so as to ensure a balance between their profitability and social welfare?

CHAPTER 2

Marketing Environment

Learning Outcomes

After studying this chapter, you will be able to:

- Identify the various micro and macro environment variables
- Explain the demographic environment variables
- Define the economic environment variables
- Classify various socio-cultural environmental factors
- Understand the impact of technological and natural environment
- Describe the significance of political-legal environment
- Restate the environmental scanning and analysis procedure

Marketing as an activity is closely influenced by the various changes taking place in the environment and it is equally capable of influencing the various factors in the environment. Therefore, it becomes important for all the successful companies to take an outside-inside view of the business. They have to continuously monitor the various marketing and environmental factors to identify the new opportunities and threats being posed by them and have to learn to adapt to them. All those companies who fail to see change as an opportunity are generally not able to survive in today's competitive environment. Companies which tend to ignore or resist change might become obsolete with time and this might put them into a disadvantageous position.

Although every manager in an organisation needs to observe the outside environment and every department has to adapt themselves to the changes taking place, but the marketing department is one which feels the maximum impact of various environmental variables as they have to interact with them on a more regular basis. At times even the success or failure of various marketing strategies depends on these variables. Thus, it becomes a major responsibility of the marketing managers to identify significant market place changes in time and ensure a speedy action.

These days the identification of significant factors is made possible with the help of marketing intelligence and marketing research systems. With the help of these systems marketers can anticipate the changes and adjust themselves accordingly. Even though marketers spend more time with their customers and competitors, they have to keep their eyes wide open to the other environmental factors as well. The various environmental factors can be broadly classified into two categories—micro-environmental variables and macro-environmental variables as depicted in Figure 2.1.

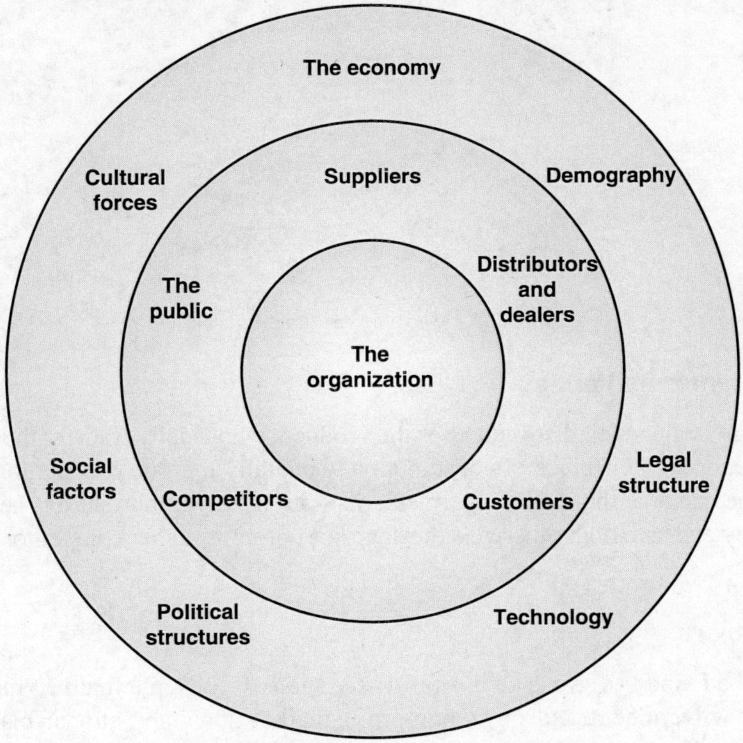

Figure 2.1 Various environmental variables.

2.1 MICRO ENVIRONMENT VARIABLES

Micro-environmental variables imply the factors and forces in the immediate environment which affect thc company's ability to serve its market. It is possible for the company to ensure proper relations with the micro-level variables and exercise control over their activities to some extent, with better management practices and fair dealing with them. Various micro-environment variables, as depicted in Figure 2.2, are listed as under.

2.1.1 Suppliers

It includes all the suppliers whether they are supplying raw material, labour or technology. It is very important for an organisation to ensure cordial relations with their suppliers because any problem with them and their supplies will get affected adversely and it will in turn have a negative influence on the production process of the organisation. Production delays can result in loss of customers and an adverse effect on the image and goodwill of the company.

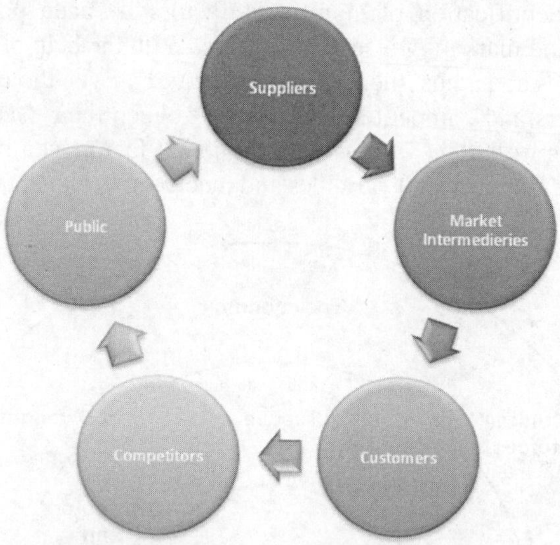

Figure 2.2 Micro-environment variables.

2.1.2 Market Intermediaries

It includes all the dealers and distributors of the products who finally transfer the goods from the place of production to their place of consumption. Generally the fate of a company's product is very much in the hands of the market intermediaries so it is very important for the organisation to keep them happy and satisfied, otherwise they can start promoting the competitor's brand instead of theirs.

2.1.3 Customers

Customers can be found in various kinds of markets, such as, consumer market, industrial market, reseller market, government and other non-profit market and international market. It is very important for an organisation to take their customers seriously and try to give them maximum value and satisfaction because their future is in the hands of the customers.

2.1.4 Competitors

It is very important for an organisation to decide whether the firm is going to compete, in what markets should they compete and how should they compete with the competitors.

2.1.5 Public

It is very important for an organisation to keep the interest of the general public into account in order to ensure their survival in the business. Philip Kotler (1999), in his book *Marketing Management,* quoted that, "companies must put their primary energy into effectively managing their relationship with their customers, distributors and suppliers, but their overall success will be affected by how other publics in their society view their activity. Companies would be wise to spend time monitoring all their publics—understanding their needs and opinions and dealing with them constructively".

2.2 MACRO-ENVIRONMENTAL VARIABLES

The firm's external environment is constituted by the various macro-environmental factors and forces that affect its consumer markets, business markets and competitors. Successful companies recognise and respond profitably to the unmet needs and opportunities prevailing in the environment. Therefore, it is very important for them to identify such opportunities and use them to their advantage. For example, it has been observed in the recent past that participation of women in the workforce is increasing rapidly, which has resulted in various opportunities, such as, the child day-care business, increased consumption of microwaveable foods, semi-processed foods and office-oriented women's clothing, etc.

2.3 IDENTIFYING AND RESPONDING TO THE MAJOR MACRO-ENVIRONMENTAL FORCES

The various micro-environmental variables, such as, companies' suppliers, market intermediaries, customers, competitors and publics, all operate in a macro-environment of forces which provide various opportunities and pose certain threats. These forces are non-controllable to a large extent so the only thing an organisation can do is to constantly monitor them and respond to the changes happening in them. There are six major forces— demographic, natural, political-legal, socio-cultural, technological and economic, as depicted in Figure 2.3. Marketers need to go and constantly monitor these forces as they provide them with new profitable opportunities as well as certain threats. It will be possible for them to take the advantage of the opportunities and handle the threats effectively only if they are able to identify them immediately and take the required action fast.

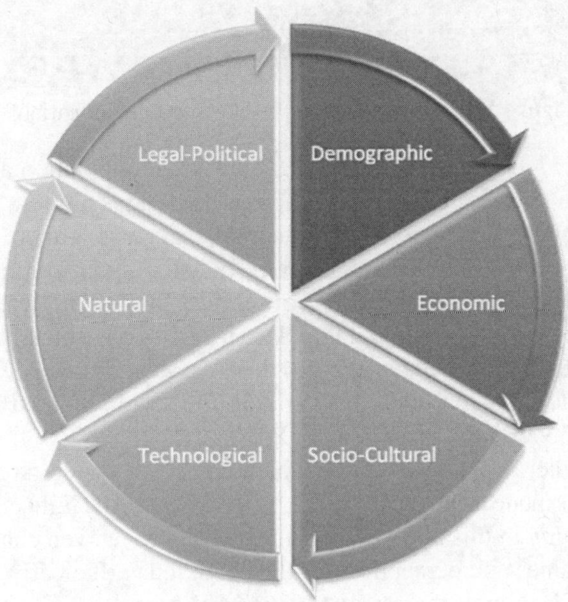

Figure 2.3 Macro-environmental variables.

2.3.1 Demographic Environment

The first and the foremost important variable for the marketer is to monitor its 'people' or, in other words, the demographic forces as they constitute their markets. It is very significant for them to get information about the overall population and the growth rate of population in different cities, regions or nations as they have to plan their production as well as the marketing activities keeping the figures into account. The anticipated rate of growth of population helps marketers in demand forecasting, but the growing population does not mean growing markets unless and until people have sufficient purchasing power. Thus, it becomes more important for them to get knowledge about the income distribution, age distribution, educational levels, sex composition, household patterns as well as the rural and urban movements in the population. All this information helps them decide about their segmentation and market targeting policies. The various parameters of demographic environmental variables are represented in Figure 2.4.

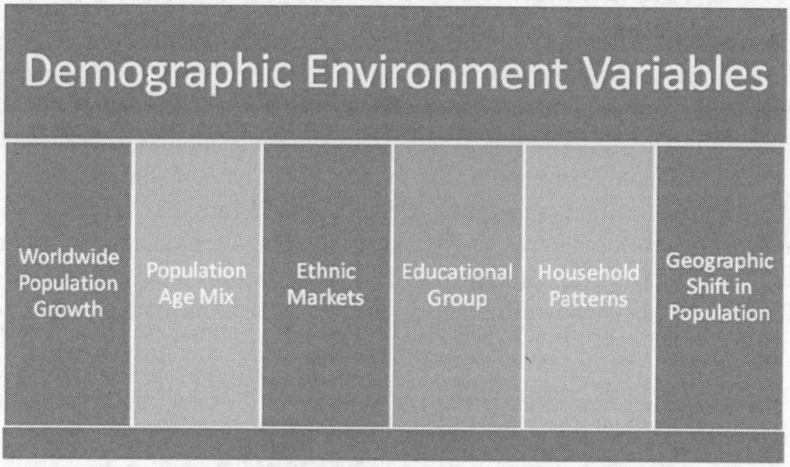

Figure 2.4 Various demographic environment variables.

1. Population age mix: Different countries have different population age mixes. A population can be sub-divided into six age groups—preschool, school age children, teens, young adults age 25 to 40, middle aged adults age 40 to 65 and older adults age 65 and up. For marketers it is very important to understand as to what percentage of the country's population lies in which age group as they have to decide about the types of goods or services they would like to produce and market. For example, the findings of 2020 National Population Survey have clearly reflected that the major percentage of India's population is in the age-group of less than 35 years, which is a very important fact for the marketers to be taken into consideration for deciding about the various products or services they like to deliver in the markets after 2020.

In a recent example, Pepsi, a company which has always been targeting its product to the youth of the country, has made a change in their advertisement in the light of the growing percentage of India's population lying in this particular segment. They have even changed the basic theme in light of the changing values and perceptions of the youth today. It clearly highlights the influence of age-group on the projection of the product in the market.

Changes in the Behavioural Implications for Consumer Market Segments: FMCG, Durables and Retail during Covid-19

Compassionate Communication	*Value of Time*	*Innovative Thinking*
Customers want to be heard and empathised with. This means crafting communication that feels personal outreach purely motivated by product marketing and targeted ads will come across as insensitive.	As more time is being spent at home and with family, customers are indulging in DIY behaviour which is also an opportunity for brands to explore DIY products and services.	This is a good time for brands to reinvent themselves, experiment with new approaches, customer offerings and take risks.
To build trust, brands will have to display good understanding of regional culture, tastes and devise an inclusive messaging that speaks to regional needs.	As extended period of work from home continues, home entertainment, home improvement, office electronics, supplies as categories will continue to get influx of attention.	Engage your customers to crowd source ideas, co-experiment to deepen your relationship and build an innovative future of your brand.
Share with your customers how you will put their health and welfare at the top, how you are taking care of your employees, vendors, and workers. This will exhibit emotional intelligence and build trust.	Brands will need to rethink products that align with home-bound behaviours. This means comfort (home bound) and quality (long lasting products) will dominate purchase behaviour.	Consumers' heightened sense of awareness around sustainable lifestyle is a huge opportunity for brands to innovate on quality, resource efficient products, extending useful life of existing products, managing waste, etc.
Consumer attitudes have shifted towards being energy consumption conscious, health conscious and having a sustainable lifestyle. Brand messaging must convey support towards making responsible choices for a sustainable future.		

Source: https://home.kpmg/in/en/home/insights/2020/12/understanding-impact-consumer-behavior-due-to-covid-19.html

Questions for Discussion

1. On the basis of the findings of the KPMG team, what are your observations regarding the impact of Covid-19 on the consumer markets?
2. How has this environmental factors impacted the consumer's buying behaviour?

2. Ethnic markets: Countries also vary in their ethnic and racial make-up. In India we do not have the problem of racial break up but our population is divided amongst various religious groups. Each religious group has certain specific beliefs and value system and it is expected from its followers to strongly believe in them. The religious beliefs strongly affect the likes, dislikes and the buying habits of people. Several companies producing food, clothing and furniture items keep these religious differences into account while promoting their goods in the market.

3. Educational group: The entire population can be divided into various categories on the basis of the level of education enjoyed by the people, such as illiterates, high school dropouts, high school pass outs, college degrees and professional degrees. All these levels of qualifications make a whole lot of difference in one's personality and perceptions. Therefore, for marketers it is very important to understand the educational standards prevailing in an economy before targeting their goods to them.

4. Household patterns: Traditional household patterns consisting of joint family system where husband, wife and their children used to live with their grandparents were different than today's nuclear family systems comprising of husband, wife and their children. Marketers have to be very careful while targeting their goods and promotional strategies to the various household patterns.

5. Geographical shift in population: Migration of people from villages to cities and from one country to another is again a very important parameter for marketers to take into consideration while deciding about the size of the target market.

The effect of all these changes is clearly visible while the companies design their segmentation and market targeting decisions. Certain goods or services are exclusively designed for consumers from specific age group, sex or religious background. The educational and occupational status, geographic distribution, lifestyle and other characteristics of people are also taken into consideration by marketers while targeting their communication and distribution decisions.

2.3.2 Economic Environment

Economic environment consists of economic forces that affect company's costs, revenues, and profits on the one hand, and customers' purchasing powers and willingness to spend on the other. For marketers it is important to understand the purchasing power of people in the market as it strongly affects their pricing and promotional decisions. The purchasing power, an economic factor, depends to a large extent on the economic growth rate, the gross domestic product, national income levels, inflation rate, bank interest rates, fluctuations of stock markets and commodity markets, industrial and agricultural growth rates, fiscal and monetary policies of the government, export import policies and policies regarding liberalisation, globalisation and privatisation. Consumer's expenditures depend to a large extent on their buying power which again gets strongly influenced by their basic nature, i.e. whether they tend to save more or spend. The rate of marginal propensity to consume and the rate of marginal propensity to save prevailing in the economy strongly determine the level of expenditure of consumers. Thus, it becomes very important for marketers to keep track of the changes taking place in all these economic spheres especially with regards to the cost of living, the interest rates by banks, saving and borrowing factors, as well as the growth rate prevailing in the economy as these factors strongly influence their marketing decisions.

2.3.3 Natural Environment

When we talk about the influence of natural environmental variables on marketers' policies we look at it from various perspectives. Some of the important ones are listed as under:

- The availability and shortage of essential natural resources
- The rate of usage or consumption of essential natural resources
- The deterioration in the natural environment
- The increasing land, air and water pollution levels
- A hole in the ozone layer due to use of certain chemicals producing 'greenhouse effect'.
- The increased cost of traditional sources of energy
- The role of government in saving the environment

It is quite evident from all the factors listed above that the natural variables exercise a strong influence on the marketers' policies. They can produce only those goods for which the essential raw materials are available easily and at low price. Moreover, they are expected to be judiciously using the various natural resources so that the resources should not get depleted completely. Industries are expected to be taking care of the fact that they are not contributing through their production and promotion processes towards any kind of pollution in the environment. We expect this as one of the social responsibilities of the business that they should behave sensibly and try to utilise natural resources judiciously. But in case some of the manufacturers do not behave in a sensible manner, we do have a strong legal machinery to keep a check on their activities. The government is playing a very active role in ensuring that the various natural resources are used appropriately without causing any harm to the overall environment. These days, companies have to invest a huge amount in pollution control equipments and more environmentally friendly fuels. One such example is the legislation passed by the government which expects all car manufacturing companies to install antipollution devices in their cars before bringing them on the road. The message is clear that the companies must understand that people want better quality products at low prices, but not at the cost of quality of life.

2.3.4 Technological Environment

Technology plays the most important role in people's lives and is quite capable of influencing the marketers' decisions. The technological factors affect a companies' production process, the quality of goods produced and the cost of production. The research and development facilities result in inventing new improved features for products which gives them a competitive edge and helps them serve their consumers better. Technology has been a great factor contributing towards the upliftment of the standard of living of people as due to technological innovations new improved sophisticated goods are being manufactured by producers and made available to consumers. Nobody could ever imagine that one day the whole world will get connected through Internet and people can talk and pass on the messages from one place to another within seconds. It is only due to the technological revolution that we have a wide variety of goods taking care of various manual chores such as, computers, fully automatic washing machines, microwave ovens, automatic dishwashers, vacuum cleaners, etc. It is important for marketers to understand whether the right kind of technology is available in their own country before they start the production process and if not, are they allowed to import the technology from outside and what is going to be the procedure for that. Hence, many times various product ideas have not been conceptualised mainly because of the non-availability of right technique at reasonable prices. For marketers it is essential to constantly monitor the trends in technology such as, the pace of change, replacement cost, opportunities for innovation, role of government in developing or importing new technology, regulations affecting technological changes and reforms and procedures for technological transfer amongst nations.

2.3.5 Political and Legal Environment

Another important factor influencing the marketing decisions is the political and legal environment of a country. This environment is composed of the legal machinery, various laws, government enforcement agencies, and voluntary organisations which constantly put pressure and limit various organisations and individuals. In a country like India, where we have the multi-party political structure, it is very important for marketers to keep track of the changes which are taking place in the ruling government. With every change in the party in power there is a change in the marketing policies and companies have to adjust to those changes. Every government in power formulates a series of legislations to regulate business operations to restrict unfair trade practices and protect consumer and social interests. These laws may create new opportunities or challenges for businessmen. A marketing manager must know the business philosophy and approach of the current government and legal provisions that he has to observe while dealing with other parties. Understanding about the working of the judiciary and administrative machinery is also a very important factor to be taken into account before arriving at any important policy decision of the organisation.

2.3.6 Socio-Cultural Environment

Society shapes our beliefs, values and norms. The moment an individual is born in a particular society he/she inherits the cultural values, beliefs, and norms of that society. These values and beliefs strongly influence their buying pattern. What to buy? When to buy? How to buy? Where to buy? These decisions get unconsciously influenced by their beliefs and societal norms. Most of the time their purchase preferences get strongly influenced by the views of other individuals, society, organisations, nature or the universe to which they belong. These relationships are very powerful in determining an individual's preference for various goods and services. The various socio-cultural variables influencing an individual have been nicely depicted in Figure 2.5.

1. Views of themselves: People are more cautious in their spending pattern and more value driven in their purchases. Most of their purchases are strongly guided by their views about themselves. They make purchases to reflect their personality or an image which they want to portray to the outside world.

2. Views of others: Many times our purchases not only get influenced by our own views about ourself but the views of others, especially the ones who are close to us like family, friends and peers. Their opinion about us also has a lot of weightage on our buying pattern.

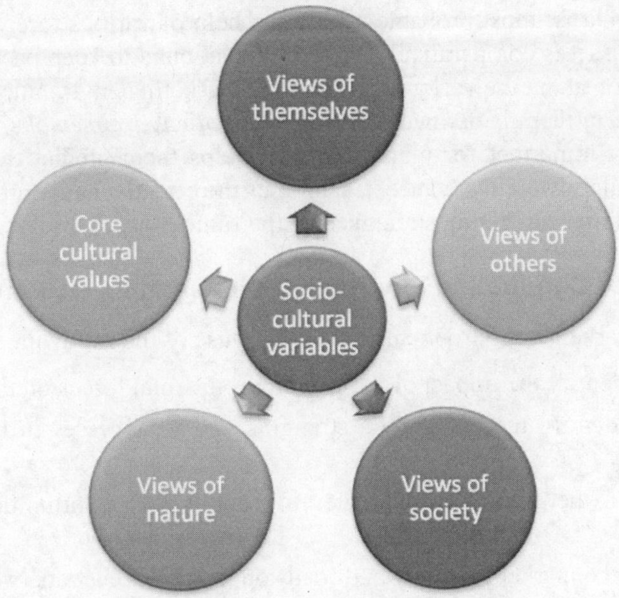

Figure 2.5 Socio-cultural variables.

3. Views of society: People vary in their attitudes towards their society. According to Philip Kotler (1999), some defend it (preservers), some run it (makers), some take what they can from it (taker), some want to change it (changers), some are looking for something deeper (seekers) and some want to leave it (escapers). Often consumption patterns of individuals reflect their social attitudes.

4. Views of nature: People vary in their attitude towards nature. For long nature has been destroyed by various human activities, but only lately people have started realising their responsibility towards nature and some awakening has taken place on the part of the marketers and individuals. Various green marketing initiatives are a step in this direction. This consciousness towards nature is also being reflected in the consumer's buying pattern as most of them have started buying green or eco-friendly products.

5. High persistence of core cultural values: People living in a particular society hold certain core values. Core beliefs and values are generally passed on from parents to their children and are reinforced by certain social institutions such as schools, colleges, business and government. Marketers always try to look for these core values and perceptions because it is always in their interest to match their product to these values. Values change with time as well. Cultural perceptions change with change in income, education, and occupation. Thus, marketers always keep a check on these cultural shifts in order to identify new marketing opportunities or threats.

2.4 ENVIRONMENTAL SCANNING AND ANALYSIS

As discussed in previous paragraphs, there are lots of micro as well as macro level environmental variables that influence marketers' policies. Therefore, it is very important for them to keep pace with the changes taking place. Although the future is not predictable, marketers can obtain information about what is 'most probable'. With the help of various forecasting techniques and computerised systems, it is comparatively easier for marketers to keep pace with these changes. Collecting information about the various forces in the marketing environment and monitoring the changes taking place in them is defined as the *process of environmental scanning and analysis.* This analysis is very important for marketers as it helps them predict the likely changes and prepare for those changes well in advance. It increases the effectiveness of their policies and helps them in developing better marketing strategies for the future.

2.4.1 Reasons for Conducting Environmental Scanning and Analysis

Marketers analyse marketing environment closely because of the following important reasons:

- To clearly identify the impact of various environmental forces on their policies
- To clearly identify the company's strengths and weaknesses in the light of changing scenario
- To lay down the marketing strategies to exploit the opportunities and threats being confronted
- To segment the market precisely and focus on the target customers effectively
- To conduct an internal analysis and formulate long-term marketing plans
- To design effective marketing strategies to beat the competition
- To adjust and readjust continuously to the changes taking place in the internal as well as external environment
- To overall improve the efficiency of marketing operations and ensure long-term profitability

LET US SUM UP

- Marketing as an activity is closely influenced by the various changes taking place in the environment and it is equally capable of influencing the various factors in the environment.
- The various environmental factors can be broadly classified into two categories—micro-environmental variables and macro-environmental variables.
- Micro-environmental variables imply the factors and forces in the immediate environment which affect the company's ability to serve its market.
- Micro environmental variables are—suppliers, market intermediaries, customers, competitors and public.
- The firm's external environment is constituted by the various macro-environmental factors and forces that affect—its consumer markets, business markets and competitors.
- There are six major macro-environmental forces, such as demographic, economic, natural, technological, socio-cultural and political-legal.
- Demographic variables include knowing about the age-distribution, educational levels, household patterns, regional characteristics and movements in the population.
- Economic environment consists of economic forces that affect a company's costs, revenues and profits on the one hand, and customers' purchasing powers and willingness to spend on the other.

- The natural variables exercise a strong influence on the marketers' policies as they are expected to be judiciously using the various natural resources so that the resources should not get depleted completely while manufacturing their products.
- The technological factors affect a companies' production process, the quality of goods and services produced, and the cost of production and innovation which gives them a competitive edge and helps them serve their consumers better.
- Political and legal environment of a country is composed of the legal machinery, various laws, government enforcement agencies and voluntary organisations which constantly put pressure on various marketing organisations and individuals.
- The moment an individual is born in a particular society, he/she inherits the cultural values, beliefs and norms of that society, and these values and beliefs strongly influence their buying pattern.
- Collecting information about the various forces in the marketing environment and monitoring the changes taking place in them is defined as *the process of environmental scanning and analysis.*
- It increases the effectiveness of marketers' policies and helps them in developing better marketing strategies for the future.

QUESTIONS TO CHECK YOUR PROGRESS

Short Answer Questions

1. List out three reasons for marketers to study marketing environment.
2. Name the various elements of micro-environment.
3. List out the various macro level environmental variables.
4. Name two elements of demographic environment.
5. Which is the most influential primary reference group?
6. What is environmental scanning and analysis?

Long Answer Questions

1. Differentiate between micro and macro level environmental variables.
2. Describe the environmental forces that affect the company's ability to serve its customers.
3. "The Indian market is gradually becoming consumer oriented". Discuss.
4. Discuss how a company can react to the changes in the marketing environment.
5. Describe the features and implications of the impact of various types of environmental factors faced by a firm in marketing its products.
6. Discuss the internal and external factors influencing the marketing mix of a company.
7. What is micro-environment of marketing? Discuss the role of various factors that constitute the micro marketing environment of a firm.
8. Explain how a marketing manager might use competitor analysis to avoid situations that involve head-on competition.
9. Give some examples of how the changing role of women has been reflected in the marketers' policies.
10. What are some of the marketing implications of the increasing public interest in health and physical fitness?
11. Explain how a firm's marketing system can be influenced by the environmental factors of technology.

12. "Every change in government regulatory environment creates adjustment problems for the marketers". Explain with suitable examples.
13. Explain the major marketing challenges facing Indian business and industry in the context of the liberal economic policy pursued by the government and suggest measures as to how to tackle them.
14. Discuss the impact of changes in economic and technological environment on the marketing mix of a consumer good company.
15. Why does a marketing manager need to study marketing environment, when he can do little to control or influence it? Briefly describe the major elements of marketing environment in India.
16. Discuss some of the socio-cultural trends prevailing in India which are likely to affect the marketing policies and operations of Indian business firms in the years ahead.
17. "Every change in the politico-legal environment creates an adjustment problem for the marketers". Explain this statement.
18. Why is it necessary to scan marketing environment? What are the various controllable and uncontrollable marketing environment variables?
19. How has the changing role of women affected the marketers of food stuff in India? Explain with suitable examples.
20. It has been said that the single most important demographic trend in India is going to be the significant percentage of population in the youth segment in the years to come. Take these three industries—automobile/computers/mobile phones, and suggest specific strategies that would help these industries being successful with this changing demographic profile.
21. How will the following demographic changes affect marketers?
    (i) An increase in the elderly population
    (ii) An increase in the working women in population
    (iii) Increasing influence of children in the family's purchase decision
    (iv) Growing health consciousness amongst people
    (v) High rate of inflation in the economy

CHAPTER 3

Marketing Information Systems and Marketing Research

Learning Outcomes

After studying this chapter, you will be able to:

- ❖ Understand the concept and significance of marketing information systems (MIS)
- ❖ Define the major components of MIS
- ❖ Explain the marketing intelligence systems
- ❖ Identify the steps to improve the marketing intelligence
- ❖ Determine the marketing research systems
- ❖ Discuss the steps in conducting marketing research
- ❖ Express the barriers to effective marketing research

To manage a business well is to manage its future and to manage the future is to manage information. As we have been saying that marketers should be future oriented and they should have the ability to anticipate changes taking place in the marketing environment. Lots of micro and macro level environmental variables as discussed already have their impact on the marketer's decisions. In order to keep pace with these environmental changes, it is important for the marketers to forecast the direction and intensity of these changes and adjust their strategic marketing planning in line with these changes. To do all this, management needs information–effectively managed information.

Many a times, marketers are not able to handle a particular situation well or are not able to make the most of the opportunities that come in their way simply because they could not have access to the right information at the right time. It is not only important to have the critical information, making it available to the concerned person at the right time is equally important to ensure its execution. Just as lack of information is a problem for marketers, so many times lots of irrelevant information can pose a bigger problem. Getting important information too late or having doubts about the accuracy of the information can be some more problems which come in the way of managing the information flows in the organisation accurately and precisely. Thus, it can be put forward that in today's information-based societies, companies with access to appropriate information enjoy a competitive advantage. They can formulate better marketing strategies and design better product offerings than their competitors. Hence, it is indispensable for organisations to ensure a smooth flow of information to all their marketing managers.

3.1 REASONS FOR MANAGING INFORMATION

Management has devoted most of its attention to managing money, material, machine and men, but the fifth critical resource of the firm—information was ignored for long time. But these days it is essential for marketers to pay serious attention to the information aspect because of the following reasons:

- Complexity of marketing decisions;
- Shifts in consumer preferences from local to national and international products;
- From buyers' needs to buyers' wants;
- Increased awareness and consciousness amongst the customers;
- Intensified competition in the marketplace; and
- An active participation and intervention by government.

Thus, MIS is the major tool used by marketing management to aid in problem-solving and decision-making, and marketing research is a major component in MIS. In simple words, a *marketing information system (MIS)* can be defined as *a structure within an organisation designed to gather, process and store data from the organisation's external and internal environment and to disseminate this in the form of productive information to the organisation's marketing decision makers in time.*

According to Philip Kotler (2011)—

> *A marketing information system (MIS) is a continuing and interacting structure of people, equipment, and procedures to gather, sort, analyse, evaluate, and distribute needed, timely, and accurate information to marketing decision-makers to improve their marketing planning, implementation and control.*

It is quite clear from the definition given that an efficient marketing information system ensures that all the people, equipment and procedures are put together to work in a coordinated manner so that the right amount of information, rightly sorted out, analysed and evaluated is made available to the right person at the right time in order to facilitate the right decision. The information is developed through internal report systems, marketing intelligence activities, marketing models, and marketing research systems. Figure 3.1 illustrates the major components of an MIS, the influence of various environmental factors on the activities of MIS and the types of marketing decisions made through MIS.

The explanation of this model of an MIS begins with a description of each of its four major constituent parts—the internal reporting system, marketing research system, marketing intelligence system and marketing models.

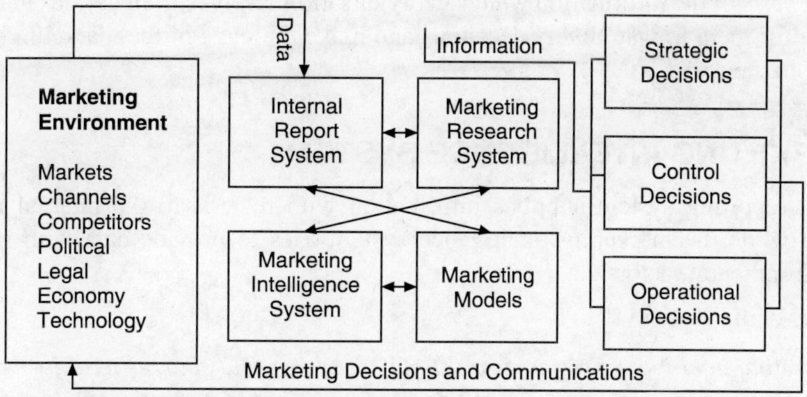

Figure 3.1 The marketing information systems and its subsystems.

3.2 INTERNAL REPORTING SYSTEMS

Internal reporting system is one of the basic sources of information. Before moving out and collecting information from outside sources, it is always important to first look at the internal reports on orders, sales, prices, costs, inventory levels, receivables, payables, and such other documents in order to arrive at effective marketing decisions. By carefully examining all these reports, the marketing managers can identify their problems and important opportunities. Some of the commonly referred internal records are listed as under—

3.2.1 The Order-to-Payment Cycle

The order-to-payment cycle represents the efficiency with which the orders received by the organisation from customers are processed and timely deliveries are ensured to them. Customers always prefer those organisations that can promise timely delivery. In order to ensure the timely delivery there has to be an effective coordination and integration between the activities of the sales representatives or dealers who dispatch orders to the firms and the sales department which prepares invoices, coordinates with the production department and ensures speedy delivery of the goods. The sales department should always keep a close check on the inventory levels and ensure proper shipping and billing procedures with the help of various computerised systems. The efficiency with which all these operations are being handled depends to a large extent on the smooth flow of information at various levels.

3.2.2 Sales Information Systems

In order to increase the market share and win over the competitors it is very important for the marketing managers to have timely information about the current and the anticipated level of sales for the organisation. These days, with the help of laptop computers and mobile data cards, it is possible for the sales representative to stay in touch with the management, have immediate access to information about prospects and customers, and provide instant feedback and sales reports to them.

On the basis of the information which an organisation receives from various internal sources, it is possible for them to take timely decisions and make the most of the marketing opportunities which come in their way.

3.3 MARKETING INTELLIGENCE SYSTEM

The internal reporting system supplies information with regards to the internal affairs of the organisation while the marketing intelligence system tries to provide data with regards to the various environmental factors.

According to Philip Kotler (2011)—

> *A marketing intelligence system is a set of procedures and sources used by managers to obtain everyday information about developments in the marketing environment.*

Marketing managers collect marketing intelligence by reading books, newspapers, trade publications, talking to customers, suppliers and distributors, and meeting with other company managers.

Steps to Improve the Quality of Marketing Intelligence

A company can take several steps to improve the quality of its marketing intelligence. Some of the important ones are highlighted in Figure 3.2.

Figure 3.2 Steps to improve the quality of marketing intelligence.

3.3.1 Train and Motivate Sales Force

Sales representatives are the company's 'eyes and ears' as they are in regular touch with customers, dealers, distributors and competitors. They can keep track of the various developments in the environmental factors. Thus, they need to be properly trained and motivated so that they should fulfil their basic responsibility of keeping their eyes and ears wide open, notice all the developments, collect all the information and report it to the concerned managers immediately.

3.3.2 Motivate Dealers and Distributors

The company can motivate dealers, distributors, retailers and other intermediaries through various incentives to pass on the first-hand information regarding the consumer's and competitor's response as they are in direct touch with them.

3.3.3 Gather Knowledge about Competitor's Moves

A company can work out a marketing strategy better than their competitors by closely observing them and keeping a check over their activities. They can learn about competitors by purchasing their products, reading their published reports, attending stockholders meetings, talking to their employees, dealers, distributors and suppliers, and going through their ads.

3.3.4 Collect Customer's Feedback

A company can set up a customer complaint cell or a suggestion box and invite their views about the company and the competitor's products. Their senior management should regularly get in touch with the company's largest customers or their most regular and loyal customers and collect their feedback about companies performance. The company gains valuable information about customer needs and the customers feel more bonded to a company that listens closely to their comments.

3.3.5 Purchase Information

The company can purchase information from outside suppliers such as various Audit Bureau of Information, specialised ad agencies or market research organisations. The research firms gather and store data regarding the market trends and changing consumer preferences.

3.3.6 Establish a Marketing Information Centre

Some companies have even established a marketing information centre to collect and circulate market intelligence information.

3.4 MARKETING MODELS

After collecting the information with the help of internal record system and market intelligence system, it becomes important to process that information with the help of various marketing models to draw meaningful interpretations out of it. Some commonly used marketing models are:

- Time series
- Sales models
- Brand switching models
- Linear programming
- Elasticity models (price, incomes, demand, supply, etc.)
- Regression and correlation models
- Analysis of Variance (ANOVA) models
- Sensitivity analysis
- Discounted cash flow models

These mathematical, statistical, econometric and financial models are the indispensable part of the MIS because only they can help to process the otherwise rough data, analyse it properly and draw meaningful conclusions from it. These days we can take the help of various computer software programmes like SPSS to execute these models effectively. A relatively modest investment in a desktop computer is enough to allow an enterprise to automate the analysis of its data.

3.5 MARKETING RESEARCH SYSTEM

Marketing research serves marketing management by providing information which is relevant to decision making. It helps to reduce the uncertainty surrounding the decisions to be made by making systematic, objective and pertinent information available to the concerned person through effective marketing research. Market researchers conduct market surveys, interview people, gather their responses and analyse the information gathered in order to find out the product performance in the market, changing marketing trends, competitors strategies, or the advertising effectiveness.

According to Philip Kotler (2011)—

> *Marketing research is the systematic design, collection, analysis, and reporting of data and findings relevant to a specific marketing situation facing the company.*

Green and Tull (1978) have defined marketing research as follows—

> *Marketing research is the systematic and objective search for, and analysis of, information relevant to the identification and solution of any problem in the field of marketing.*

From both the definitions, it can be gathered that the basic objectives of conducting a marketing research is to collect relevant information, analyse it, interpret it and provide it to the concerned marketing personnel to help them provide solutions to their problems. Some of the common problems addressed by market research are listed as under:

- Determination of market characteristics
- Measurement of market potential
- Market share analysis
- Sales analysis
- Studies of business trends
- Short range forecasting
- New product acceptance and potential
- Pricing studies
- Long-range forecasting
- Competitive product studies

3.5.1 Designing the Market Research Brief or Design

Marketing research can be conducted for any of the purposes listed above. Since the researcher cannot investigate everything about a market, he/she must be selective. It is very important for them to understand as to which specific aspect and with what dimensions they would like to study. Therefore, before the research begins, researchers are given the outline regarding the research objectives, methodology, guidelines, resource allocation and the time frame through a document called *research brief*. The brief must inform the researcher as to what aspects of the market are particularly important to be covered.

Thus, once the clarity is attained about the purpose of research, the marketing research team sets the objectives clearly, to be achieved within a specific time period. This is from where the actual process of conducting the market research begins, but identifying the various suppliers of information for conducting research is the first and the foremost important activity before all other activities of research process start.

3.5.2 Suppliers of Marketing Research

A company can conduct marketing research in a number of ways. Most large companies have their own marketing research departments. These departments provide information on industries, markets and competitors with the help of regular research and information services. Small companies can hire the services of a marketing research firm or conduct research in creative and affordable ways, such as, engaging students or professionals to design and carry out projects, using Internet or checking out competitors.

3.5.3 The Marketing Research Process

As discussed earlier, marketing research is undertaken to understand a marketing problem better and find a viable solution to it. In order to carry out an effective marketing research, it involves six steps as depicted in Figure 3.3.

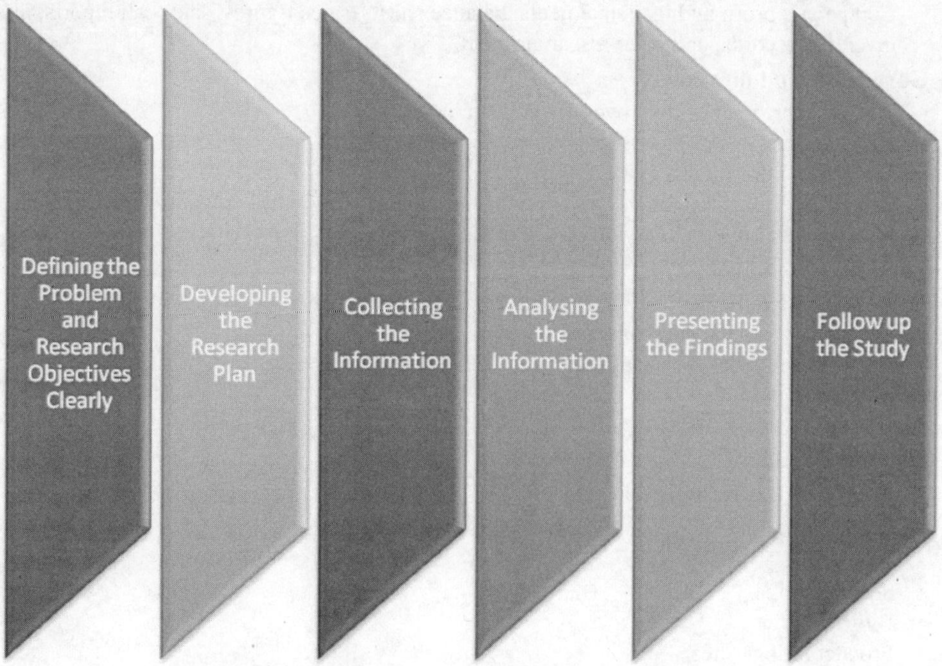

Figure 3.3 Steps in marketing research process.

Step 1: Define the Problem and Research Objectives Clearly

A market researcher must have a clear idea about the problem and the objectives to be achieved. It is often said that a problem well-defined is half solved and at times it is even more important to identify whether the firm actually has a problem. Therefore, it becomes very important for marketers to define a problem clearly and precisely, and go down to the root of the problem in order to arrive at the best possible solutions.

Step 2: Develop the Research Plan

The second stage of marketing research calls for developing the most efficient and economical plan for gathering the needed information. It is important for them to analyse whether the cost incurred is going to be worth the effort or not. Designing a research plan calls for decisions on the data sources, research approaches, research instruments, sampling plan and contact methods.

1. Data sources: The researchers can gather information through secondary as well as primary data, or both. Secondary data are data that were collected for another purpose or by another person and already exist somewhere, while primary data are data gathered for a specific purpose or for a specific research project.

(a) *Secondary data*. Researchers usually start their investigation by examining secondary data to see whether the problem can be partly or wholly solved without collecting costly primary data. It provides a starting point for research and offers the advantages of low cost and ready availability. Information can also be gathered from various secondary data sources as mentioned in Table 3.1.

Table 3.1 Secondary Sources of Data-Collection

A. Internal sources

- Company's profit and loss statements, balance sheets, sales figures, sales call reports, invoices, inventory records, and prior research reports.

B. Government publications

- Statistical abstract of the government of India
- Industry data
- Marketing information guide
- Other government publications include the annual surveys of government, Census reports, reserve bank bulletin and vital statistics reports.

C. Periodicals and books

- Business periodicals
- Technical journals and magazines
- Encyclopaedias of associations
- Marketing journals
- General business magazines like business world business today the Economist etc.

D. Commercial data

- Audit Bureau of Circulation data, etc.

E. Internet

- Web sites
- Search engines
- Blogs
- Product ratings sites
- Podcasts and other digital platforms

(b) *Primary data.* When it is not possible for researchers to collect the required information through secondary sources, or information available is outdated, inaccurate, incomplete, or unreliable, the researcher will have to rely on primary data. Most marketing research projects involve some primary data collection. The normal procedure is to interview some people individually, or in groups, and gather their view point on the subject in question and then develop a formal research instrument or a questionnaire. After that a survey is conducted and the researcher gets the questionnaire filled by the respondents and collects the data. This data is later compiled, analysed, interpreted and stored for further references.

2. Research approaches: In order to collect the primary data, the researcher can take the help of any of the five methods—observation, focus groups, surveys, behavioural data, and experiments as depicted in Figure 3.4.

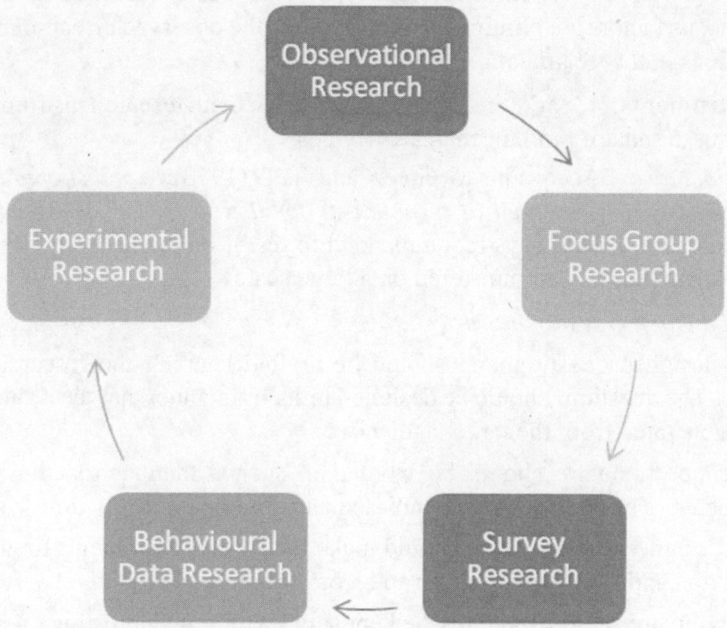

Figure 3.4 Various research approaches.

(a) *Observational research.* In this method, the researcher simply observes the behaviour of the respondents and makes a note of the information gathered.

(b) *Focus group research.* This method is used to collect information from a target group of audience, who are invited to discuss with each other and give their views about a product, service, idea, or any other preposition. They are left free to discuss at length whatever they want to regarding the issue being discussed. The research is coordinated by a moderator, whose job is simply to observe and note the proceedings. He will intervene only to ensure that the discussion goes on uninterrupted and everyone gets a chance to speak and give their observation. The discussion, recorded through note taking or on audiotape or videotape, is subsequently studied to understand consumer beliefs, attitudes, and behaviour.

(c) *Survey research.* Surveys are the best method for descriptive research. Companies undertake surveys to learn about people's knowledge, beliefs, preferences and satisfaction about their product or services. In surveys the information is collected by getting the questionnaires filled by respondents.

(d) *Behavioural data research.* Customer's actual purchases are better indicators of their preferences and often are more reliable than the verbal statements they offer to market researchers. Some of the companies try to trace customer's purchase behaviour in retail stores and draw meaningful conclusions out of it by closely observing them.

(e) *Experimental research.* It is the most scientifically valid research. The purpose of experimental research is to find out the cause-and-effect relationships by conducting the research in a controlled environment. It calls for inviting a target group of audience and subjecting them to different treatments, controlling extraneous variables and checking whether observed response differences are statistically significant. To the extent that extraneous factors are eliminated or controlled, the observed effects can be related to the variations in the treatment.

3. Research instruments: Marketing researchers use two main research instruments in collecting primary data—questionnaires and mechanical devices.

(a) *Questionnaires.* According to Green and Tull (1978), *a questionnaire consists of a set of questions presented to respondents for their answers.* Before designing a final questionnaire, it is always recommended to test it on a small representative audience. Once approved, it is administered on a large scale.

The Qualities of a Good Questionnaire

- A well-designed questionnaire should be drafted keeping the research objectives into account. The questions should be designed in such a manner that the right kind of response can be generated from the target audience.
- A good questionnaire should be worded in such a manner that it should encourage respondents to provide accurate, unbiased and complete information.
- A well-designed questionnaire should make it easy for respondents to give the necessary information and for the interviewer to record the answer properly.
- A questionnaire should generally be kept small with few interesting questions so that the respondent's interest can be retained and they should answer them honestly.

Preliminary Decisions in Questionnaire Design

There are nine steps involved in the development of a questionnaire:

- Decide the information required clearly
- Define the target respondents precisely
- Choose the method(s) of reaching your target respondents carefully
- Decide on question content
- Develop the question wording
- Put questions into a meaningful order and format
- Check the length of the questionnaire

- Pre-test the questionnaire
- Develop the final survey form

While designing the questions for the questionnaire, the marketing researchers have to be very careful regarding their form, wording and sequence. There can be various types of questions asked to the respondents as projected in Figure 3.5.

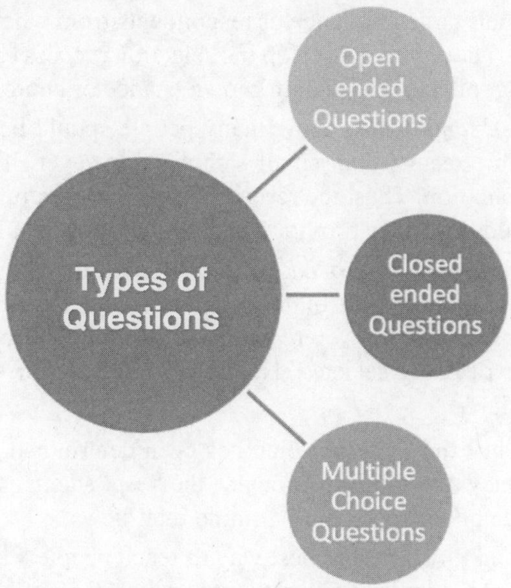

Figure 3.5 Types of questions.

(i) **Open-end questions.** These questions give respondents a liberty to answer in their own words and give whatever response they want to on a particular question. These questions often reveal more because the respondents are not constrained by a specific answer. Open-end questions are especially useful in exploratory research, where the researcher is looking for insight into how people think.

(ii) **Closed-end questions.** These questions specify all the possible answers and expect the respondents to pick and choose any one of the options provided to them. These questions provide answers that are easier to interpret and tabulate.

(iii) **Multiple choice questions.** In these questions, respondents are provided with a variety of options for a question and they are expected to select one best option out of those given.

Finally, the questionnaire should be kept simple, direct, easily worded and should be pretested with a sample of respondents. The lead question should attempt to create interest. Difficult or personal questions should be asked toward the end so that respondents do not become defensive early. To conclude, the questions should flow in a logical order.

(b) *Mechanical instruments*. Various mechanical devices are occasionally used in marketing research to measure the consumer's response, such as, Galvanometer to measure the interest or emotions aroused by exposure to a specific ad or picture, Eye movement cameras to study the respondent's eye movements to see where their eyes landed first, how long they linger on a given item, and so on. An audio meter is attached to television sets in participating homes to record when the set is switched on and to which channel it is tuned.

4. Sampling plan: According to Green and Tull (1978), while working out the sampling plan, a researcher has to make three important decisions, which are explained as under:

(a) *Decide about the sampling unit.* Who is to be surveyed? The market researchers must be clear about their target audience or respondents from whom they are going to collect the information. They should develop the selection process carefully so that everyone in the target population has an equal or known chance of being sampled.

(b) *Decide about the sample size.* How many people should be surveyed? Large samples give more reliable results than small samples. However, it is not easy to sample the entire target population. Thus, the researchers have to carefully decide about the sample size which should be able to provide them with reliable results.

(c) *Decide about the sampling procedure.* How should the respondents be chosen? While choosing the respondents out of the population, researchers generally make use of random sampling procedure, where each and every individual in the population stands an equal chance of being selected. However, the randomness has to be ensured in the selection procedure.

5. Contact methods: Once the sampling plan has been determined, the marketing researchers must decide as to how they are going to contact the respondents. Generally respondents are contacted through mail, telephone, personal or online interviews.

(a) *The mail questionnaire.* It is the best way to reach people who would not give personal interviews or whose responses might be biased or distorted by the interviewers. These questionnaires require simple and clearly worded questions, which should be easily understandable by the respondents.

(b) *Telephone interviewing.* This is the best method for gathering information quickly. The interviewer is also able to clarify questions if respondents do not understand them. The response rate is typically higher than in the case of mail questionnaires. The main drawback is that the interviews have to be short and not too personal.

(c) *Personal interviewing.* It is the most versatile method. The interviewer can ask more questions and record additional observations about the respondent by judging their body language. Personal interviewing is the most expensive method and requires more administrative planning and supervision than the other three. It is also subject to interviewer bias or distortion.

(d) *Online interviewing.* In this case, a company can include a questionnaire at its webpage and offer an incentive to answer the questions. Those people who do not use Internet or who don't want to answer a questionnaire can bias the results.

Step 3: Collect the Information

After designing the questionnaire, selecting the sample size, identifying the respondents and choosing the contact methods, the researcher's job is to go to the field and collect the data. This is one of the most difficult stages as most of the respondents refuse to cooperate with the researcher and give the information asked for. Some of them do not give true and accurate information, while others might not be willing to part with their personal details. Despite these problems, data collection methods are improving these days because researchers are able to take the help of computers, internet, telecommunications, etc. With the help of these technological innovations it is comparatively easier to collect the information from the respondents.

Step 4: Analyse the Information

The next step in the marketing research process is to draw meaningful inferences from the collected data. The researchers will have to tabulate the data and develop frequency distributions. Then, with the help of various statistical methods, such as, averages, measures of dispersion, etc., researchers would like to find out the cause and effect relationship existing between the various variables.

Step 5: Present the Findings

As this stage, the researcher presents the relevant findings to the concerned person in the required format. Findings are to be presented in a manner which is easily understandable by the concerned marketing executive so that they should be able to take speedy action on those findings and make the most of it.

Step 6: Follow-up Study

After submitting the findings to the concerned person it is important for the researchers to determine whether their recommendations are being followed or not. Unless there is a follow-up, the company people may not pay much attention to the report submitted. It may be filled and forgotten and the entire effort of the market research team can go waste.

Thus, to conclude the above discussion, it can be said that the researcher has to go through all the steps carefully in order to arrive at meaningful inferences from raw data and help the management solve various problems effectively.

3.5.4 Barriers to Effective Marketing Research

Despite the rapid growth of techniques and technologies in marketing research, many companies still fail to use it sufficiently or correctly because of several reasons. Some of the important barriers to effective market research are listed as under:

1. Inefficient marketing researchers: The effectiveness with which the research is conducted and the findings arrived after the research, depends to a large extent on the competency of the market researchers. Less competent market researchers are generally hired and because of their weak training and deficient creativity, they are not able to arrive at impressive results, so in that case the whole exercise of marketing research turns out to be a futile exercise.

2. Late submission of findings by marketing research: Most of the time it has been observed that the marketing researchers fail to submit the information at the right time to the concerned person. Thus, in that case again, the whole purpose of conducting the research is not served.

3. Lack of clarity regarding the research objectives: Most of the time the entire exercise of conducting the research goes waste because the researchers are not clear about the basic objective of conducting the research. They often design a questionnaire, choose a sample, conduct interviews, and report results, often without even carefully understanding the basic problem.

4. Presentational differences: There can be difference of presentational style between the line managers and the market researchers. At times, the final report submitted by the researcher is not very well appreciated and clearly understood by the line managers, resulting in confusion and chaos.

To sum up, it can be said that marketing research is an essential activity used by organisations these days for effective decision-making purposes. It helps the management to understand where they stand in the industry and what industry trends are likely to be in the future. It also helps in appraising and improving sales force management by measuring variations in territorial sales yield, market share and an analysis of salesman's activities. It even helps the management to stand the competition prevailing in the markets effectively and achieve the various marketing objectives successfully.

LET US SUM UP

- To manage a business well is to manage its future and to manage the future is to manage information.
- A marketing information system (MIS) can be defined as a structure within an organisation designed to gather, process and store data from the organisation's external and internal environment and to disseminate this in the form of productive information to the organisation's marketing decision makers in time.
- The information is developed through internal report systems, marketing intelligence activities, marketing models and marketing research systems.
- Marketing managers rely on internal reports on orders, sales, prices, costs, inventory levels, receivables, payables, and such other documents for deciding about important marketing issues.
- A marketing intelligence system is a set of procedures and sources used by managers to obtain everyday information about developments in the marketing environment.
- Various mathematical, statistical, econometric and financial models are the analytical subsystems of the MIS which is used to analyse and interpret the data.
- Marketing research is undertaken to understand a marketing problem better and find a viable solution to it.
- Effective marketing research involves six steps—defining the problem and research objectives clearly, developing the research plan, collecting the information, analysing the information, presenting the findings and conducting follow-up study.
- A market researcher must have a clear idea about the problem and the objectives to be achieved.
- The second stage of marketing research calls for developing the most efficient plan for gathering the needed information. It calls for decisions on the data sources, research approaches, research instruments, sampling plan and contact methods.
- The questionnaire is the most common instrument used to collect primary data. It consists of a set of questions presented to respondents for their answers.
- Data collection phase of marketing research is generally the most difficult phase and is prone to errors.
- The next step in the marketing research process is to extract meaningful findings or inferences from the collected data.
- At the next stage, the researcher presents the findings to the relevant parties.
- After submitting the findings to the concerned person, it is important for the researchers to determine whether their recommendations are being followed or not.
- Finally, it can be said the researcher has to go through all the steps carefully in order to arrive at meaningful inferences from raw data and help the management solve various problems effectively.

QUESTIONS TO CHECK YOUR PROGRESS

Short Answer Questions

1. What is marketing information system?
2. Name the three key words used in the definition of marketing research by Green and Tull.
3. Define the term 'hypothesis'.
4. List out the four basic constituents of MIS.
5. Define marketing intelligence system.
6. How is marketing research system a very important constituent of MIS?
7. List out the various stages in the marketing research process.
8. What are the main items of information which should be included in a research brief?
9. What are the various sources of collecting data?
10. Name the three advantages of open-ended questions.
11. Define experimental research.
12. What is a questionnaire?
13. What are the various types of questions included in the questionnaire?
14. Differentiate between mail interviews and personal interviews.

Long Answer Questions

1. Define marketing information systems. How is it different from marketing research?
2. What is marketing intelligence system? What are the various steps to improve the quality of its marketing intelligence?
3. Enunciate the objectives of marketing research. What benefits can be achieved by conducting marketing research?
4. Describe the nature and significance of marketing research in modern business. How will you conduct market research for a company?
5. Discuss the various sources of data for conducting marketing research.
6. It has often been said that one does not start by writing questions. How should the researcher begin?
7. Explain the various types of research approaches with examples.
8. What is a questionnaire and what are the primary requirements for designing an effective questionnaire?
9. Summarise the qualities of a good questionnaire.
10. What are the various barriers to effective marketing research?
11. Write short notes on:
    (a) marketing research versus marketing information system
    (b) primary data collection
    (c) survey research

CHAPTER 4

Consumer Buying Behaviour

Learning Outcomes

After studying this chapter, you will be able to:

- Define the concept and significance of consumer buying behaviour
- Understand the stimulus and response model
- Express the major factors influencing consumer's buying behaviour
- Explain the various stages in the consumer's buying decision process
- Illustrate the consumer's buying behaviour models

Consumer is the most important entity in every business. The success or failure of any organisation depends, to a very large extent, on the effectiveness with which they are able to entertain their present and potential customers. The concept of consumer's sovereignty has been there for long, but in today's scenario, where there is cutthroat competition in the market, keeping the customer satisfied is one of the prerequisites for every marketer to survive. Thus, for every marketer, the aim of marketing is to meet and satisfy the customers' needs and wants. But 'knowing customers' is never simple. They vary tremendously on the basis of age, income, perceptions, preferences, educational background, occupational status, culture and religion. Nevertheless, marketers must study their target customers' wants, perceptions, preferences, shopping and buying behaviour closely to position their product effectively in the market and increase their sales. According to Philip Kotler (1999)—

> *Consumer buying behaviour refers to the buying pattern of final consumers, individuals and households who buy goods and services for their personal consumption or for household usage.*

By now we have understood that different consumers purchase the same product for different reasons. Therefore, it becomes essential for marketers to understand the buying behaviour of consumers so that they should be able to position their products, services or ideas effectively in the market.

4.1 WHY SHOULD MARKETERS STUDY CONSUMER BUYING BEHAVIOUR

Positioning Guru Jack Trout (2000) called India 'The land of non-standard marketing' because according to him, for all the talk about the promise of the Indian market, it remains an extremely difficult challenge for companies that are mostly used to marketing strategies born in the West. It has been observed by him that marketing strategies that serve global markets efficiently often need to be modified or even prepared afresh to serve the Indian consumers' needs. As Indian markets are scale and volume-driven markets, marketers have to learn to communicate with masses and generate sales in bulk.

It is very much evident from Jack Trout's comment that Indian consumers are different in nature from their western counterparts and if marketers want to target their goods to them they have to study them closely, understand the differences in their perceptions and design their goods as well as their marketing strategies keeping those differences into account. Marketers need to study consumers' buying behaviour in order to ensure their survival in the market because if they will not do it their competitors will do it and will be able to win over the entire market share. The various reasons which make it important for marketers to study the buying behaviour are listed in Figure 4.1.

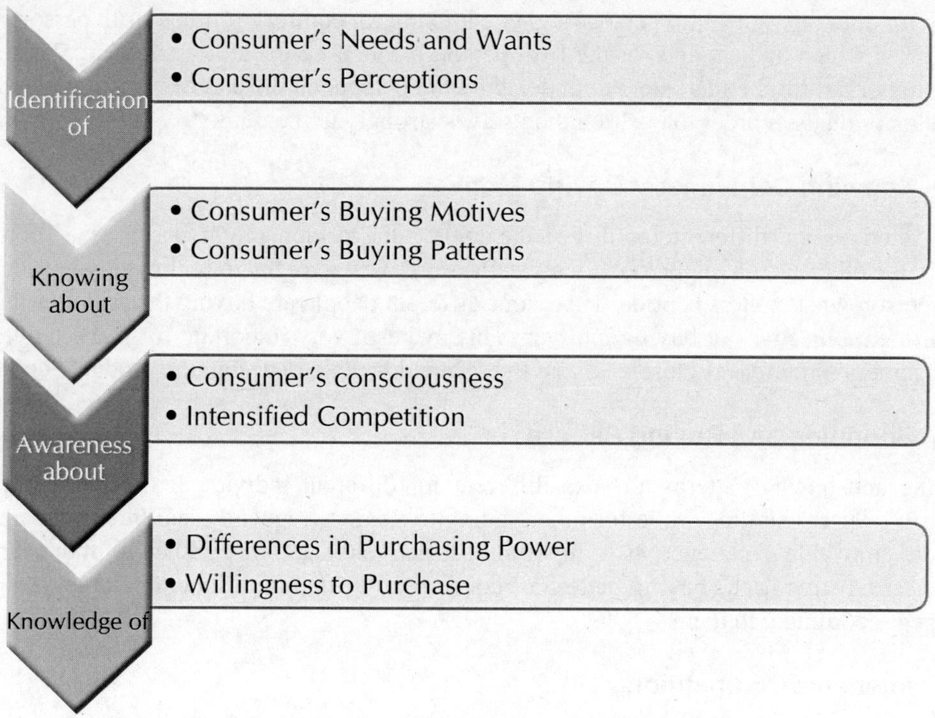

Figure 4.1 Reasons to study consumer buying behaviour.

4.1.1 Clear Cut Identification of Consumer Needs and Wants

Marketers must identify the needs and wants of the consumers clearly so that they can provide them with better products and services and also ensure constant upgradation. The more closely they will be able to relate their products to the consumer, the better it will be for them to win over their loyalty. For example, global fast food chain McDonald's typically maintains a menu that is 70 per cent original and 30 per cent local in all markets except in India, where the ratio is, just the opposite (original: 30 per cent; local: 70 per cent). McDonald's has adopted its menu to the Indian consumer's taste and preferences and has been able to achieve success.

4.1.2 Understanding Consumers' Perceptions

According to Philip Kotler (1999)—

> *Perception is the process by which an individual selects, organises, and interprets information to create a meaningful picture of the world.*

Perception is a mental process, it is a process through which an individual is able to relate the various stimuli which he/she receives from the environment and draw some meaningful inferences out of it. Different people perceive different situations differently, for example, a glass half full of water can be perceived by one as half full while the other person might look at it as half empty. In a similar manner, when it comes to targeting the goods to different consumer segments in the markets, it is important for marketers to understand as to how are they going to perceive their products because for some it might be the quality which is more important while others might be looking for durability, the third person might be looking for comfort, for the fourth person it might be the price which matters and for the fifth person it might be the style statement. Therefore, it is very important for the marketers to understand the perceptual differences existing between the various individuals in order to position themselves strongly in the market.

4.1.3 Knowing Consumers' Buying Motives

Buying motives are different for different people. One person might purchase a product for comfort, the other person might look for style, the third person might go for brand value and for the fourth person what matters is price. Thus, four different people are buying the same product with four different objectives or buying motives. This makes it very important for marketers to study the consumers' preferences closely so that they should be able to design the product accordingly.

4.1.4 Shopping and Buying Pattern

Shopping and buying patterns are also different for different individuals. Some people prefer buying in bulk at one time while for others going to market frequently and buying in small lots is a more enjoyable experience. It is important for marketers and middlemen to understand such differences existing in the buying pattern of consumers, so that they should be able to direct the messages accordingly to them.

4.1.5 Intensive Competition

The cutthroat competition prevailing in the market is one big reason as to why marketers need to study the consumers' buying behaviour. As these days a shift has taken place from the product orientation to consumer orientation, it will not be feasible for the marketers to try to sell whatever they make. If they do not give preference to the choice of the customers, their competitors will be able to take the market share away from them.

4.1.6 Awareness and Consciousness Amongst the Customers

Today the consumers are highly aware about various product options available to them as they have access to information from various media options. Moreover, they like to seek lots of information about the product before they make a final purchase decision. Thus, the marketers have to be prepared to handle all the queries beforehand so that they should be able to satisfy the consumer properly and win over their purchase decision.

4.1.7 Differences in Purchasing Power

We all know that no two individuals are alike, different individuals have different tastes and different purchasing power depending on various environmental factors. It becomes really important for marketers to know the income brackets of the people carefully so that they should be able to price their product appropriately and target them to the right segment. For example, keeping the Indian consumer into account, majority of the companies are selling their shampoos in single serve sachets, so that it falls into the purchasing power of majority of people.

4.1.8 Willingness to Spend

Earlier people used to be conservative in nature, they preferred saving a lot and spending little, while these days a new generation of consumers have come up which is more than keen to spend money and buy whatever new products are there in the market. Therefore, it is worthwhile for the marketers to know the consumer well and give them better products with better features and motivate them strongly to purchase the product and add on to their standard of living.

Finally, we can conclude that the amount of time, energy, and money spent by marketers on studying the consumers' buying behaviour is worth as the returns which they get from them far exceeds the effort put in by them.

4.2 A MODEL OF CONSUMER BUYING BEHAVIOUR

The starting point for understanding the buyer is the stimulus response theory given by Philip Kotler (1999) as shown in Figure 4.2.

According to the stimulus-response theory, consumer's learning occurs as a consumer responds to some stimulus by behaving in a particular way and is rewarded for a correct response or penalized for an incorrect one. Thus, a consumers' buying behaviour starts with the marketing stimuli's provided by marketers and ends with the important product decisions which give them utmost satisfaction. The consumer can buy only if a marketer first manufactures a product, prices it appropriately, places it right next door to the consumer and promotes it aggressively. Besides the marketing stimuli there are various environmental stimuli also which enter into the buyer's consciousness. The economic environment prevailing in the country sets their purchasing power. The technological factors determine the quantity of goods and services that can be made available to the consumers. The political stability in the economy determines the overall environment

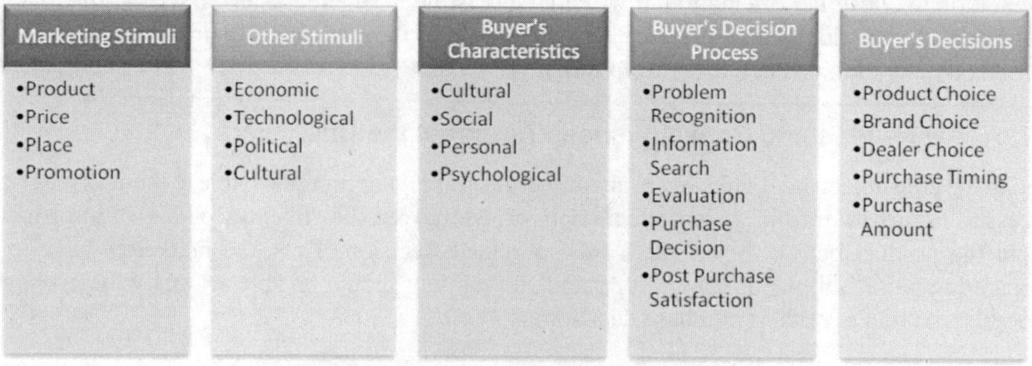

Figure 4.2 Stimulus response model.

for purchasing. The social and cultural factors of the country affect consumers' basic values, perceptions, preferences, and behaviours. Their relationship with themselves, with society, with nature and with the universe determines their buying pattern.

Besides these basic stimuli from outside, another set of factors affecting the consumer's buying behaviour are their own characteristics. There are various cultural, social, personal and psychological factors influencing consumers' purchase decisions. After being exposed to all these factors and variables, a consumer finally takes his own buying decision, where they have to go through various stages before finally arriving at the important product decisions. The product decisions can be regarding the choice of a product, a specific brand, a specific dealer, a decision about the purchase time, as well as the purchase amount. The stimulus response model given by Philip Kotler (1999) has very nicely summarised the entire buying behaviour of the consumers in a nutshell. In the following paragraphs we are going to discuss all these factors in detail.

4.3 MAJOR FACTORS INFLUENCING BUYING BEHAVIOUR

Major factors influencing buying behaviour can be broadly categorised into four categories: cultural, social, personal, and psychological. The various factors are depicted in Figure 4.3.

4.3.1 Cultural Factors

Cultural factors exert a deep influence on consumer behaviour. The marketer needs to understand the role played by the buyer's culture, subculture, and social class in their buying behaviour.

Culture

An individual's buying behaviour gets strongly influenced by his or her cultural background. *Culture* is the set of values, norms, ideas, and perceptions which are transmitted from one generation to other. The moment a child is born, he or she acquires a set of values, perceptions, preferences and behaviours through his or her family and other key institutions. Children growing up in different countries or with different religious backgrounds develop different set of values. Cultures do change over time, as old patterns gradually give way to the new.

For example, the cultural shift towards greater concern about health and fitness has created a huge industry in India for health and fitness services, exercise equipment, fitness clothing, and fat-free foods and nutritional diet supplements.

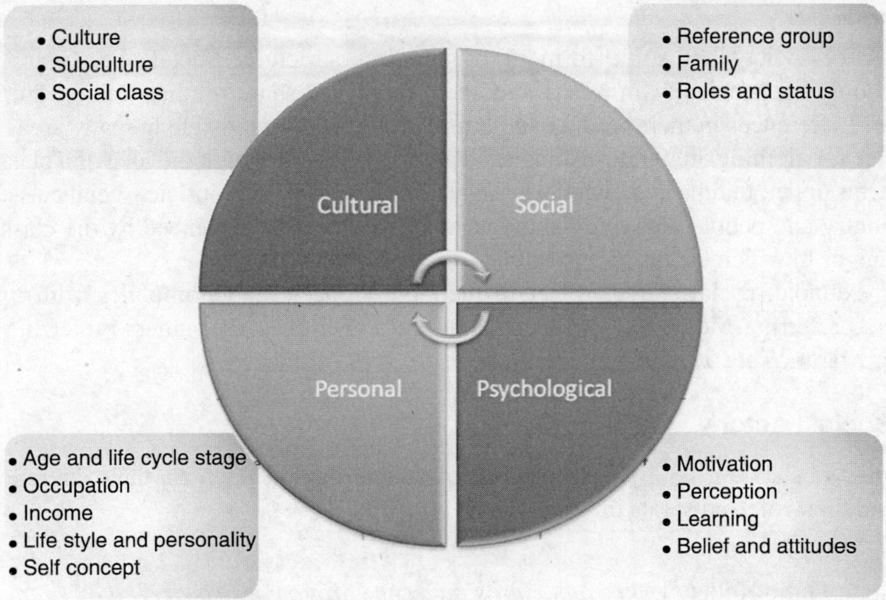

Figure 4.3 Factors influencing buyer's behaviour.

Another good example of a cultural shift which has taken place recently is the changing perception of mothers towards their children. The depiction of mothers in advertisements is changing from a 'caring mom' to a 'cool mom' and now to a mother who wants to stand by her child and make him learn to take the challenges in life. The recent Bournvita TV advertisement stands out significantly and reflects an emerging discourse in society. It not only takes the mother out of the realm of a kitchen and the dining table, it also shows how breaking the 'easy-to-give in mother' mould to become a strict goal-oriented trainer. Here is a mother who instead of making her child happy by losing, competes fiercely to make him understand the value of winning. The visual depiction of the mother also moves beyond the traditional to track pants and athletics swiftness. All this clearly reflects as to how changes in cultural perceptions affect the products and their projection in the mind of consumers.

Subculture

Subcultures are groups in a culture that exhibit characteristic behaviour pattern sufficient to distinguish them from other groups within the same culture. The behaviour patterns that distinguish subcultures are based on factors such as, nationalities, religions, racial groups, and geographical regions. India is a huge country divided into various geographical regions. The preferences of people in northern India are different from those in the southern India. Because a huge population resides in both the zones, it becomes significant for marketers to keep these changes into account and design goods exclusively for people living in those areas. For example, in case of a basic product like coffee, people in North India like the sweeter taste of coffee while people down south prefer the bitter taste of coffee. Thus, all the coffee manufacturing companies are trying to provide different variants in coffee in order to suit the preferences of people from different geographical regions.

Social Classes

Almost every society has some form of social class structure. Social classes are relatively homogeneous, hierarchically ordered, and their members share similar values, interests and behaviour. Differences in their product and brand preferences are visible in many areas including their choice for clothing, home furnishings and automobiles. Although the idea of a class structure and the terms upper, middle and lower class may not sound very appropriate, social classes do exist in our country and people's buying behaviour is often strongly influenced by the class to which they belong or to which they aspire to belong.

For example, social classes differ in their preferences for automobiles with upper class consumers preferring Mercedes, BMW or Audi and lower class consumers preferring the basic models of Maruti, Tata, Hyundai, and Honda.

4.3.2 Social Factors

A consumer's behaviour is influenced by various social factors such as, their reference groups, family, and their role and status in society.

Reference Groups

According to Philip Kotler (1999), *a person's reference group consists of all the groups that have a direct or indirect influence on the person's attitude or behaviour*. There are various types of membership groups having an influence on the consumer's buying behaviour, such as, primary groups, comprising of one's family, friends, neighbours and colleagues with whom the person interacts on a regular and informal basis. The other influential group is the secondary group which are defined as religious, professional and trade union group which tends to be more formal and require less continuous interaction. These reference groups influence the buyer's behaviour to a large extent as they create a certain pressure on them to conform to their norms, values, perceptions and lifestyle, and people adhere to such norms because of the fear of losing the membership of the group.

Family

Family is the most basic unit of a society. It is the most important reference group of two or more people related by blood, marriage, or adoption living together in a household. Most of us in the course of our life belong to at least two families—the one into which we are born and the one we acquire at marriage. The family of orientation is the one into which we are born. It consists primarily of our parents and siblings. From this family, we acquire the core values and attitudes towards religion, politics, and economics. The family of procreation—namely our spouse and children, in contrast, has a more direct influence on our specific purchases. Examples include the increasing influence of women in the household and the emerging role of children in the family's purchase decision. It is very important for marketers to understand these influences as they have to learn to target goods to them to find an easy transition into the families buying pattern.

For example, when it comes to buying a car for the family, every member in the family plays an important role. Even children come up with their specific preferences regarding the brand or the colour of the car. For marketers it is very important to understand as to whom they are going to target their product to in their advertisements.

The Role of Family

The role of family has been very nicely depicted in the recent advertisements of KurKure, a snack item, where with the introduction of the new Kurkure family, the brand is trying to establish its Indian roots again. Last year PepsiCo brought on board five new brand ambassadors. A list that includes actors Parineeti Chopra, Boman Irani, Farida Jalal and Kunal Kapoor, among others. This new family (taking over from actress Juhi Chawla) will introduce Indian consumers to new variants of Kurkure. According to Vidur Vyas, Marketing Director–foods, PepsiCo India, it was time to refresh the snack brand's identity. *The snack category has grown exponentially over the past few years. Different consumers have varied snacking needs and we will introduce more products, flavours and packs, covering everything from bite experience to packaging and eventually create occasions of consumption. With this campaign we are on our way to create a Kurkure umbrella brand.*

The campaign began with one simple brief *Tedha Hai Par Mera Hai*, a tagline that has been around for a while now, since 2008 to be precise. *We were particular about just one thing—it had to be a family*, says Vyas. The Kurkure bunch may not be a mirror image of the average soap family; it is however a caricature of the modern Indian family and its changing dynamics, a modern twist on tradition

Source: The Brand Equity, the Economic Times, September 9th 2011.

Questions for Discussion

1. Explain the significance of the role of family in an individual's buying patterns.
2. "PepsiCo's strategy of focusing on family values has helped their brand to perform better in the market". Do you agree with the statement?

Roles and Status in the Society

The role and status enjoyed by a person in the society get reflected in the kind of lifestyle they enjoy, goods they own, and the way they project themselves to the outside world. As discussed in the previous points, an individual is a member of various groups and organisations, their position in each group gets reflected by the role and status enjoyed by them and it strongly influences their buying behaviour. It has been rightly said that the decor of the office of an executive clearly reflects the role and status of that executive to the organisation. People choose products that clearly reflect their status in the society.

For example, the company president often drives a Mercedes, wears expensive suits, and keeps designer goods. Marketers are aware of the status symbol potential of products and brands.

4.3.3 Personal Factors

A buyer's purchase decision is also influenced by personal characteristics. These include the buyer's age and stage in the life cycle, occupation, economic circumstances, lifestyle, personality and self-concept.

Age and Stage in the Life Cycle

The buying behaviour of consumers is determined strongly by their age-group and the life cycle stage (as depicted in Table 4.1) they are going through. For example, the buying preferences regarding cloths, accessories and recreation of children are going to be different than young people and mature people. Hence, it becomes important for marketers to understand such age related differences as it helps them in segmenting the marketing accordingly and positioning the product therein. Buying is also shaped by the stage of the family life cycle, as has been given to us by William D. Wells and George Gubar (1966) and depicted in Table 4.1. It lists out nine stages of the family life cycle along with their financial situation and typical product interest in each group. Marketers often define their target markets in terms of the life cycle stage and develop appropriate products and marketing plans for each stage.

For example, children's products are targeted to all young parents.

Table 4.1 Stages in Family Life Cycle Buying or Behavioural Pattern

Bachelor's stage—young; Single; Not living at home.	Few financial burdens; Fashion opinion leaders; Recreation oriented; Buy basic home equipments, furniture, cars, vacations.
Newly married couple—young; No children.	Highest purchase rate and highest average purchase of durables—cars, appliances, furniture, vacations.
Full nest I—youngest child under six.	Home purchasing at peak; Liquid assets low; Interested in new products, advertised products. Buy—washing machines, television, baby food, baby medicines and toys.
Full nest II—youngest child six or over.	Financial position better; Less influenced by advertising; Buy larger size packages, multiple-units deals; Buy many food items, bicycles, music lessons, etc.
Full nest III—older married couples with dependent children.	Financial position still better; Some children get jobs; Hard to influence with advertising; High average purchase of durables—new improved furniture, luxury cars, unnecessary appliances, dental services, magazines.
Empty nest I—older married couples; No children living with them; Head of household in labour force.	Most satisfied with financial position and money saved; Interested in travel, recreation, self education; Make gifts and contributions; Not interested in new products; Buy—vacations, luxuries, home improvements.
Empty nest II—older married couple; No children living at home; Head of household retired.	Drastic cut in income; Buy—medical appliances, medical care products.
Solitary survivor; In labour force.	Income still good but leading a simple lifestyle.
Solitary survivor; Retired.	Same medical and product needs as other retired group; Drastic cut in income; Special need for attention, affection, and security.

Occupation and Economic Circumstances

Product choices are greatly affected by the economic circumstances of consumers as it determines their purchasing power. While the purchasing power of an individual gets affected by various factors, such as, their disposable income, savings and assets, debts, borrowing power, and attitude towards spending versus saving. A person's buying behaviour gets strongly influenced by the type of occupation they are in, such as, whether they are in the blue-collar jobs or white-collar jobs. It does make a difference in their purchases as it is reflected in their economic circumstances as well. Marketers try to identify certain occupational groups and segment their market accordingly. They might design certain exclusive products for them, such as designer shirts for successful corporate executives. In case the economy is going through recession, it directly affects the purchasing power of people. At that time marketers can take steps to redesign, reposition, re-price and replace their products so that they continue to offer value to the target customers.

Lifestyle

People from the same subculture, social class and occupation may lead quite different lifestyles. According to Philip Kotler (1999)— *a lifestyle is the person's pattern of living in the world as expressed in their activities, interests and opinions.* Lifestyles portray 'the whole person' interacting with his or her environment. For marketers it is very important to search for relationships between their products and lifestyle groups because only then they will be able to arrive at appropriate positioning strategies. There are generally four major types of lifestyles:

1. Actualizers: These are successful, sophisticated, active, 'take-charge' people who generally prefer buying expensive, niche oriented products, such as, I-phone, Apple Mac Book, etc.

2. Fulfilled: These are mature, satisfied, and contended people who favour durability, functionality and value in products. They prefer buying products, such as, Maruti's car.

3. Achievers: These are successful, career-oriented people who favour established, prestigious products that demonstrate success to their peer. Examples include luxury cars and expensive mobile phones.

4. Experiencers: They are young, vital, enthusiastic, impulsive and rebellious people who spend a comparatively high proportion of their income on clothing, fast food, music, movies and mobile phones.

Personality and Self-concept

Each person has a distinct personality that influences their buying behaviour. According to Philip Kotler (1999)—*personality means distinguishing psychological characteristics that lead to relatively consistent and enduring response to environment.* Personality is usually described in terms of certain traits, such as, self-confidence, dominance, authority, aggressiveness, shyness, dynamism, security, introversion, flexibility, friendliness and adaptability. Related to personality is one's self-concept which determines as to how they want to project themselves to the entire world. Hence, marketers have to learn to give their products a certain image which can match with the personality of their target audience.

For example, premium luxury cars are meant for people who are dynamic, secure and successful.

4.3.4 Psychological Factors

A person's buying choices are influenced by four major psychological factors as depicted in Figure 4.4—motivation, perception, learning, and beliefs and attitudes of people.

Motivation

It is what makes people behave the way they do and purchase what they want to. The basic reason behind every purchase is a felt need. All behaviour starts with a need. Physiological, security, social acceptance and prestige are examples of needs. A need has to be strong enough to become a motive. Thus, a *motive* is a need that is sufficiently pressing to drive the person to act in different situations. Identifying the motives for behaviour is generally very difficult. Psychologists have developed theories of human motivation where they have made attempts to identify the motives underlying the various types of purchase behaviour. Some of the important motivational theories have been given by Maslow, Herzberg and Mcgreger. The focus in all these theories have been on understanding the buying behaviour of people getting affected by various sets of needs at various stages in their lives. With a greater understanding of motives, marketers are better prepared to design appealing products for consumers.

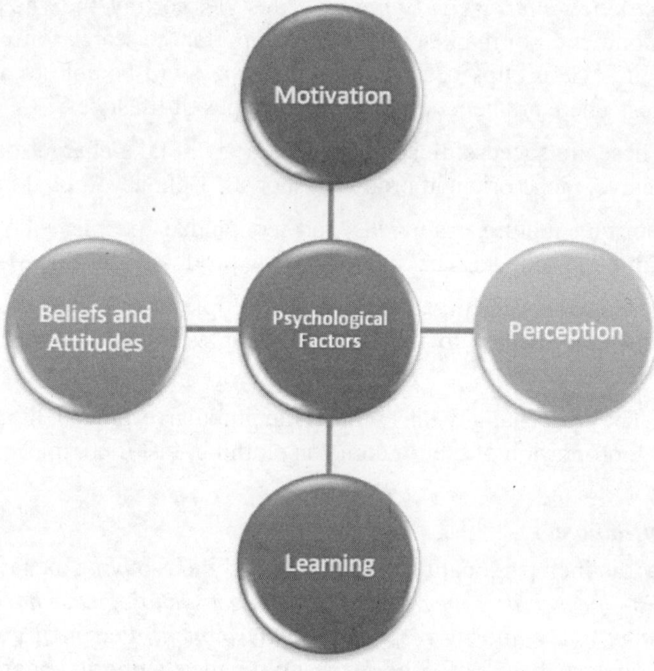

Figure 4.4 Various psychological factors.

Perception

It is the process by which an individual selects, organises, and interprets information inputs to create a meaningful picture of the world. As discussed earlier different people perceive different products and situations differently. It plays a major role when a consumer has to identify various alternatives. Differences in perception of people can be attributed to three major reasons—selective attention, selective distortion and selective retention.

1. Selective attention: People are exposed to a number of stimuli from the environment. For example, an average person may be exposed to over 500 to 1000 advertisements per day. But a person cannot possibly attend to all of these, so they pay attention to some of them while ignoring the rest—a process called *selective attention.* In order to overcome the problem of selective attention, marketers have to work hard to attract consumers' notice. They should design bold, colourful messages and try to relate to the current needs of the consumers to attract their attention.

2. Selective distortion: *Selective distortion* is the tendency to twist information as per the personal preferences and interpret information in a way that will fit into their perceptions.

3. Selective retention: As people tend to forget what they learn, it becomes important for the marketers to ensure that their messages are retained by consumers. It is because of this reason that marketers repeat their messages again and again and try to relate them to the consumer's beliefs and attitudes.

Learning

Involves changes in an individual's behaviour arising from experience. Learning theories teach marketers that they can build up demand for a product by associating it with strong drives, using motivating cues and providing positive reinforcements.

Beliefs and Attitudes

A *belief* is a descriptive thought that a person holds about something. It may be based on knowledge, opinion or faith. Marketers are always interested to know about people's beliefs because their beliefs make up the product and brand images, and determine people's response.

An *attitude* is a person's favourable or unfavourable feelings and action tendencies towards some object or idea. People have different attitudes towards things and their attitudes put them into a frame of mind of liking or disliking an object. Thus, it can be suggested to marketers that they should fit their products into consumer's existing attitudes rather than trying to change their attitude.

To conclude, it can be rightly said that consumer's buying behaviour gets strongly influenced by the various personal factors already discussed. It is for the marketers to identify the specific set of factors depending on the nature of the product, the nature of the consumer, and the particular situation. Besides knowing these factors, it is important for the marketers to understand the buying motives of consumers to understand their buying behaviour perfectly.

4.4 CONCEPT OF BUYING MOTIVES

Buying motives are defined as the basic instinct or the genuine reason for which a consumer purchases a product. These are the most selfish reasons behind the purchase of any product by a consumer. Buying motives differ from person to person and even in the life of one person, motives differ from time to time depending on the various reasons. Everyone has different sets of goals and aspirations. And they decide, in the light of their goals, as to what they want from life and then pay the price for those particular satisfactions. Therefore, it is important for the marketers to discover that the buying motives vary in strength and that this variation can from person to person and from time to time.

4.4.1 Variations in Buying Motives

Person to person variation in buying motives reflect the fact that no two individuals are alike. Each sets up his own goals and scale of values. Factors that help explain why A's buying motives are different from B's are:

- Hereditary background
- Personality and capability
- Training and education
- Experience
- Environment
- Social status
- Occupation and income

Even the same individual buyer, however, experiences changes in his motivation patterns from time to time, due to the following reasons:

- Age affects what he wants to do and what he can do.
- Season of the year affects and changes what buyer considers desirable.
- Phase of business cycle—whether times are good or bad can affect buyer's buying pattern.
- Change in marital status.
- Immediate circumstances can compel a person and play an important role influencing their buying pattern.
- A slight change in the buyer's mood can also alter his feelings.

Thus, the marketer's job is all the more challenging and complicated because at times it might be very difficult for them to understand the difference in the buying patterns of different individuals, such as, Mr. A buys insurance from fear, Mr. B buys it out of affection for his family. Miss A buys a dress early in the season in order to be distinctive while Miss B buys late in the season for reasons of economy.

4.4.2 Knowledge of Buying Motives

Nothing is more essential in marketing than the knowledge of what the prospect wants. Hence, a successful marketer will always try to assimilate as much of information as possible, about the various motives which guide the purchase decisions of their customers. Some of the benefits which they seek from gathering the knowledge about the consumer's buying motives are:

(a) It helps them to decide as to which appeal is to be used.

(b) Ideal for the marketers to be able to project themselves into the prospect's circumstances to determine what motives will influence the prospect towards buying and then to be able to set those motives in action.

(c) When the salesman knows what the prospect wants from the product and how much the prospect will hope to benefit from purchase, he can emphasize the specific advantage of his merchandise, which will appeal most to that prospect.

(d) His sales story will be more complete and sound.

4.4.3 Kinds of Buying Motives

Buying motives can be divided into two major groups—Rational and Emotional.

Rational Buying Motives

These concern such matters as price, cost-in-use, durability, servicing, reliability, length of useful usage and, in general, any consideration affecting the full long-run cost of the article to the purchaser. Rational motives play a very important role as many, if not most, people like to believe that they are behaving rationally even though the real drives underlying their actions are emotional. In general, business executives attempt to buy as rationally as possible, but they, too, frequently fail to be completely rational. Personal friendships, brand names, reciprocity and status symbols may influence their buying decisions.

Emotional Buying Motives

A complete classification of all emotional buying motives is impossible. Our emotions are so complex that it is difficult to isolate each motive and classify it. Some of the more common emotional buying motives are—physical pleasure, comfort, ego, pride, sex, recreation and avoidance of effort. However, the "motive mixes" underlying the two purchases could be quite different. Two executives may purchase exactly the same luxurious office for ostensibly the same emotional motive of ego gratification. The first executive may have purchased her furniture to prove to her fellow employees that she possesses certain status within the organisation. The other executive may have purchased his office furnishings to impress such outsiders as competitors, other business executives, and customers—to convey an image of success, largely for business reasons. The salesperson must be able to detect these differences in buying motives, because it is a serious mistake to appeal to the first executive in terms of external prestige when internal status is desired. Similarly, the second executive would not respond to appeals dealing with internal prestige alone. Some of the more common emotional buying motives are given as under:

1. Physical pleasure, comfort, avoidance of effort: Every human being has the same physiological needs. Humans require food, drink, sleep, and a temperature that is not too hot or too cold. Many humans spend most of their effort in acquiring these basic necessities; others are able to satisfy these with a portion of their effort and go on from there to acquire other desirable things. This urge is basic and accounts for the purchase of food, a good mattress, shelter, clothes and conveniences about the home or place of work. Washing machines, vacuum cleaners, cars with automatic transmission, power brakes, air conditioning, are all examples of things which we value because they satisfy this urge.

2. Aesthetic pleasure: We derive strong satisfaction or pleasure from the impact of the beauty on our senses and emotions. This may be beauty of form, colour or sound. It may be found in art, music, literature or nature in the home or at work. We have only to look around us to realize how strongly this motive has influenced the design of thousands of items such as automobiles, washing machines, kitchen utensils, stove, furniture, architecture, clothing and interior decorating of home, factory office, etc. The purely utilitarian and functional approach has been modified by this determination to produce things that will also appeal to the aesthetic motive.

The smart salesperson capitalizes on this drive by selling particularly well-designed products and by displaying them in such a way that they are able to make people buy the product on the basis of those virtues. And it does no harm to point out to the prospect, "Isn't it beautiful?", "It's the best-looking model", etc.

3. Self esteem, pride, ego striving, power status: Whatever we call it, all of us have it. We want to be appreciated, complimented, to be made to feel important. Many times marketers use this approach to catch the attention of the prospective customers and impress upon them as to how a particular product will make them more powerful and important in their society.

4. Imitation or emulation: Pure imitation, such as that displayed by monkeys and small children, is found to a certain extent in adult human beings, but most people imitate others in the purchase of certain things with the idea that by doing so they are showing themselves superior to others. We imitate those who are, in our opinion, more important in this respect than we are. A young girl styles her hair like some prominent woman. A man buys a more expensive car than what he can afford simply because many men whom he admires drive that car. This is *emulation*.

5. Acquisitiveness: The *acquisitive* or possessive urge may manifest itself in many ways. A few of us hoard things, more of us collect things, and most of us like to own things. We seem to have an urge to possess, to call things "mine". The automobile salesperson plays upon this motive when he allows his prospect to test drive the car. Once behind the steering wheel, the automobile driver imagines himself the owner of the car and rebels at the idea of giving it up.

6. Romantic and sexual drives: The desire to be with, or to appeal to, members of the opposite sex accounts for the purchase of many things such as cosmetics, cloths, hair styling, and tickets to movies and concerts. We struggle to retain our hair, our complexion, our figure in the hope that romance will remain in our life and we will be able to constantly attract people from opposite sex to us. Many times, illustrations showing the presence of the opposite sex in some relationship to the product being sold will do the job better than words.

7. Physical and mental health, physical fitness: People have an inborn urge to live as long as they can. As young people, we do not worry much about dying or being ill. But after forty, it is different. We tend to rationalize, to explain our purchases on the ground that they will promote health. We join golf or fitness clubs; we eat a more balanced diet; we buy "natural foods"; we visit the dentist regularly. It should be pointed out that in discussing health we include not only the negative aspect of avoiding illness but the positive aspect of physical fitness, of a condition in which we possess energy and zest for living. Health appeal has gained considerable strength. We are spending more money on preventive health activities—health spas, vitamins and exercise equipment. It's a powerful motive. In order to support this point we would like to quote a famous example of Parle G—a brand known in the biscuit market, which is trying its level best to target to the health conscious consumers.

Parle G – Retaining the Leadership Position

For long time, one of the largest-selling biscuit brands in the world is now facing a tough competition from Britannia and Sunfeast from ITC. Parle G has been in business for more than 75 years and has practically captured the near monopoly situation for long. But amidst the tough competition, the company is trying its level best to retain its market share.

Perhaps with tomorrow in mind, Parle Products recently launched an advertising campaign—the first in a decade—to hunt down Kal ke Genius. Created by Ogilvy India and shot by Chrome Pictures, the campaign made waves online overnight—or perhaps even before that. Law and Kenneth, who managed the social media campaign for the brand, used the tagline, 'Be Curious', to talk about the campaign and it was among the Top five trending topics on Twitter.

If Parle has to make a noise in the market, it is because of the presence of two formidable rivals in the glucose segment–Britannia and ITC. As of June 2012, Nielsen data indicates the former had a share of 8.7 per cent and ITC 8.3 per cent. Parle still rules the roost with a 79.4 per cent share, but with both the competitors armed with deep pockets, the battle is going to rage on for some time to come.

Along with competition, the glucose segment itself stands the risk of getting crowded out by a basket of newer healthier options, from oat and ragi cookies to digestive and milky biscuits. Agrees Ajay Chauhan, executive director, Parle Products—*Consumers today have acquired a taste for 'variety', which is seen by the success of multiple biscuit variants across price points. As consumer preferences evolve, the market for biscuits as a whole will increase and Glucose has a healthy imagery in consumers' minds and today the health platform has gained more voice than ever.*

The new advertisement campaign will immediately draw a larger number of customers into the space as well as refresh the connection with the existing customers.

Source: An article by Preethi Chamikutty, "Will Parle-G be relevant to the next generation?", in Brand Equity, The Economic Times, 16th January 2013.

Questions for Discussion

1. What, in your point-of-view, should have been the marketing strategy of Parle-G, a one time leader in the biscuit category to protect their leadership position?
2. In the midst of the newer and healthier options of oat and ragi cookies, will Parle-G be able to survive with the same glucose biscuits?
3. Parle-G is trying to encash on people's desire to be intelligent and physically fit and moreover they are trying to capture the mind share of youth through social networking cites. Can you comment on the success of their strategy?

8. Curiosity or the desire for new experience: We like to go places and do things, to travel and visit new scenes, to extract new thrills from life. This urge is found more strongly in the young than in the old. The salesperson often appeals to raw curiosity to get initial attention and interest but does not utilize this appeal so often in closing the sale, as it is rarely the motive that finally prompts the purchase.

9. Desire for justice and right, sense of duty, love of others: These may be acquired motives, but we cannot deny their power. People have died for what they thought was right; they fight to obtain justice for themselves or others; they forgo pleasures for the higher satisfaction of feeling that they have done their duty. Parental or romantic love, a selfless devotion to others, is a motive prompting millions of purchases daily.

10. Fear or Caution: We fear the loss of life, of health, of friends, of reputation, of security, of job, of money, of freedom, of comfort, of everything which we value. To fail to gain the things we crave or to lose them causes pain. It may be physical or mental, but it is pain and we strive to avoid it. The fear motive is closely allied to caution and the desire for security. People buy insurance, homes, and bonds and stocks, or put money in the bank because they are trying to gain security for their old age or for a 'rainy day'. Fire extinguishers, locks for doors and windows, and a thousand items are bought because the buyer fears the consequences of not buying them and prefers the security they hope to gain by having them.

Thus, the knowledge of all the above listed buying motives can be of great help to the marketers to understand their consumer's buying pattern properly.

4.4.4 Various Types of Buying Roles

Different people in a family play different roles in the family's purchase decisions. Hence it becomes very important for the marketers to understand the different types of roles being played by different family members in initiating the purchase, influencing the purchase, and finally taking the purchase decision. Some of the important types of buying roles being played by different people are listed as under:

- **Initiator** is a person who first suggests the idea of buying the product or service.
- **Influencer** is a person whose views or advice influences the decisions.
- **Decider** is a person who takes the final decision of buying a product. He decides about whether to buy, what to buy, how to buy or where to buy.
- **Buyer** is the person who goes to market, makes the payment and finally materialises the actual purchase.
- **User** is a person who consumes or uses the product or service and draws satisfaction out of it.

All these buying roles, as shown in Figure 4.5, are of great significance while discussing the purchasing patterns of people. People play different roles in different situations, for instance, a person may be an initiator for a certain purchase, an influencer in another case, and might be a purchaser for the purchase of certain products and ultimately the user for most of the purchases.

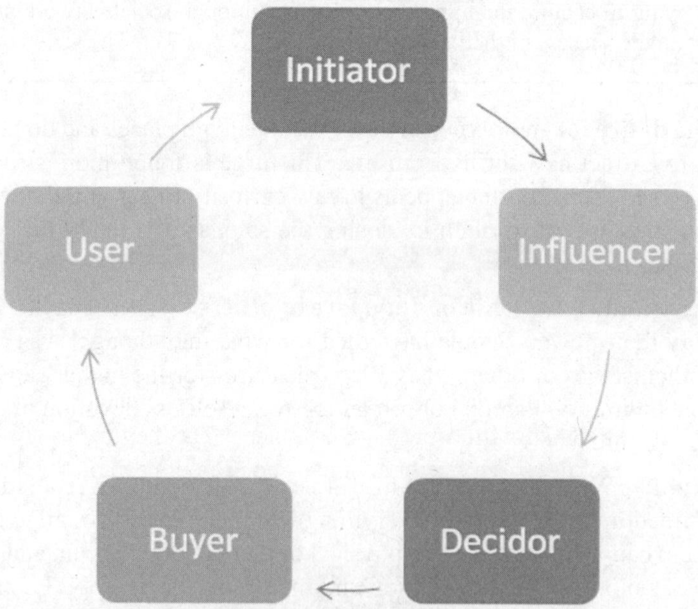

Figure 4.5 Types of buying roles.

4.4.5 The Buying Decision Process

Making a purchase decision is not an easy task for the consumer. They need to gather facts from various sources, pay attention to each and every detail, work out the various possible options available and then take the purchase decision. Generally the consumer has to pass through various stages before finalising the purchase decision. Figure 4.6 shows a model of the typical buying process. Typically, the consumer passes through five stages—problem recognition, information search, evaluation of alternatives, purchase decision and post purchase behaviour. Thus, it is quite clear that the buying process starts long before the actual purchase is made and has consequences long afterwards.

The model in Figure 4.6 implies that consumers pass sequentially through all the five stages in buying a product. But this is not the case—consumers may skip or reverse some stages. This depends to a large extent on the type of the product being purchased by the consumer, their level of involvement in the purchase and the money involved. When it comes to buying any of the fast moving consumer goods, such as, toothpaste, detergents, deodorants, etc., the consumer may directly go to the purchase decision stage skipping information search and purchase evaluation. However, we will discuss this model because it captures the full range of considerations that arise when a consumer faces a purchase decision in which he is highly involved.

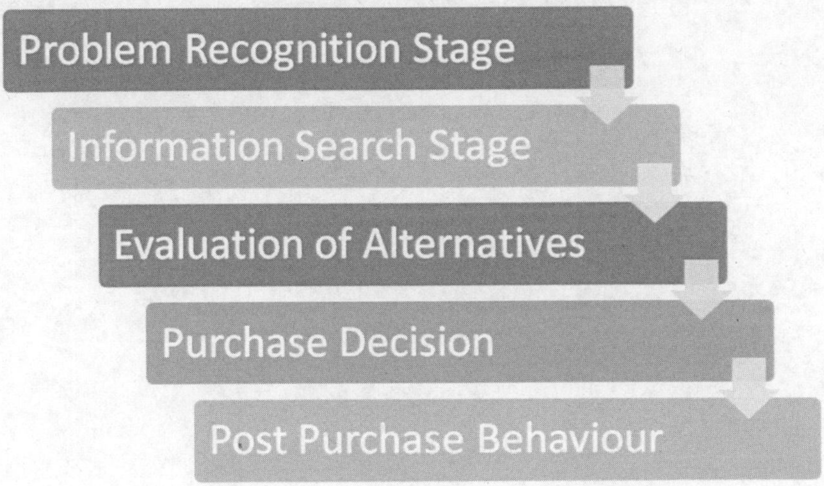

Figure 4.6 The buying decision process.

Problem Recognition Stage

Consumers buying process starts with the recognition of a particular problem or need. Its only when consumers are confronted with a problem or a need that they try to find a solution in the form of a purchase of a product or service or an idea. The problem can be basic in nature, i.e. need for food, shelter and clothing or it can be something which is aroused by an external stimulus, such as, an advertisement coming on television for a new mobile phone or a friend acquiring a new car. A problem once identified needs to be understood clearly. A consumer has to go down to the root of the problem and find out the main cause responsible for it so that the solution can be worked out. Therefore, at the first stage the consumer has to identify the problem clearly with all its dimensions. For marketers it is important to understand the factors which initiate a particular need or problem.

Information Search

Once the problem is clear then search for solution gets started. Consumer has to look for information from various possible sources. An effort should be made to identify all the sources and gather as much of information as possible so that the chances of committing a mistake can be reduced to the minimum. It is very important for the marketer to understand the major information sources for consumers which can influence their purchase decision. Various sources from which a consumer can gather information are depicted in Figure 4.7:

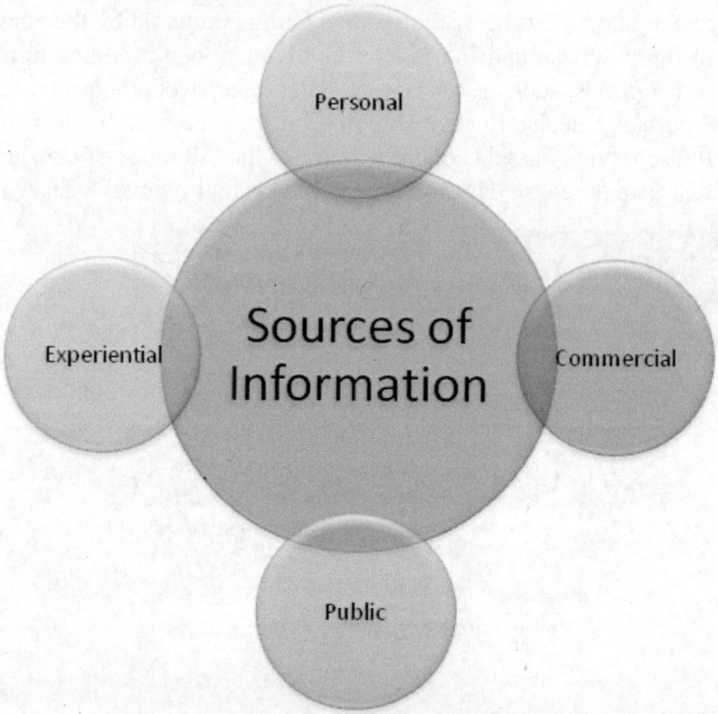

Figure 4.7 Sources of information.

1. Personal sources: To begin with, the first and the foremost important source from which information flows in are generally from the various family members, friends, neighbours and acquaintances. It is expected from the consumer to talk to all these people and seek as much of information as possible regarding the solutions to the problems being faced by them.

2. Commercial sources: Another important source from which a consumer is able to gather information about the various alternatives available is advertisements coming on various mediums, through salespersons, dealers and distributors, trade shows and exhibitions.

3. Public source: Information coming from various mass media options, marketing research organisations and consumer rating organisations is another source on which the consumer can rely.

4. Experiential sources: In some cases a consumer would like to go and experiment with new products, handle them themselves, examine carefully, use the sample product and draw their own conclusions.

Through gathering information, the consumer can learn about the various features of the product as well as about the competing brands and their features. Therefore, it becomes very important for the company to gather information about the competing brands so that they should be able to position their product as superior to the consumers.

Evaluation of Alternatives

After acquiring information about the various brands from various sources listed above, the consumer is expected to process that competitive information and make a final value judgement. There is no single evaluation process used by all consumers or by one consumer in all buying situations. But whatever the case may be, the consumers' evaluation process follows set attributes they have in mind for rating the product. They make final decisions, judgements and preferences towards the various brands through an attribute evaluation procedure, where they try to rate the various brands on the basis of their desired attributes and brand image. It is important for the marketers to understand the various attributes the consumers are looking for in the purchase of their product so that they should bring in those attributes in their products to meet the consumer's choice.

Purchase Decision

At the evaluation stage, the consumer forms preferences among the various brands available in the market. A consumer's decision to purchase, postpone or avoid a purchase decision is heavily influenced by various factors, such as, his income levels, convenient timings, convenient purchase location and urgency of requirement. In executing a purchase decision, the consumer may have to make five purchase sub decisions—a brand decision, i.e. what to buy? (Maruti Car); vendor decision, i.e. from whom to buy? (Bagga Links); quantity decision, i.e. how much to buy? (One Swift car); timing decision, i.e. when to buy? (Weekend); and payment method decision, i.e. how to pay for it? (Credit card). Purchases of everyday products involve fewer decisions and less deliberation.

Post Purchase Behaviour

After purchasing the product, the consumer will experience some level of satisfaction or dissatisfaction. The marketer's job does not end when the product is sold. They must monitor post purchase satisfaction, post purchase actions and post purchase uses and disposal of products. It is important for the marketers to determine the level of satisfaction of the buyer with the purchase. The buyer's satisfaction is a function of the association between the buyer's expectations and the product's delivered performance. If performance falls short of expectations, the consumer is disappointed; if it meets expectations, the customer is satisfied; if it exceeds expectations, the customer is delighted. These feelings make a lot of difference in deciding whether the buyer will buy the product again and talk favourably or unfavourably about the product to others. Marketers should also monitor how buyers use the product and finally dispose it off so that it should not cause any harm to the overall environment.

4.4.6 Types of Consumer Buying Behaviour

Consumer decision-making varies with the type of product to be purchased. The decisions to buy an FMCG, a personal computer, a mobile phone or a new luxury car are all very different. Complex and expensive purchases are likely to involve more deliberation and more participants. According to Henry Assael (1987), there are four types of consumer buying behaviours based on the degree of buyer involvement and the degree of differences among brands as depicted in Table 4.2.

Complex Buying Behaviour

Consumers engage in complex buying behaviour when they are highly involved in a purchase and are aware of significant differences among brands. This is usually the case when the product is expensive, bought infrequently and highly self expressive. Complex buying behaviour involves a three-step process:

(i) The buyer develops beliefs about the product.
(ii) He or she develops attitudes about the product.
(iii) He or she makes a thoughtful choice.

In this case the marketer should follow the following strategies:

(i) As generally in this case, the consumer does not know much about the product category. Therefore, the marketer of a high involvement product must understand consumers' information-gathering and evaluation behaviour.
(ii) They need to develop strategies that assist the buyer in learning about the product's attributes and their relative importance.
(iii) The marketer needs to differentiate the brand's features, use print media to describe the brands benefits, and motivate store sales personnel and the buyer's acquaintances to influence the final brand choice.

Finally, the marketer has to reassure the consumer about their buying decision to give them maximum satisfaction.

Table 4.2 Types of Consumer Buying Behaviour

	High Involvement	**Low Involvement**
Significant differences between brands	Complex buying behaviour	Variety seeking buying behaviour
Few differences between brands	Dissonance-reducing buying behaviour	Habitual buying behaviour

Dissonance-reducing Buyer Behaviour

Sometimes the consumer is highly involved in a purchase but sees little difference in brands. The high involvement is based on the fact that the purchase is expensive, infrequent and involving. For example, carpet buying is a high involvement decision because carpeting is expensive and self expressive, yet the buyer may consider most carpet brands in a given price range to be the same. In this case marketer should follow the following strategies:

(i) The buyer for such products will shop around to learn what is available but will buy fairly quickly, perhaps responding primarily to a good price or to purchase convenience.
(ii) Marketers should communicate effectively with consumers and give them reason to feel good about their product choice.

(iii) The consumer will like to gather as much of information as possible to support his or her decision.

(iv) After the purchase, the consumer might experience dissonance that stems from noticing certain disquieting features or hearing favourable things about other brands.

(v) Finally, marketers should give reinforcing advertisements to reassure the consumer that they have bought the right product.

Habitual Buying Behaviour

Many products are bought under conditions of low involvement and the absence of significant brand differences. Consider salt–consumers have little involvement in this product category. They go to the store and reach for the brand. If they keep reaching for the same brand, it is out of habit, not strong brand loyalty. There is good evidence that consumers have low involvement with most low-cost, frequently purchased products. In this case marketer should follow the following strategies:

(i) With these products, consumer behaviour does not pass through the normal sequence of beliefs, attitudes and behaviour.

(ii) Consumers do not search extensively for information, evaluate characteristics and make a decision on which brand to buy.

(iii) They are passive recipients of information in television or print advertisements. Advertising repetition creates brand familiarity rather than brand conviction.

(iv) After purchase, they may not even evaluate the choice because they are not highly involved with the purchase.

(v) Marketers of such products find it effective to use price and sales promotions to stimulate product trial.

(vi) Television advertising is more effective than print because it is a low involvement medium that is suitable for passive learning.

Variety Seeking Buying Behaviour

Some buying situations are characterised by low involvement but significant brand differences. Here markets are flooded with brands and consumers often do a lot of brand switching. For instance, in case of shampoos, the consumer simply likes a particular brand of shampoo, purchases it without much evaluation, and the level of satisfaction attained on consumption will determine that whether they will be going in for repeat purchase or they might try out a new brand. Brand switching occurs for the sake of variety rather than dissatisfaction. In this case marketer should follow the following strategies:

(i) The market leader and the challenger firms in this product category have different marketing strategies.

(ii) The market leader will try to encourage variety seeking buying behaviour by dominating the shelf space, avoiding out of stock conditions, and sponsoring frequent reminder advertising.

(iii) Challenger firms will encourage variety seeking by offering lower prices, deals, offers, free samples, and advertising that presents reasons for trying something new.

(iv) Aggressive advertising and sales promotion incentives are used by all to attract the customers towards their products.

Finally, to conclude, consumer is the most important person for a marketer and it is necessary for them to keep them happy, satisfied and loyal towards their product at any cost.

LET US SUM UP

- Consumer buying behaviour refers to the buying pattern of final consumers, individuals and households who buy goods and services for their personal consumption or for household usage.
- According to stimulus-response theory, consumer learning occurs as a consumer responds to some stimulus by behaving in a particular way and is rewarded for a correct response or penalized for an incorrect one. Thus, a consumers' buying behaviour starts with the marketing stimuli provided by marketers and ends with the important product decisions which give them utmost satisfaction.
- Major factors influencing buying behaviour can be broadly categorised into four categories—cultural, social, personal, and psychological.
- Cultural factors exert a deep influence on consumer behaviour. The marketer needs to understand the role played by the buyer's culture, subculture and social class in their buying behaviour.
- A consumer's behaviour is influenced by various social factors such as, their reference groups, family, friends, and social roles and statuses.
- Family is a group of two or more people related by blood, marriage, or adoption living together in a household. Family plays a very important role in influencing the purchase decisions of the individuals.
- A buyer's purchase decision is also influenced by personal characteristics. These include the buyer's age and stage in the life cycle, occupation, economic circumstances, lifestyle, personality and self-concept.
- People from the same subculture, social class and occupation may lead quite different lifestyles and their lifestyle is quite capable of influencing their buying decisions.
- A person's buying choices are influenced by four major psychological factors—motivation, perception, learning, beliefs and attitudes of people.
- Different people in a family play different roles in the familie's purchase decisions. Therefore, it becomes very important for the marketers to understand the different types of roles being played by different family members in initiating the purchase, influencing the purchase and finally taking the purchase decision.
- In order to make a purchase decision, the consumer passes through five stages—problem recognition, information search, evaluation of alternatives, purchase decision and post purchase behaviour.
- There are four types of consumer's buying behaviour based on the degree of buyer involvement and the degree of differences among brands—complex, habitual, dissonance-reducing and variety seeking buying behaviour.
- Complex buying behaviour involves a three-step process. First, the buyer develops beliefs about the product. Second, he or she develops attitudes about the product. Third, he or she makes a thoughtful choice.
- In dissonance-reducing buying behaviour, the consumer is highly involved in the purchase as it is expensive, infrequent and risky, and at the same time there is very little choice available. Therefore,

the consumer tries to select the best out of the variety available so as to minimise their overall dissatisfaction.

- Many products are bought under conditions of low involvement and the absence of significant brand differences, such as, in case of salt consumers have little involvement in the product category and they buy it only out of habit resulting in habitual buying behaviour.
- Some buying situations are characterised by low involvement but significant brand differences. Here consumers often do a lot of brand switching and resort to variety seeking buying behaviour.

QUESTIONS TO CHECK YOUR PROGRESS

Short Answer Questions

1. Define consumer buying behaviour.
2. What do we call the process by which an individual selects, organises, and interprets information to create a meaningful picture of the world?
3. Define the concept of buying motives.
4. What are the various types of buying motives?
5. Name some of the emotional buying motives.
6. Differentiate between rational and emotional buying motives.
7. Name the first stage in the buying decision process.
8. Name the four major factors that influence consumer buying behaviour.
9. List out the various stages involved in the buying decision process.
10. What are the various sources of information to study consumer behaviour?
11. What is dissonance reducing buying behaviour?
12. Many products are bought under conditions of low involvement and the absence of significant brand differences. What is this kind of a behaviour called?

Long Answer Questions

1. Explain consumer buying behaviour. Discuss the recent developments in the field of consumer behaviour.
2. What do you understand by buying motives? Briefly discuss the buying motives which lead a consumer to buy a product and illustrate them with relevant examples.
3. Explain the concept of consumer buying behaviour. Why should marketers study consumer buying behaviour?
4. Define the consumer market and construct a simple model of consumer buying behaviour.
5. Draw and explain a neatly labelled diagram of stimulus response model.
6. Briefly discuss Kotler's model of consumer behaviour, identifying its various determinants.
7. Briefly explain the various factors affecting the consumers' buying behaviour. Briefly explain the role of attitudes in influencing the consumer behaviour.
8. Examine the role of a reference groups and personality in assisting the marketer.
9. "The personality traits and attitudes are important guides to consumer behaviour". Explain.
10. "In India family and social class regulates consumer behaviour". Do you agree? Give reasons for your answer.

11. Explain psychographics and lifestyle analysis. Explain how they might be useful for planning marketing strategy to reach college students as opposed to an average consumer.
12. How should social class influences affect the planning of a new restaurant in a large city? How might the 4Ps be adjusted?
13. Explain the major psychological factors influencing the consumer behaviour.
14. Briefly explain the consumer buying decision process. How can a marketing manager benefit from the study of consumers post purchase behaviour?
15. In what ways is the buying behaviour of a consumer affected by his family? List out certain products where family plays a very important influencing role.
16. What is cognitive dissonance? How can a marketer help a consumer reduce his cognitive dissonance?
17. Explain the various stages through which a consumer has to pass through before making a buying decision. Do they pass through all the stages when it comes to buying toothpaste or a laptop computer?
18. Describe the various types of consumer buying behaviour and examine their usefulness as well as limitations with examples from the current market scenario.
19. In designing an advertising campaign for a soft drink, which would you find more useful: information about consumer demographics or information about consumer lifestyle? Give an example of how would you use each type of information.
20. Think about a very good or a very bad experience you have had with a product. How did this experience shape your beliefs about the product, the purchasing process or shopping in Stores? How long will these beliefs last? What could make you change these beliefs?
21. There are four types of consumer buying behaviours based on the degree of buyer involvement and differences among brands. Which of the four types of consumer buying behaviour is involved in each of the following situations: (a) you are about to purchase a new Lexus automobile; (b) you go into a candy store in the mall and purchase a new brand of candy bar; (c) you go to the retailer to purchase a set of tires; and (d) during a break from class you purchase a soft drink from a vending machine. Explain your choices with sufficient explanation.

CHAPTER 5

Market Segmentation

Learning Outcomes

After studying this chapter, you will be able to:

- ❖ Understand the concept of target marketing
- ❖ Define the levels and patterns of market segmentation
- ❖ Determine the market segmentation procedure
- ❖ Discuss the bases for segmenting consumer goods market
- ❖ Classify the various patterns for market targeting
- ❖ Explain the concept and types of product positioning strategies

India is a big country with a population of billions and a large geographic territory. It is not easy for any organisation to design a product which meets with the requirements of people from different social and cultural backgrounds, perceptions, languages and buying habits. People look for different attributes, features, functions and quality levels from the same product. Some people are ready to pay a high price for quality products, while for others the economical pricing matters a lot. Thus, it becomes important for the marketers to identify the consumer segments that they can serve most effectively. Therefore, instead of producing a common product and targeting it to all, the organisation might be willing to design an exclusive product for a specific consumer segment. In simple words, *market segmentation* can be defined as a process of dividing a total market into different sub-markets, segments, or parts by using some definite criteria or bases. It is also called as *target marketing*. Many companies are embracing target marketing these days. Renowned marketers have defined market segmentation as:

Philip Kotler (1999), has defined target marketing as—

> *The process were sellers distinguish the major market segments, target one or more of those segments, and develop products and marketing programmes tailored to each. Instead of scattering their marketing efforts (a shot gun approach) they can focus on the buyers they have the greatest chance of satisfying (a rifle) approach.*

According to William J Stanton (1994)—

> *Market segmentation consists of taking the total heterogeneous market for a product and dividing it into several sub-markets or segments, each of which tends to be homogeneous in all significant aspects.*

5.1 CHARACTERISTICS OF MARKET SEGMENTATION

From both the definitions discussed above, some of the important characteristics of market segmentation have emerged, such as:

(a) The concept of market segmentation is based on the principle of consumer sovereignty, i.e. treating consumer as the king and giving him the best value-based product.

(b) It is a process of dividing the total market into small manageable segments and selecting one or more segments which can be served well.

(c) Instead of focusing on all and ensuring an average satisfaction to all the customers, the concept of market segmentation believes in giving maximum utility, value and satisfaction to the few selected customers.

(d) It includes dividing the market on the basis of certain common parameters, grouping them together and serving them well.

(e) It involves designing exclusive products for the selected segments and positioning them effectively in those segments.

(f) Effective product positioning ensures maximum value to be delivered to the consumer.

5.2 STEPS IN TARGET MARKETING

According to Philip Kotler (1999), target marketing requires marketers to take three major steps as depicted in Figure 5.1.

A. **Step one**—Identify and profile distinct group of buyers who might require separate products or marketing mixes (market segmentation).

B. **Step two**—Develop measures of segment attractiveness and select one or more market segments to enter (market targeting).

C. **Step three**—Develop product positioning for each target segment, design marketing mix for them and communicate the product's key distinctive benefits in the market (market positioning).

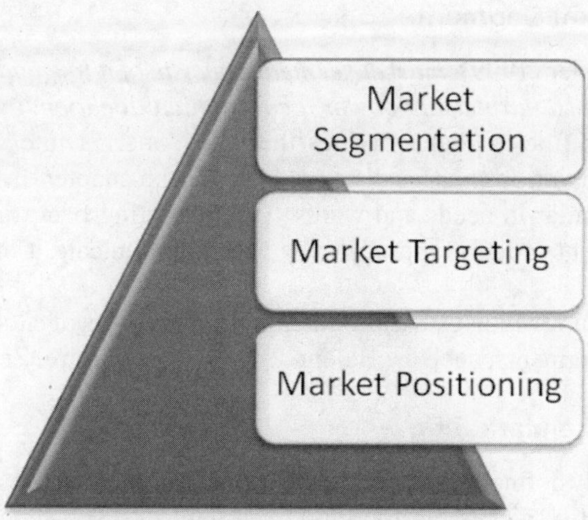

Figure 5.1 Steps in target marketing.

5.3 LEVELS OF MARKET SEGMENTATION

The starting point of any segmentation discussion is mass marketing. In mass marketing, the seller engages in the mass production, mass distribution and mass promotion of one product for all buyers. Mass marketing gives the advantage of targeting the product to a huge population and increasing the market share. This can give the benefit of bulk production, economies of scale, lower prices and higher margins to the marketers. But in today's competitive environment, with more informed and demanding consumers, it is not possible for marketers to design a product that meets with the expectations of all. Therefore, in order to create a loyal and committed clientele, the marketers have started turning to micro-marketing at one of the four levels given by Philip Kotler (1999). These levels are— segments, niches, local areas and individuals as projected in Figure 5.2.

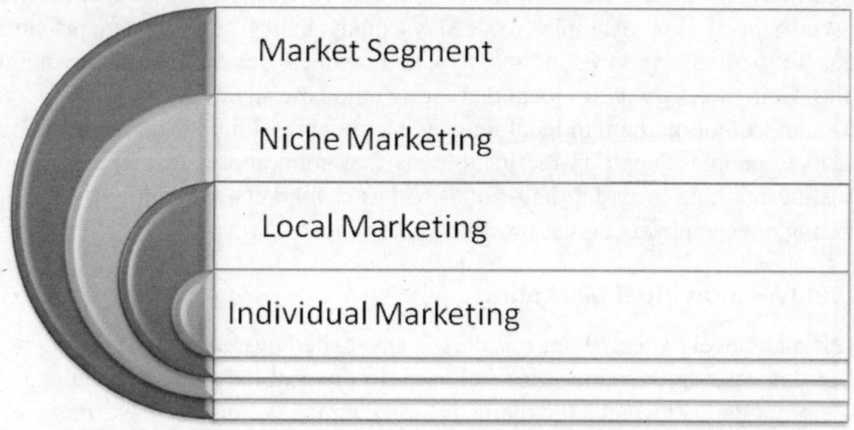

Figure 5.2 Levels of market segmentation.

5.3.1 Level I—Market Segment

According to Philip Kotler (1999), *market segment consists of a large identifiable group within a market with similar wants, purchasing power, geographical location, buying attitudes, or buying habits.* In segmentation, the marketer divides the whole market into small identifiable market segments on the basis of various factors discussed later in the chapter. In each segment, buyers are assumed to be quite similar in needs and wants. The marketing firm tries to design an exclusive product for each segment, price it appropriately and communicate it effectively with the target audience.

For example, Maruti Udyog Ltd. is producing different types of cars to meet the requirements of people in different segments, such as, Baleno, Swift, Swift Desire, Zen, Wagen R, Alto, etc.

5.3.2 Level II—Niche Marketing

Niche is a more narrowly defined group, typically a small market, whose needs are not well served. Marketers usually identify niches by dividing a segment into sub-segments or by identifying a group seeking exclusive benefits. These consumers are willing to get their exclusive needs fulfilled and are willing to pay a premium price for the product. Generally, the niche is so small that it does not attract competitors. Marketers gain certain economies through specialisation, size, profit and growth potential.

For example, in continuation to the above example, if Maruti Company plans to produce a sports car for all the sports car lovers in India, it will be a niche being carved by the company as the number of prospective buyers is going to be few but they will be more than keen to pay the high price as their exclusive demand is being met.

5.3.3 Level III—Local Marketing

Local marketing is going a step closer to consumers and taking care of their needs in a better way than competitors. According to Philp Kotler (1999), *it is leading to marketing programmes being tailored to the needs and wants of local customer groups (trading areas, neighbourhoods, even individual stores).* For example, these days many banks have started providing various combinations of banking services in their local branches depending on the neighbourhood demographics. Companies going for local marketing enjoy the advantage of giving a local touch to the products and promoting them in local language and expressions, which helps them in coming close to the local people. People in the local areas feel good about such local products, but the organisations are not able to target their goods to larger markets and enjoy economies of scale. Local marketing does not have a great prestige value in it as well.

5.3.4 Level IV—Individual Marketing

This is the ultimate level of segmentation. This is also called *customized marketing* or one to one marketing. In this case the marketer tries to look into the problems of each and every consumer and design the goods exclusively for them. In our country we do not have many examples of individual marketing at the corporate level, but for centuries consumers are being served as exclusively when it came to designing the tailor-made suit and the cobbler designing shoes for the individuals. Much business to business marketing today is customised, in that a manufacturer will customise the offer, logistics, communications and financial terms for each major account. With the help of new technologies, for example computers, databases and e-mails, it has been made possible for companies to resort to customised marketing or what is called mass customisation. *Mass customisation* is the ability to prepare on a mass scale individually designed products and communications to meet each customer's requirements.

Thus, it can be concluded that the degree of segmentation and customisation increases as marketers move from market segments to individual marketing.

5.4 PATTERNS OF MARKET SEGMENTATION

Buyer's preferences in the markets can be segmented in three different patterns by identifying their liking for various product attributes, such as, homogenous preference, diffused preference and cluster preference as depicted in Figure 5.3.

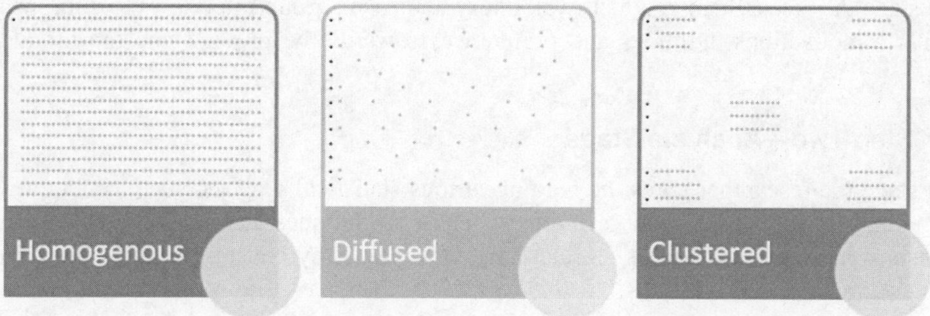

Figure 5.3 Patterns of market segmentation.

5.4.1 Homogenous Preference

These are products where all consumers have roughly the same preference. There does not exist any difference regarding the consumer's choice for certain products. In such markets no natural segments exist and generally it is very difficult for the organisation to work out the segmentation strategy. Therefore, generally organisations prefer designing a common product with common features and target it to all. Examples include products like salt, sugar, pulses, rice, etc.

5.4.2 Diffused Preference

This is the other extreme where consumer's preference may be scattered throughout the space, indicating that consumers vary greatly in their preferences. It again becomes difficult for the marketers to decide as to how they should segment the market and design the products for the consumer. Generally, companies design their products with average features and target them somewhere in the middle so as to reduce the overall dissatisfaction of the consumers. The second or the third competitors can position their brands at certain exclusive corners with some specialised features and show real differences to match consumer's preferences.

5.4.3 Clustered Preference

In certain markets, marketers might be able to identify distinct preference clusters called *natural market segments*. In such cases, marketers might decide to design products exclusively for a specific cluster and go for niche marketing or they can design several brands, each targeted to different clusters. For example, Hindustan Unilever has designed Dove, a bathing soap, for the target audience looking for a rich creamy soap. At the same time they have launched various other brands of soaps in the market meeting the requirements of different consumers, such as, Lifebuoy for health-conscious consumers, Lux the beauty soap, and Breeze for the younger segment of the population.

5.5 MARKET SEGMENTATION PROCEDURE

It is a three step procedure—survey, analysis, and profiling as depicted in Figure 5.4.

5.5.1 Step One—Survey Stage

At this stage the researchers conduct exploratory and focus group interviews to gain insight into consumer's motivations, attitudes and preferences towards the product and the product usage patterns, etc.

5.5.2 Step Two—Analysis Stage

At this stage the researcher takes the help of various statistical devices, such as, factor analysis, cluster analysis and co-relation techniques. These techniques are used to find out certain relationships between the various product attributes quoted by consumers and cluster them into different segments.

5.5.3 Step Three—Profiling Stage

At this stage each segment is profiled in terms of its attractiveness, distinguishing attributes, consumer's behavioural patterns, demographic profiles, psychographics and media preferences. In the light of the observations attained, marketers have to judge whether designing products for such segments will prove to be profitable in the long run and then work out their segmentation strategy.

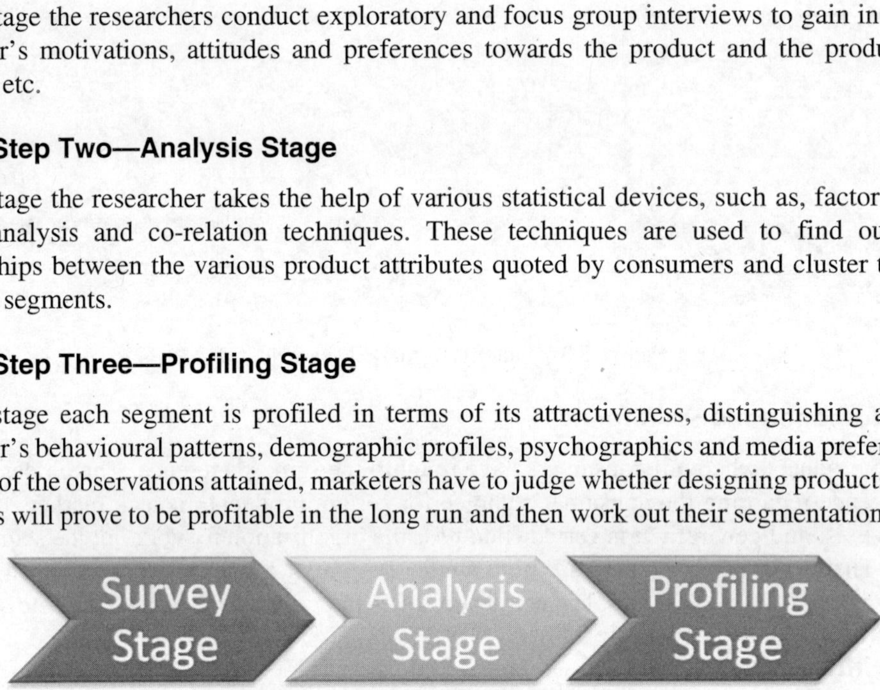

Figure 5.4 Market segmentation procedure.

5.6 BASES FOR SEGMENTING CONSUMER MARKETS

There are differing bases used for segmenting consumer goods markets. According to Philip Kotler (1999), the major amongst them are—geographic, demographic, psychographics and behavioural segmentation variables as depicted in Figure 5.5.

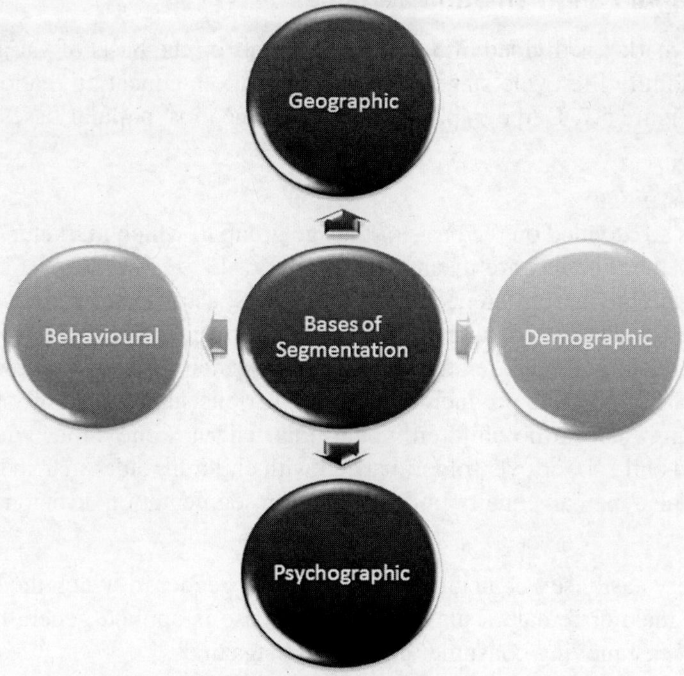

Figure 5.5 Bases for segmenting consumer markets.

5.6.1 Geographic Segmentation Variables

This calls for dividing the market into different geographical units, such as, nations, regions, states and cities. This is one of the most commonly used segmentation variable as marketers can decide about the geographic dimensions of their market depending upon the availability of resources. They can decide to operate in one or few geographic areas or operate in all as illustrated in Figure 5.6.

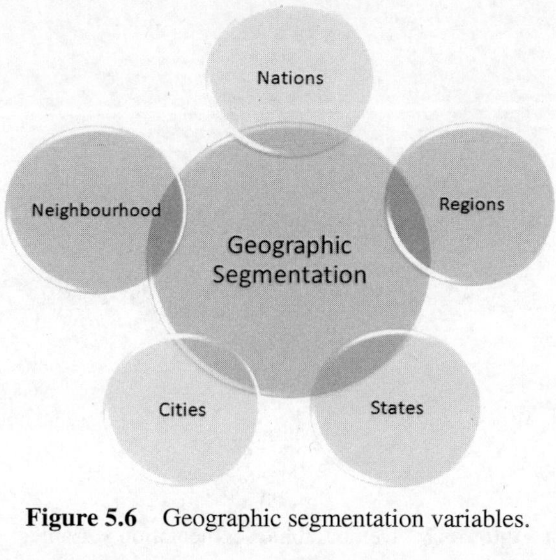

Figure 5.6 Geographic segmentation variables.

5.6.2 Demographic Segmentation Variables

In such cases, the market is divided into various segments on the basis of variables, such as, age, sex, family size, family life cycle stage, income, occupation, education, nationalities and social class as given in Figure 5.7. Demographic variables are the most popular bases for distinguishing customer groups.

Age and Life Cycle Stages

Generally markets are divided on the basis of the age group to which marketers are targeting their products. Whether the products are meant for under 6, 6–11, 12–19, 20–34, 35–49, 50–64, 65+, etc. For example, the buying preferences regarding cloths, accessories and recreation of children are going to be different than young people and mature people. Thus, it becomes important for marketers to understand such age related differences as it helps them in segmenting the markets accordingly and positioning the product therein. The various stages of family life cycle, such as, young single, young married no children, young married with one child, youngest child under six, young married child six or over, older married with children, older married no children, older single, and others also play an equally important role in segmentation decisions.

Gender

Markets can be very easily segmented on the basis of the gender to which the products are being targeted, such as, male or female. This segmentation base is applied generally in clothing, hair styling, cosmetics, fast moving consumer goods and magazines.

Income

Income brackets serve as a very important basis for segmenting the target market. This base is generally used in case of automobiles, mobile phones, cosmetics and travel.

Social Class

Many companies design products and services for specific social classes. This base is generally used in case of cars, clothing, home furnishings or leisure activities.

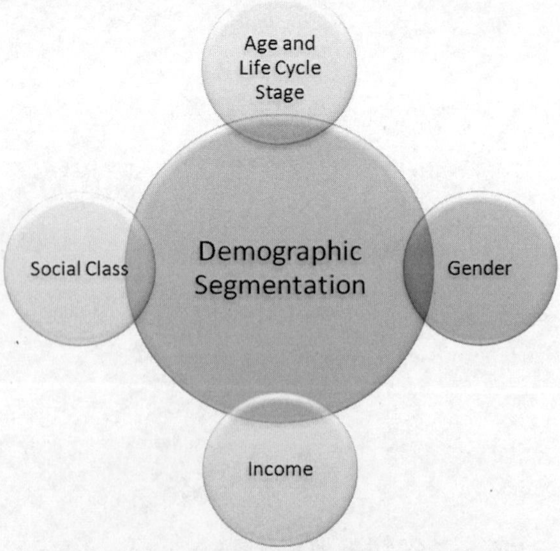

Figure 5.7 Demographic segmentation variables.

5.6.3 Psychographic Segmentation

In these cases buyers are divided into different groups on the basis of their values, perceptions, lifestyle or personalities as projected in Figure 5.8. People within the same demographic group can exhibit very different psychographic profiles.

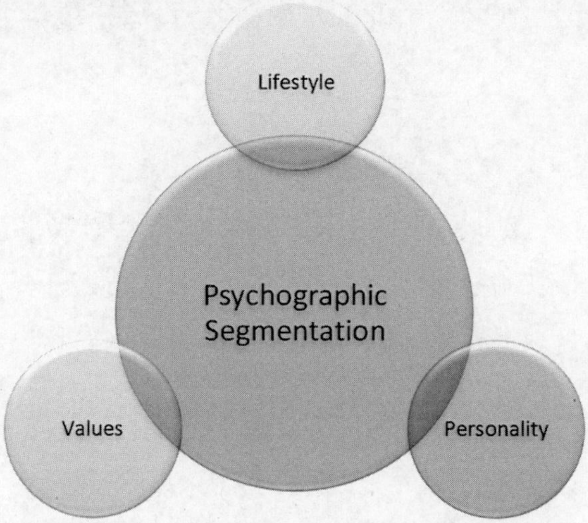

Figure 5.8 Psychographic segmentation variables.

Lifestyle

Different people maintain different lifestyles. As discussed in the previous chapter, lifestyles portray 'the whole person' interacting with his or her environment. For marketers it is very important to search for relationships between their products and lifestyle groups because only then they will be able to arrive at appropriate positioning strategies.

Personality

There are different personality traits enjoyed by people, such as, authoritarian, compulsive, ambitious, innovative, conservative, broad-minded, etc. Different people possess different personality traits and one's personality is one's self-concept which determines as to how they want to project themselves to the entire world. Thus, marketers have to learn to give their products a certain image which can match with the personality of their target audience.

Values

The core values or the belief systems underlie consumers' attitudes and behaviour. Marketers believe that by appealing to people's inner selves, it is possible to influence their outer selves and their purchase behaviour.

5.6.4 Behavioural Segmentation

Buyers can also be divided into groups on the basis of their loyalty status and attitude towards the product, their usage pattern, benefits which they seek from the product and the occasion of their purchase as given in the Figure 5.9.

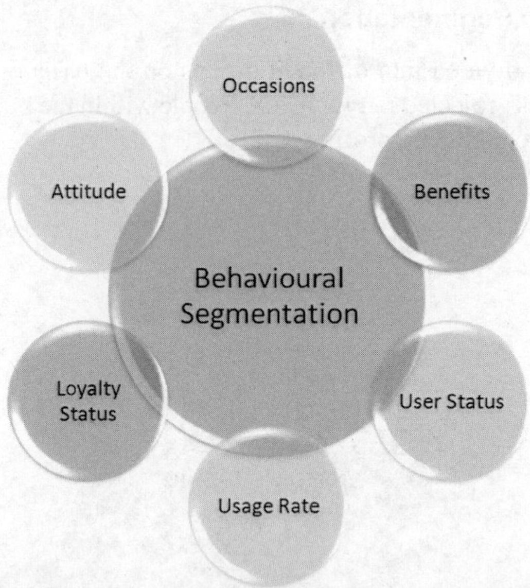

Figure 5.9 Behavioural segmentation variables.

Occasions

Occasions matter a lot in case of the purchase of a product especially in our country. There are many purchases which are made at the time of joining a new job, marriage, child birth, festivals, etc.

Benefits

Different people seek different benefits in purchases. There are some people who travel for fun, for others the purpose of travel is to be with family, or there are people who travel for adventure or educational purposes. The basic purpose is to travel but different people are seeking different benefits out of it, so marketers have to learn these differences and provide such benefits to the consumers.

User Status

Target consumers can be categorised into non-users, ex-users, potential users, first-time users and regular users of a product. Marketers have to decide as to which user status they would like to target their goods to.

Usage Rate

Markets can also be segmented on the basis of the consumption pattern of the consumers, such as, wholesale markets targeting to bulk purchasers and retail markets targeting to light and medium purchasers.

Loyalty Status

Consumers have varying degrees of loyalty to specific brands, stores, and other entities. On the basis of loyalty status, buyers can be divided into four groups:

(a) **Hard-core loyal**—they would buy only one brand all the time;

(b) **Split loyal**–where consumers loyalty is divided between two or three brands;

(c) **Shifting loyal**–where consumers shift from one brand to another;

(d) **Switcher**–where people have no loyalty to any brand.

A company can learn a great deal about consumers by analysing their degree of brand loyalty. They might have to put efforts to ensure the loyalty amongst the consumers and target the goods to them accordingly.

Attitude

It is a person's favourable or unfavourable feeling and action tendency towards some object or idea. People have different attitudes towards things, such as, some are enthusiastic and positive, while others can be indifferent, negative and hostile. Thus, it becomes important for the marketers to segment the market on the basis of consumers' existing attitudes rather than trying to change their attitude.

5.6.5 Multi Attribute Segmentation (Geo-Clustering)

Marketers are increasingly combining several variables in an effort to identify smaller, better defined target groups. Geo-clustering takes into consideration various factors in order to arrive at the precise definition of the market. It captures the increasing diversity of the population. Marketing to micro-segments has become accessible and more effective for marketers.

5.7 ESSENTIALS FOR EFFECTIVE SEGMENTATION

In order to be effective and useful, market segments must be:

(a) **Measurable**—The size, purchasing power and characteristics of the segment can be measured.

(b) **Substantial**—The segments are large and profitable enough to serve.

(c) **Accessible**—It should be easier for marketers to access those markets and make their goods available to the consumers in those markets.

(d) **Actionable**—It should be easier for marketers to implement their segmentation strategies and measure the results.

5.8 MARKET TARGETING

After segmenting the market into various sub-segments, it is essential for marketers to identify as to how many segments they would like to target keeping their marketing objectives and overall resources into account. The various factors which are taken into consideration to evaluate the market segments while deciding about market targeting are:

- The segments overall attractiveness; and
- The company's objectives and resources.

A company would like to finally select a market segment which will help them to achieve their objectives within their resources and in the best possible manner.

5.9 PATTERN FOR MARKET TARGETING

Having evaluated different segments, the company can consider five different patterns of target market selection as depicted in Figure 5.10.

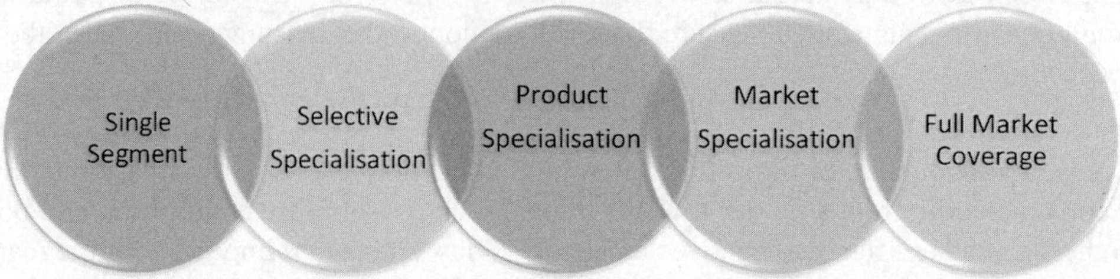

Figure 5.10 Pattern for market targeting.

5.9.1 Single Segment Concentration

In this case the organisation will put all their concentrated marketing efforts in a single segment and would like to ensure a strong market presence. For example, Royal Enfield specialises in manufacturing and selling heavy motor cycles to people. In this case the organisation is taking a big risk as they are putting all their eggs in one basket.

5.9.2 Selective Specialisation

In this case the organisation selects a number of segments, each objectively attractive and appropriate and designs a product exclusively for them. This multi-segment coverage strategy has the advantage of diversifying the firm's risk. For example, Maruti Udyog Ltd. is producing different types of cars to meet the requirements of people in different segments, such as, Baleno, Swift, Swift Desire, Zen, Wagen R, Alto, etc.

5.9.3 Product Specialisation

In this case the organisation concentrates on making one product and selling it to several segments. For example, Nokia selling mobile phones to various segments of the target audience.

5.9.4 Market Specialisation

This is where the organisation concentrates on serving many needs of a particular customer group or a specific segment. For example, Lakme, the cosmetic company, is serving the various needs of females by providing them with talcum, lipsticks, creams, moisturisers, nail paints, etc.

5.9.5 Full Market Coverage

In this case the organisation is willing to serve all the customer groups with all the products they might need in a particular market segment. Only very large firms can undertake a full market coverage strategy, such as, IBM is trying to take care of all the computer related needs of the consumers by providing them with various computer hardware and software.

5.10 PRODUCT POSITIONING

After segmenting the market and deciding to target the segments, it is very important for firms to develop a distinctive positioning strategy for each segment. Philip Kotler (1999) has defined, *positioning as the act of defining the company's offering and image to occupy a distinctive place in the target market's mind.* It is the basic reason as to why the target market should buy the product.

Positioning according to Al Ries and Trout (2000)—

> *Positioning starts with a product, a piece of merchandise, a service, a company, an institution, or even a person, but positioning is not what you do to a product. Positioning is what you do to the mind of the prospect. That is, you position the product in the mind of the prospect.*

Ries and Trout argue that in an over advertised society the consumers always remember the number one brand existing in the market. The top firm is remembered best. For example when asked, "Who was the first person to fly alone across the Atlantic Ocean successfully?", we answer "Charles Lindbergh". When asked, "Who was the second person to do it?", we draw a blank. That is why companies fight for the number one position. The second brand should invent and lead in a new category.

5.11 DIFFERENT POSITIONING STRATEGIES

Companies can position their products in the market on the basis of different strategies as given by Philip Kotler (1999). Some of them are listed in Figure 5.11 as under:

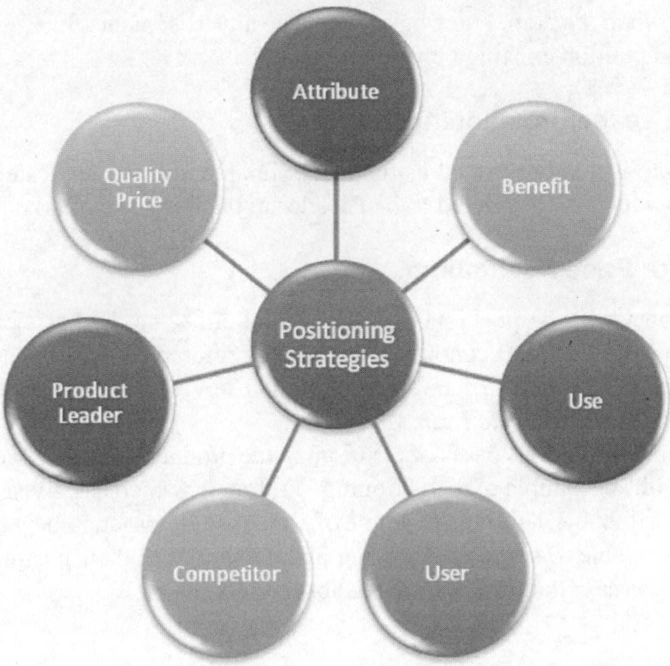

Figure 5.11 Different positioning strategies.

5.11.1 Attribute Positioning

In this case a company positions itself on the basis of an exclusive attribute, such as, the size or the number of years in existence. Disneyland can advertise itself as the largest theme park in the world.

5.11.2 Benefit Positioning

In this case the product is positioned as the leader in a certain benefit category. For example, Tide detergent claims to wash the clothes whitest.

5.11.3 Use or Application Positioning

In this case the product is positioned as best for some specific use or application. For example, Harpic advertises its product as a toilet cleaner which cleans the toilet in the best possible manner and ensures 100 per cent germ free toilet seat.

5.11.4 User Positioning

This calls for positioning the product as best for some users group. The advertisements for Mountain Dew show people performing thrilling activities and in the end they show them sipping the drink with a tagline *Dar Ke Age Jeet Hai* that means the drink is meant for those who want to seek thrill in their life.

5.11.5 Competitor Positioning

In this case, companies try to position the product in such a manner that they can prove their product to be better than the competitor's product. The advertisements for Complan and Horlicks showed a direct competition existing between the brands.

5.11.6 Product Leader Positioning

This is where the product is positioned as the leader in a certain product category. For example, Sony is a company which is considered to be a leader in the television market.

5.11.7 Quality or Price Positioning

In this case the product can be positioned in the market either on the basis of claiming the best quality or on the basis of the most economical price being offered by the company. Nirma washing powder was successful to generate a market share for themselves on the basis of the price advantage with their tagline *Wahi Safedi Saste Dam Me*.

After discussing the various bases of positioning the product in market, we would like to sum up the discussion with an example of repositioning—a strategy which has given life to an otherwise dying soap brand—Lifebuoy. This is an example of a smart strategy adopted by Hindustan Unilever where they have been able to successfully bring about changes in their positioning strategies for Lifebuoy soap and increase their market share substantially.

Brand Positioning Strategies of some Successful Companies

1. Coca-Cola: Coca-Cola is a pioneer in the field of product positioning. The brand is highly successful and has been able to survive for more than 125 years. It has always tried to bring out the values of happiness, friendship, joy, and sharing to position itself in the market. This has helped to promote engagement in consumers and in turn encouraged them to share happy experiences and moments.

Source: https://thisisnotadvertising.files.wordpress.com/2012/02/coke_connect_land.jpg

2. Starbucks: Starbucks has positioned itself well by focusing primarily on giving the best consumer experience. This brand introduced a new culture of writing the name of the client on the glass before serving them the drink. This was received well with millions of postings on social media networks. The brand was able to convey a simple message that buying a coffee can be a pleasant experience. The brand also allows customers to request through the mobile app. This helps to optimise the customer's time and lets him choose his coffee calmly which in turn helped to reinforce and improve the brands positioning.

Source: http://mydigitalinsight.blogspot.com/2019/11/starbucks-three-main-benefits-for.html

3. Amazon: The leading e-commerce company is also doing well when it comes to brand positioning. The relationship that the brand has with its customers to take shopping to an altogether new level is what drives its brand positioning. Agility in delivery, low prices, and freedom to like or dislike the product gives the brand a unique identity.

Source: https://digitalmarketinginstitute.com/blog/corporate-16-brands-doing-corporate-social-responsibility-successfully

Questions for Discussion

1. What do you think about the Starbucks brand positioning strategy?
2. Collect few more examples from the corporate world and discuss their positioning strategies.

LET US SUM UP

- Market segmentation can be defined as a process of dividing a total market into various sub-segments or parts by using some definite criteria or bases.
- Instead of focusing on all and ensuring an average satisfaction to all the customers, the concept of market segmentation believes in giving maximum utility, value and satisfaction to the few selected customers.
- Target marketing requires marketers to take three major steps—market segmentation, market targeting and market positioning.
- Many companies are turning to micro-marketing at one of the four levels—market segments, niche marketing, local marketing and individual marketing.
- Market segment consists of a large identifiable group within a market with similar wants, purchasing power, geographical location, buying attitudes or buying habits.
- Niche is a more narrowly defined group, typically a small market, whose needs are not well served. Marketers usually identify niches by dividing a segment into sub-segments or by defining a group seeking a distinctive mix of benefits.
- Local marketing is designing the marketing programmes being tailored to the needs and wants of local customer groups.
- Ultimate level of segmentation leads to segmentation of one—customized marketing or one to one marketing. This is where a manufacturer will customise the offer, logistics, communications and financial terms for each major account.
- Buyer's preferences are generally segmented in the market in the three different patterns, such as, homogenous preference, diffused preference and cluster preference.
- There are differing bases used for segmenting consumer markets. The major amongst them are—geographic, demographic, psychographics and behavioural segmentation variables.
- Geographic segmentation variables call for dividing the market into different geographical units such as, nations, regions, states, cities or neighbourhoods.
- In demographic segmentation, the market is divided into groups on the basis of variables, such as, age, family size, family life cycle, gender, income, occupation, education, nationalities, social class, etc.

- In case of psychographics segmentation, buyers are divided into different groups on the basis of lifestyle or personalities and values.
- Behavioural segmentation calls for dividing buyers into groups on the basis of their knowledge of, or attitude towards, or use of, or response to a product.
- Once the firm has identified its market segment opportunities, it has to decide how many and which ones to target keeping in mind their objectives and resources and is called *market targeting*.
- After segmenting the market and deciding to target the segments, it is very important for firms to develop a distinctive positioning strategy for each segment. *Positioning* is defined as the act of defining the company's offering and image to occupy a distinctive place in the target market's mind.
- Companies can position their products in the market on the basis of different strategies, such as, attribute, benefits, user, competitor, quality or price positioning.

QUESTIONS TO CHECK YOUR PROGRESS

Short Answer Questions

1. Explain target marketing.
2. Give two examples of niche marketing.
3. List out the factors in behavioural segmentation.
4. Explain one-to-one marketing.
5. What is clustered marketing?
6. Define geo-clustering.
7. Name the considerations for selecting target markets.
8. Name three patterns followed for market targeting.
9. Define the concept of product positioning as given by Al Ries and Trout.
10. List out the bases for product positioning.

Long Answer Questions

1. What is market segmentation? Discuss the different criterias for market segmentation.
2. Why is it important for marketers to go for market segmentation? Explain the various levels of market segmentation with examples.
3. What is market segmentation? What variables would you use in segmenting the consumer goods market?
4. List and discuss the major levels of market segmentation and bases for segmenting consumer goods market.
5. Briefly describe the three steps of target marketing—market segmentation, market targeting and market positioning.
6. Distinguish between mass marketing and target marketing with the help of an example.
7. What is target marketing? How will you classify the segment and what marketing strategy will you suggest in case of—(a) five-star hotel rooms; (b) ice creams; (c) baby foods; (d) books; (e) furniture; (d) computers; and (f) expensive cameras.

8. "Firms have shown different strategies towards the existence of market segments-some ignoring them, some developing the variety of products and marketing programmes to meet their needs, and some going after only a few segments". Illustrate this statement and bring out the relevant merits and demerits of the above three strategies. What characteristics influence the firm's choice of a marketing strategy?
9. "Market segmentation and product positioning are the bases for marketing planning and control". Comment upon the statement.
10. Suggest a successful way to segment the market for the following products— (a) detergent soap; (b) automatic dishwasher; (c) designer jewellery; (d) carpets; and (e) breakfast cereals.
11. What are the factors that affect the choice of an appropriate segmentation strategy for a company manufacturing consumer goods?
12. What is market segmentation? How is it different from product differentiation and product positioning?
13. Explain the major demographic bases for segmenting of consumer goods market. Give suitable examples.
14. Explain how companies identify attractive market segments and choose a market coverage strategy.
15. What is positioning? How does it differ from segmentation? List out the various bases for product positioning.
16. Discuss how companies can position their products for maximum competitive advantage in the marketplace.
17. Why is it important to position the product carefully in the minds of consumers? Explain by listing three positioning strategies used by marketers with example.
18. Write short notes on—(a) niche marketing; (b) one-to-one marketing; (c) market segments; (d) behavioural segmentation; and (e) value-based segmentation.

CHAPTER 6

Product Decisions

Learning Outcomes

After studying this chapter, you will be able to:

- ❖ Define the concept of product
- ❖ Illustrate the composition and classification of the product
- ❖ Explain the stages involved in the new product development process
- ❖ Understand clearly the marketing strategies for various stages of the product life cycle
- ❖ Discuss the concept of product mix and product line
- ❖ Determine the significance of packaging, branding and labeling in the success of a product

Marketing is an indispensable activity for every business to succeed in today's competitive environment. But for marketers to succeed and to enter in the market, it is very important to have a product, service or an idea. After segmenting the markets and understanding the behaviour of the prospective consumers, it is very important for the marketers to produce or procure a product and launch it in the market. In a very narrow sense, a *product* is a set of tangible physical attributes assembled in an identifiable form. However, in marketing, the concept of a product is much wider. A product can be more than a physical thing and it may be a service, a feeling, a pleasure, a reputation, or an experience. In reality, the consumer obtains a bundle of satisfaction as a result of buying a product. Thus, the organisations have to consider the product from the customer's perspective. For example, the cosmetic companies are combining chemicals to make lipsticks, vitamin manufacturers produce little pills, watch makers produce mechanical devices that keep time—but for a customer, a lipstick becomes a hope to look young and beautiful, vitamins become a hope for a healthier life and watches become status symbols.

According to Philip Kotler (1999)—

> *A product is anything that can be offered to a market for attention, acquisition, use or consumption that might satisfy a need or want. It includes physical objects, services, persons, place, organisations or ideas.*

According to William J. Stanton (1994)—

> *A product is a set of tangible and intangible attributes, including packaging, colour, price, manufacturer's prestige, retailer's prestige, and manufacturer's and retailer's services, which the buyer may accept as offering want-satisfaction.*

Therefore, it should be clear that a product is not only a bundle of physical and chemical attributes, but also includes various intangible attributes that have the potential to satisfy the present and future customer's needs and wants, and is received in exchange for money or money's worth. In addition to the physical good itself, other elements include packaging, branding, labeling, manufacturer's prestige, wholesaler's and retailers' prestige, guarantee, warranty, installation, after sales services, etc., which add tremendous value to the product. For example, a customer buying an air-conditioner with a maintenance contract from *Samsung* is buying a different product than another who buys some unbranded air-conditioner without the maintenance agreement.

6.1 COMPOSITION OF A PRODUCT

Let us understand the composition of a product. Generally speaking, a product is compared to an onion, which has various layers. As the top layer is peeled, the next layer comes out. In the same manner, a product has five layers or levels. At each layer or level, marketers add more customer value by adding some more features or services to the product. The various product levels have been listed out in Figure 6.1.

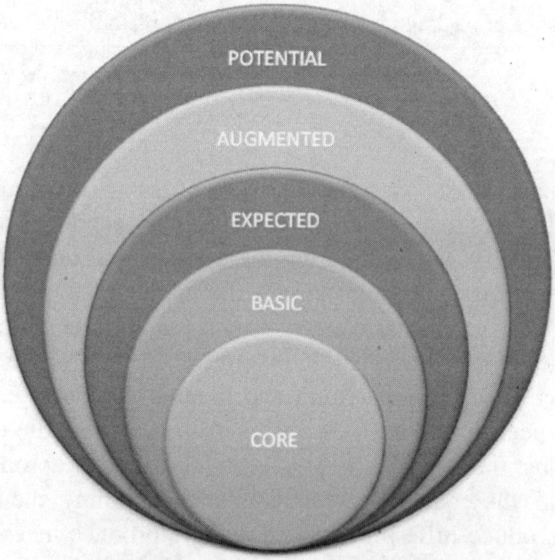

Figure 6.1 Composition of a product.

6.1.1 Core Product

The first and the most fundamental level is the Core product which provides core benefit—the fundamental service or benefit that the customer is really buying for. It is the genuine reason for which the product is purchased or the basic satisfaction a consumer is looking for in the purchase of that product. For example, a woman buying a lipstick is not buying simply lip colour or the physical and chemical attributes but is buying a hope or feeling of looking pretty. In other words, a product in its pure raw or natural form is called the *core product*, as in the case of tea leaves, which are freshly plucked from the tea gardens and after processing get converted into the core product.

6.1.2 Basic Product

At the second level, the marketer has to turn the core product into a basic product. Core product is generally in a very raw form, so marketers have to add a certain quality level, some more features, design the product's packaging, give it a label and a brand name to convert it to the basic level. For example, tea leaves plucked from the tea garden and processed simply in raw form is the core product, but when these leaves are graded, packed, labeled and are given a brand name, they get converted into the basic product.

6.1.3 Expected Product

At the third level, the marketer prepares an expected product, wherein another set of attributes and conditions are added to the product, to make it more valuable to the customer, for example the convenience of a product purchase and economical prices. As explained in the previous level, varieties of tea leaves are made available to the customer at convenient locations in the market with different levels of pricing, keeping the quality levels and the cost of packaging into account.

6.1.4 Augmented Product

At the fourth level, the marketer prepares an augmented product that exceeds customer expectations. At this level, new improved features are added to the product, which are not being offered by any competitor. The tea producers launch various flavours of tea in the market, such as ginger tea, green tea, honey lemon tea, premium tea, etc. Thus, in today's scenario, competition essentially takes place at the product augmentation level because at this stage different features are added by marketers in their products to give their product a distinct identity than that of their competitors. This view has been supported by the renowned marketing author Theodore Levitt (1969). According to him—

> *The new competition is not between what companies produce in factories, but between what they add to their factory output in the form of packaging, services, advertising, customer advice, financing, delivery arrangements, warehousing, and other things that people value.*

6.1.5 Potential Product

At the fifth level stands the potential product. This is where companies try to add certain exclusive features in their product. They search for new, innovative and creative ways to satisfy customers and give their product a distinct identity from that of the competitor. Successful companies add benefits to their offering that not only satisfies the customer, but also surprises and delights them. Delighting is a matter of exceeding expectations. This is one of the reasons that banks provide their customers with e-banking or some other online services, so that they do not have to travel long distances to perform banking transactions. These are the added benefits which add tremendous value to the marketers' goods or services. Thus, a product can have all these levels, as it is introduced in the market.

6.2 PRODUCT CLASSIFICATION

Product classification can be done on a variety of perspectives.

6.2.1 Tangibility and Durability

Based on the tangibility and durability, the product can be classified into three main groups as depicted in Figure 6.2.

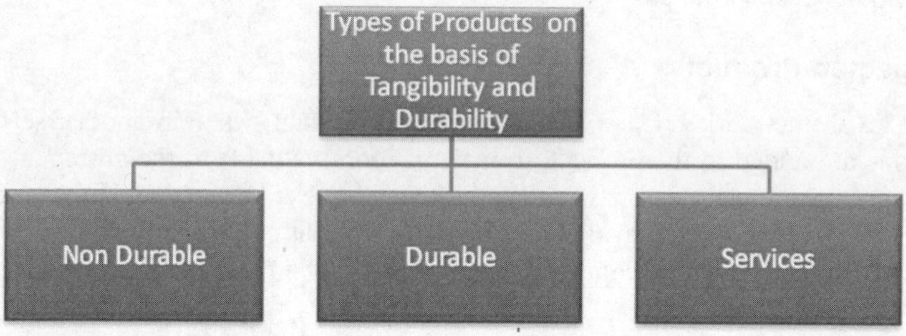

Figure 6.2 Types of product on the basis of tangibility and durability.

Nondurable Goods

Nondurable goods are tangible goods that are normally consumed in one or few uses. Examples include fruits, vegetables, toothpaste, soaps, talcum powder, etc. Because these goods are consumed quickly and purchased frequently, the marketer tries to make them available at various locations, keep low prices and advertise aggressively to induce trial and purchase, and build preference.

Durable Goods

Durable goods are tangible goods that normally survive many usages and generally last for a year or more. Examples include various furniture and household items, cars, mobile phones, computers, clothing, etc. In general, these types of goods require more personal selling, unique features, are high margin products, require more quality control and lots of after sales services, such as guarantee/warranty, etc.

Services

Services are intangible, inseparable, variable and perishable products. They are delivered by the service provider directly to the recipient. The quality of the service depends on the service provider. It might vary from person to person. As a result, services normally require more quality control, supplier credibility and adaptability. Examples include travel and tourism, hospitality, medical and educational services, banks and financial institutions, etc.

6.2.2 Consumer Goods Classification

The products can also be classified on the basis of, type of consumer and the purpose for which the products are being consumed. Thus, they fall into two categories—Consumer goods and Industrial goods. Their classification is nicely depicted in Figure 6.3.

Consumer Goods

Consumer goods are consumed by final consumers for their own interests (individuals and households) and not for commercial purposes. The vast array of consumer goods can be classified on the basis of shopping habits of consumers into four types:

1. Convenience goods;
2. Shopping goods;
3. Specialty goods; and
4. Unsought goods.

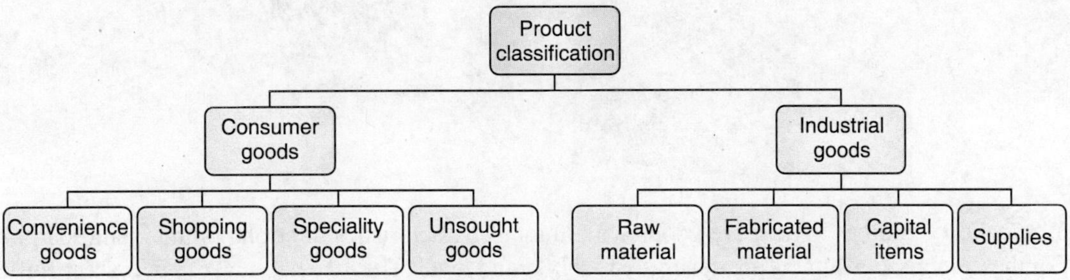

Figure 6.3 Product classifications on the basis of consumption pattern.

1. Convenience goods: Convenience goods are those products that a customer purchases frequently, immediately and with a minimum of effort in comparison and buying. Examples include soaps, toothpaste, batteries, candies, newspapers, etc.

2. Shopping goods: These are goods for which a consumer will not mind shopping around and making a thorough comparison on the basis of their price, quality, style, uniqueness, etc. They do not mind spending time in purchase and travelling long distances for making such comparisons. Examples include home furnishings, shoes, purses, mobile phones, accessories and major electronic appliances.

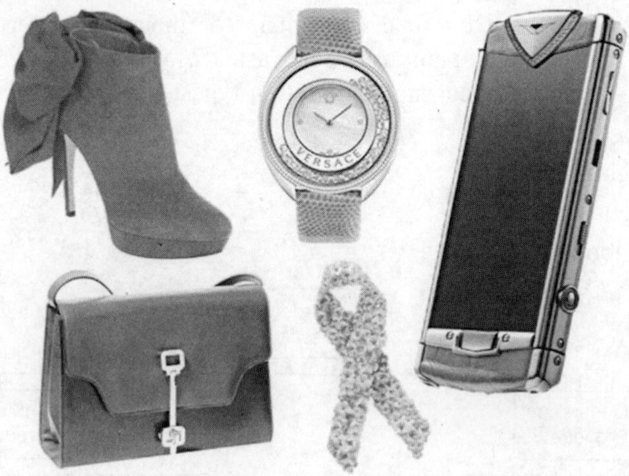

3. Speciality goods: These are goods with unique characteristics or strong brand identification. For these goods, consumers are generally highly brand loyal. They are habitual of buying a specific product and are willing to make special purchasing efforts for them. They do not mind travelling long distances, waiting long periods and even paying premium prices to acquire such products. Examples include luxury cars, designer watches, designer clothing, expensive mobile phones, etc. But it is not necessary that only expensive goods fall in the category of speciality goods. A commonly quoted example in this case is cigarettes where it has been observed that people are generally loyal to a specific brand of cigarettes and prefer having that only.

4. Unsought goods: Unsought goods are goods that are not purchased frequently in normal course. In case of such goods, most of the times the consumer does not know about them, or knows about but does not normally think of buying. These goods can also be of two kinds:

(a) *Unsought regular products* are goods which exist in the market and are known to consumers, but are not purchased by them in the normal course of time, such as medicines, life insurance policies, etc.

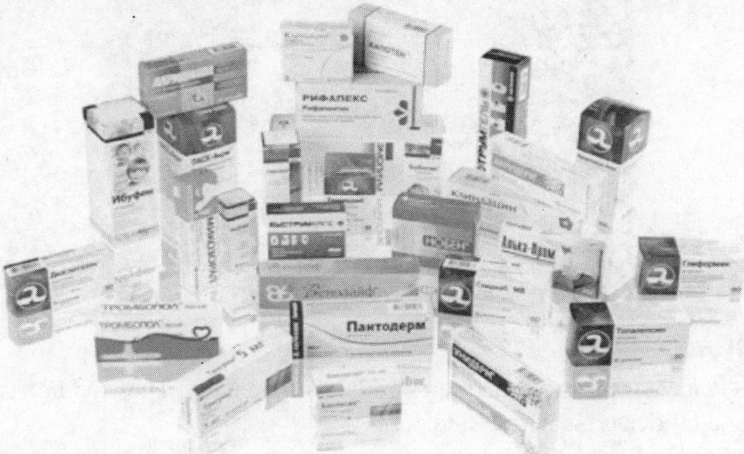

(b) *Unsought new products* are products which are new to the market and consumers do not know much about them or have some misconceptions about them. Therefore, they won't be purchasing them unless they get full information about the product. For example, smoke detectors, automatic dish washers, etc.

6.2.3 Industrial Goods Classification

Industrial goods can be classified in terms of how they enter the production process and their relative costliness. They can be divided into three groups—materials and parts, capital items, supplies and business services.

Materials and Parts

These are goods that enter the manufacturer's product completely. They fall into two categories—raw materials, and fabricated materials and parts.

1. Raw materials: These are taken from nature. Examples include wheat, cotton, livestock, fruits and vegetables. These are supplied by many producers, who turn them over to marketing intermediaries, who provide assembly, grading, storage, transportation and selling services, and finally make them available to the manufacturers.

2. Fabricated material and parts: These are manufactured products of one production unit such as iron, yarn, cement, wires, etc., and are required by another production unit to be processed further and finally become part of the finished goods.

Capital Items

Capital items are long lasting goods or in other words, basic goods which facilitate the production of the finished goods. They include two groups—installations and equipment.

1. Installations: Consist of buildings (factories, offices) and heavy equipment (generator, elevators, mainframe computers).

2. Equipment: Factory equipment and tools (hand tools, lift trucks) and office equipments (personal computers, desks, tables).

These types of products do not become part of the finished product, but are very important to produce finished goods. They provide the basic infrastructure which facilitates the smooth production of goods and services. While buying such products, companies look for their quality, utility, durability, exclusive features and price.

Supplies and Business Services

Supplies and business services are short-lasting goods and services that facilitate developing or managing finished product.

1. Supplies: They are of two kinds—operating supplies (lubricants, coal, writing paper, pens, etc.), and maintenance and repair items (paints, nails, vacuum cleaners).

2. Business services: These include maintenance and repair services (window cleaning, computer maintenance, etc.) and business advisory services (legal, management consulting and advertising services).

6.3 NEW PRODUCT DEVELOPMENT PROCESS

It has been rightly said that nothing happens unless somebody sells something. Therefore, it is very important to first have something to sell—a product, a service or an idea and that 'something' must be developed carefully. There are certain stages through which every company has to go before arriving at the final product. Figure 6.4 nicely depicts the stages to be followed.

Figure 6.4 New product development process.

As shown in the figure, the development of a new product proceeds through a series of seven stages that are listed below. During each stage, management must decide carefully whether to move on to the next stage, abandon the product, or seek additional information. While it is not necessary for all the companies to follow the step-by-step approach, but still it is always recommended, as this approach helps them in minimizing the risk of product failure at a later stage.

6.3.1 Idea Generation Stage

The first stage in the new product development process is to generate various ideas which can be later evaluated as potential product options. At this stage the focus is on inviting as many ideas as possible and from whatever source within or outside the organisation, so that the manufacturer should not repent at a later stage that some ideas were not explored. Customer's needs and wants are the logical places to start in the search for new product ideas. Ideas can be generated by organising focus group interviews with consumers, middlemen, feedback from sales personnel, consumer feedback and suggestions, and acquiring knowledge about competitor's product strategies through various sources.

6.3.2 Idea Screening Stage

At this stage the ideas generated at stage one are critically evaluated by the senior management in order to select the most attractive option. While selecting the ideas, the opinion of people at various levels is sought so that the chances of committing an error can be reduced to the minimum. At the screening stage, the company must avoid two types of errors—a drop error, which occurs when the company dismisses an otherwise good idea, or a go—error, which occurs when the company permits a poor idea to move into the development and commercialization stage. The purpose of screening is to analyze the ideas carefully and avoid committing both the types of errors.

6.3.3 Concept Development and Testing Stage

At this stage, few selected ideas are discussed at length with customers, distributors and the company employees by showing them a detailed concept note or a storyboard displaying drawings of product ideas, so that their suggestions can be incorporated while designing an excellent product. During discussions with everyone, an effort is made to elicit their response in terms of their likes and dislike of the concept, the various features to be included in the product, their level of interest in purchasing the product and the likely price they would like to pay for the product.

6.3.4 Business Analysis Stage

At this stage, when marketers are left with one or two options, lots of efforts are made by them to check out the commercial viability of those product ideas because no organisation would like to move to the next stage with a loss-making proposition. Even though the idea still remains on paper, an effort is made by marketers to estimate the tentative market size or the expected market demand of the product, calculations are made regarding the estimated cost of manufacturing the product and the resultant sales and profit figures are calculated. It is at this stage that the ideas are discussed with the purchase and production department personnel. So that it should be convenient for them to arrange for the necessary raw materials, machinery and infrastructure to ensure a smooth production process.

6.3.5 Product and Marketing Mix Development Stage

Ideas passing through business analysis enter into product and marketing mix development stage. At this stage, with the help of the research and development department of the organisation, the basic design of the product is prepared and certain prototypes of the idea are developed. Lots of functional tests are performed on these prototypes under laboratory and field conditions to check their performance levels and safety standards. Decisions regarding the other three Ps, namely, Price, Place, and Promotion are also taken at this stage. Once the prototype is ready, a representative group of customers are invited to the company premises and are shown the real product. They are also encouraged to discuss the pricing strategy and give their comments on the sample advertisements. Customer's suggestions at this stage help the company to arrive at appropriate marketing-mix decisions and the product is finally ready to be launched in the market.

6.3.6 Market Testing Stage

Products surviving up to step six are ready to be tested as real products in the market. At times when the marketers are confident about the success of the product after the concept testing stage, they can skip this stage but generally when their stakes are higher, they go for market testing before finally going for commercialization of their product. At this stage, the product is finally packed, priced, promoted and introduced in a.small geographical area. The response of the consumers is sought from the test marketing area and the required adjustments are made in the various marketing-mix elements. Once finally approved by the larger segment of target customers, the product is ready to move to the seventh stage, i.e. commercialization.

6.3.7 Commercialisation Stage

This is a stage where the product is ready to be introduced to a wider market. Some firms introduce the product in phases to different parts of the market. This allows the company to plan the production in a more controlled way and to fine tune the marketing mix as the product is distributed to new areas. But before the product is distributed to new areas, certain important decisions are taken such as—

When to Introduce the Product (Timing)?

Marketers have to decide about the right time to introduce the product in the market at a large scale, keeping the time factor into account, such as the seasonal nature of the products, festivities and the flow of disposable income with consumers.

Where to Introduce the Product (Geographical Distribution)?

Marketers decide about the geographic dimensions of the market, i.e. whether to launch the new product in a single locality, a specific region, several regions, the national market or at the international market?

To Whom to Target the Product (Target Market Prospects)?

Within the markets, where the products have been introduced, the company must target its distribution and promotion policy to the best prospect group of customers.

How to Introduce the Product in the Market (Introductory Marketing Strategy)?

Companies must develop a plan for introducing the new product in the market. Various marketing mix decisions are taken carefully to introduce the product in a big way in the markets. Sometimes attractive introductory offers are made to attract present and potential customers towards the new product, such as distribution of free sample, buy-back guarantee, etc.

Finally to conclude, it can be said that it is very important for marketers to follow all these stages carefully if they want to avoid costly mistakes at a future date.

6.4 PRODUCT LIFE CYCLE

The moment a product is commercialized, it enters into its life cycle. A product is like a human being. It is born, grows up fast, matures and then finally passes away. The product life cycle discusses the stages which a product has to go through since the day of its birth to the day it is taken away from the market. A new product progresses through a sequence of stages from introduction to growth, maturity and decline. This sequence is known as the Product Life Cycle and is associated with the changes in the marketing situation, thus impacting the marketing strategy and the marketing mix. Companies have to design different marketing strategies for their products as they enter the various stages of the product life cycle. Figure 6.5 depicts the various stages in the Product Life Cycle of a product.

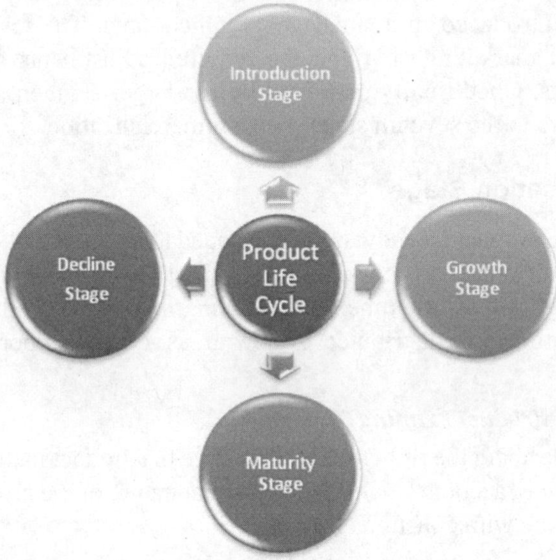

Figure 6.5 Product life cycle.

6.4.1 Theory of Diffusion and Adaptation

The theory of diffusion and adaptation of innovations provides the basic rationale for the Product Life Cycle. As depicted in Figure 6.6, when a new product is launched in the market, people hardly know about it. Therefore, it becomes important for the company to—

(i) First spread awareness about the product;
(ii) Generate interest in them;
(iii) Induce trial of the product; and
(iv) Finally initiate purchase action.

This whole process takes time, and in the introductory stage only a few persons (innovators) generally buy the product. These are enthusiastic people who would like to buy a new product. If the product is satisfying, a positive message spreads and a larger number of buyers (early adapters) are drawn in. At this stage, the competitor enters the market resulting in increasing the market's awareness and causing the prices to fall. As a result of this, more buyers start buying the product at the growth stage (early majority), and after listening to their positive feedback some more (late majority) buyers also join in. But after a certain point of time, generally at the maturity stage, the number of potential new buyers approaches zero, as all those who were interested to buy the product are already buying, sales become stagnant and only few (laggards) join the customer base. Eventually, sales decline as new and better product choices emerge in the market and divert the consumer's interest from the existing products and they start buying the newer options. That is how the product life cycle is explained by normal developments in the diffusion and adaptation theory of new products.

Figure 6.6 Theory of diffusion and adaptation.

6.4.2 The Product Life Cycle Stages

There are four basic stages in the product life cycle— Introduction, Growth, Maturity and Decline. Figure 6.7 nicely depicts the sales and profit levels during the four stages of the Product Life Cycle.

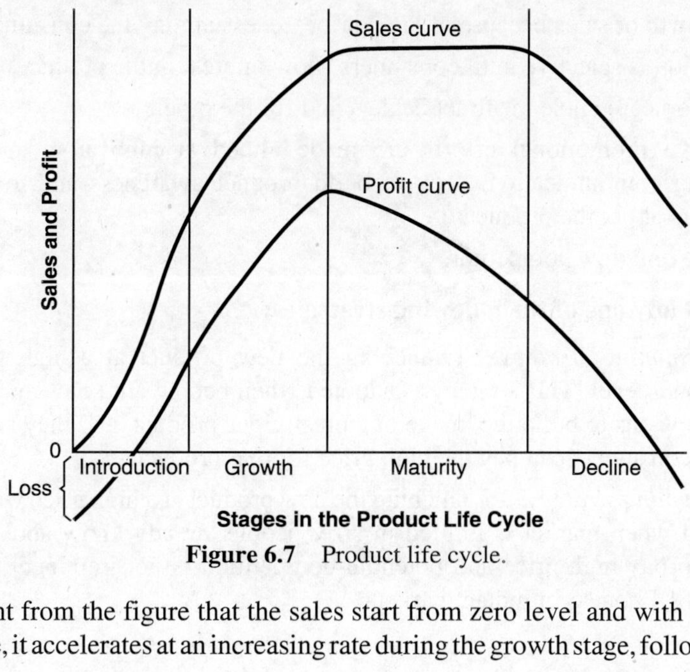

Figure 6.7 Product life cycle.

It is quite apparent from the figure that the sales start from zero level and with a slow start in the introduction stage, it accelerates at an increasing rate during the growth stage, followed by stagnation at the maturity stage and falling sales during the decline stage. Similarly, the profit curve starts from the initial losses, reaches the breakeven level and then starts increasing at the introduction stage, increases at a rapid pace during the growth stage, reaches its highest point somewhere near the maturity stage, starts declining during the stable maturity stage and continues to decline at the decline stage. As the sales and profit curve behave differently during the different stages, it becomes important for the marketers to design appropriate strategies to handle the product during the various stages.

Stage one: Introduction Stage

Stage one is where the new product is launched in the market. As the product is new, nobody knows about it and the marketers have to work very hard to get the product introduced and noticed in the market. The length of the introduction stage varies from product to product depending on various factors discussed in the preceding paragraphs.

Characteristics of introduction stage:

- Decisions regarding the product branding, packaging and labeling are made, and patents (if any) and trademarks are obtained.
- As the product is new and the company is not sure of its success, it introduces the basic version of the product in the market.
- Huge investments are made in the production, distribution and promotion of product in the market.
- Costs are high due to low initial sales.
- Pricing may be low-penetration pricing to build market share rapidly, or high-skimming pricing to recover developmental costs fast.
- Slow growth of sales because of lack of awareness among the consumers.
- Distribution is selective until consumers show interest in the product.
- Huge efforts are made to attract dealers and fill the pipelines.
- Aggressive promotional efforts are made aimed at innovators and early adopters. Marketing communications seek to build product awareness and to educate potential consumers about the product.
- There are only few competitors.

Marketers adopt any one of the following strategies:

- *Rapid skimming strategy*: Launching the new product at a high price with a high promotional level. This strategy is adopted when people are unaware about the product, company wants to build the image of a prestigious product, and they are confident of the fact that consumers can pay the high price for that product.
- *Slow skimming strategy*: Launching the new product at a high price with low promotion. It is used when market is limited in size, people already know about the product, are willing to pay high price and potential competition is not imminent. For example, the launch of I-Phone 5 in Indian markets.

- *Rapid penetration strategy*: Launching the product at a low price and spending heavily on promotion. This strategy works when the market is large, unaware of the product, and buyers are highly price sensitive. There exists a strong potential competition and the marketer is planning to reduce the unit manufacturing cost with increasing turnover. Thus, the focus is on targeting a large market share and earning profits through generating volume. For example, the introduction of new breakfast cereals in the market.
- *Slow penetration strategy*: Launching the new product at a low price and low level of promotion. Marketers use this strategy in case when market is large and people are highly aware of the product. The product is generally basic in nature and people want to buy it on their own. It is price sensitive and there is very little potential competition existing, such as in case of selling salt, sugar, pulses, etc.

Stage 2: Growth Stage

The growth stage is marked by a rapid climb in sales and profits of the company. Early adapters like the product and the middle majority consumers start following their leads. The firm seeks to build brand preference and increase market share. There is increasing demand in the market, sales curve starts moving upwards and the product starts showing profits. This is a stage which attracts competitors as they would also like to take the advantage of increasing profitability in that product category. Thus, special care is needed to ensure that it does not affect the growth stage of the product.

Characteristics of growth stage:

- Rapid climb in sales; early adaptors and middle majority can follow the leader.
- New competitors enter the market attracted by large scale production and profit.
- Pricing is maintained as the firm enjoys increasing demand with more and more customers coming forward and buying their products.
- Some of the companies may purposefully lower the prices in order to discourage the entry of competitors.
- Profits increase during this stage as promotion costs are spread over a large volume and unit manufacturing cost falls faster.
- Promotion is aimed at a broader audience.
- Companies maintain their promotional expenses at the same level or slightly raised level to meet competition and continue educating the market.
- Sales rise much faster, causing a decline in the promotion-sales ratio.

Marketers use the following strategies at this stage:

- Product quality is maintained, and additional features and support services may be added.
- New improved models of the product may be introduced.
- Companies tend to enter new market segments and increase their distribution network as demand increases and customers accept the product.
- The nature of advertising shifts from product awareness to bringing about product's conviction and purchase.

- The company may lower prices at the right time to attract the next layer of price sensitive consumers.

Stage 3: Maturity Stage

At the maturity stage, the rate of sales growth slows down and the product enters a stage of relative maturity. This stage poses formidable challenges to marketing management.

The maturity stage can be divided into three phases.

In the first phase, growth-maturity, the sales-growth rate starts to decline because of distribution saturation. There are no new distribution channels to fill, although some laggard buyers still enter the market.

In the second phase, stable maturity, sales come at par on a per capita basis because of market saturation. Most potential consumers have tried the product and future sales are governed by population growth and replacement demand.

In the third phase, decaying maturity, the absolute level of sales now starts to decline and customers start moving towards other products and substitutes.

Characteristics of maturity stage:

- The slowdown in the rate of sales growth creates overcapacity in the industry, which leads to intensified competition.
- The industry eventually consists of well-entrenched competitors whose basic drive is to gain competitive advantage.
- Sales become stagnant.
- Profits start to decline.

Marketers have to resort to the following strategies:

- In order to sustain the sales at a constant level, the company might have to add new or improved product features to differentiate their product from that of the competitors.
- They will have to convert non-users into users—for example, try to encourage non-coffee drinkers to drink coffee.
- They can suggest frequent uses of their products—for example, the shampoo company tries to introduce frequent uses of shampoo to have nice, silky and glowing hair.
- Even more usage per occasion can be recommended—for example, *Milkmaid* distributing Milkmaid recipe books free to the customers to suggest frequent and more usage of their product in various recipes.
- A company will have to try hard to win over the competitors customers.
- Prices may have to be reduced to attract the price-sensitive consumers away from the competitor.
- Distribution becomes more intensive and incentives may be offered to the middlemen, to encourage them to hold their product over competing products.
- Promotion emphasizes product's differentiation over that of the competitors'.
- Various sales promotion incentives are introduced for the consumers as well as dealers to maintain their interest in the product.

One of the recent examples of a company which has made an effort to come out of their decaying maturity and has tried to give a new lease of life to their product is Blackberry, as discussed below.

Blackberry's Revival Strategy

Blackberry—a name to be reckoned with for long time all over the world, was going through its worst time in the last one or two years mainly because of their sluggish approach to innovation. This practically moved the company into the decaying maturity stage, with market shares falling constantly. In the US, its market share, according to figures from Kantar World panel Com tech data, dropped from 6.1 per cent to a mere 1.1 per cent from the quarter ending December 2011 to the quarter ending December 2012. Shares in the UK were down from 16 per cent to 6.4 per cent. The overall scenario in India was also not comfortable, with growing competition from other mobile service providers.

But with an exhaustive launch of devices powered by the BlackBerry10 operating system, the company is making an effort to revive and is optimistic about its future. Armed with a tagline 'Keep Moving', BlackBerry is making lots of promises to their customers to popularise devices based on BB10. Backed by the huge financial support from the management, company is making lots of efforts to achieve market transformation. 'Keep Moving' is a line that the team expects to resonate with BlackBerry users across the globe, particularly in markets like India where technology has emerged as an enabler for a new generation of strivers. It's also going in for a lot of celebrity firepower. Thus, with technological improvements, celebrity endorsements, and lots of incentives, Blackberry is trying hard to win back its market share and come into the game again.

Source: Ravi Balakrishnan, "BlackBerry 10 arrives with a bang; can it grab the No 3 slot in each market it's launched in?" An article in Brand Equity, The Economic Times, February 13th 2013.

Questions for Discussion

1. Explain the reasons for the decline in the BlackBerry's market share all over the world.
2. Will the company be able to revive with new and improved technology, or do they need a new promotional policy to regain their lost market share?

Stage 4: Decline Stage

At this stage, market is saturated. Sales and profits eventually decline. Decline may be slow or rapid.

Characteristics of the decline stage:

- Sales may plunge to zero or they may remain at a low level and continue for many years.
- Sales decline for a number of reasons, including technological advances, consumers' shift in taste, and increased domestic and foreign competition, overcapacity, increased price cutting and profit erosion.
- Profits start declining and at times become negative.

As sales and profits decline, the firm can resort to the following marketing strategies:

- The product can be maintained in the market for some more time by adding certain new features and finding new uses.
- The company can continue to offer the product to its loyal customers at a reduced price.
- They can even discontinue the product.
- Use the product as replacement product for launching another new product successfully in the market.
- The various marketing decisions in the decline phase will depend on the fact that, whether it is being rejuvenated, or given a new lease of life, or left unchanged if it is being liquidated.
- The price may be maintained or reduced drastically if liquidated.

6.4.3 Summary of the Product Life Cycle

Table 6.1 Objectives of the Product Life Cycle

Stages	Introduction	Growth	Maturity	Decline
Objectives	Create product awareness and trial	Maximize market share	Maximize profits and defend market share	Reduce expenses and milk brands

Table 6.2 Characteristics of the Product Life Cycle

Stages	Introduction	Growth	Maturity	Decline
1. Sales	Low sales	Rapidly increasing sales	Peak sales followed by stability in sales	Declining sales
2. Costs	High cost per customer	Average cost per customer	Low cost per customer	Low cost per customer
3. Profits	Negative	Rising profit	High profit	Declining profit
4. Customer	Innovators	Early adopters	Early majority, late majority	Laggards
5. Competitor	Few	Growing number	Stable number, beginning to decline	Declining numbers

Table 6.3 Strategies of the Product Life Cycle

Stages	Introduction	Growth	Maturity	Decline
1. Product	Offer basic product	Offer product extension, service, warranty	Diversify brands/ models	Phase out weak products
2. Price	Charge cost plus profit	Price to penetrate market	Price to match better competition	Cut price
3. Distribution	Build selective distribution	Build intensive distribution	Build more intensive distribution	Selective phase-out of unprofitable unit
4. Advertising	Build product awareness among early adopters and dealers	Build awareness and interest in mass- market	Stress on brand difference and benefits	Reduce to retain hard core loyal
5. Sales Promotion	Use heavy sales promotion to induce trial	Reduce sales promotion due to increased consumer demand	More sales promotion to encourage brand switching	Reduce to minimum level

6.5 PRODUCT MIX AND PRODUCT LINE

Product mix is sum total of all the products manufactured or traded by some business house to reinforce their presence in the market, increase market share and increase the turnover for more profitability. For example, if we take the case of Hindustan Unilever, their product mix consists of fabric wash segment, hair care, skin care, oral care, household cleaning and other product lines. The Product Mix and Product Line of Hindustan Uniliver Ltd. (HUL) are depicted in Figure 6.8. Product mix and product line are two expressions used in connection with the range and variety of the products of a firm.

6.5.1 Product Mix

It is a larger entity. It denotes the complete set of all products offered for sale by a company. The product mix of a company is composed of all the product lines it carries.

6.5.2 Product Line

It is a group of closely related products that are considered to be a unit because of marketing, technical or end-use considerations. For example, all the toilet soaps of Hindustan Unilever like Dove, Pears, Lux, Liril, Rexona, Hamam, Lifebuoy and Breeze form a product line under personal wash category.

6.5.3 Width of Product Mix

This denotes the number of product lines it carries. It can also be termed as line extension, which means introducing a new product line, just like Mercedes was manufacturing cars; when it started to manufacture its bikes, it was line extension. Line extension can be upward or downward. In case of Mercedes, it was downwards.

6.5.4 Length of Product Line

This is decided by the number of items in a product mix.

6.5.5 Depth of a Product Line

It denotes the total number of items under each brand in the line in terms of variants, shades, models, pack sizes, etc.

> Product mix = all of the products we offer for sale
> Product line = a group of closely related products
> Length of product mix = the number of items in the product mix
> Width of product mix = the number of product lines carried
> Depth of product mix = number of variants offered in a product line

Figure 6.8 HUL's product mix and product line.

6.5.6 Constant Appraisal of Each Product/Brand in the Line

It is very important for a growing business to undertake constant appraisal of their existing product lines. Appraisal is required to check the validity of the products in light of the changes in business environment and the competitive forces. With time, some of the products become obsolete, while at times the entire product line may become outdated. Companies try to measure the market acceptance of their products from time to time in order to find out their popularity amongst the consumers. Some of the products are required to be withdrawn from the market due to functional obsolescence, which can occur because of the changing fashion or the upcoming of new/improved substitute products due to new and improved technologies. Therefore, there should be constant appraisal of each product in the product line and of each member/brand in the line.

The decisions may include withdrawal of the product in one case, stricter quality control in respect of another, giving an independent brand name to a product, and improving the utility of a product by adding a few features to it, or introducing a new product altogether, in yet another case.

6.6 PACKAGING

In a world where there is tremendous competition and all the brands are almost parallel to each other, it becomes very essential for the package to attract the attention of the target audience and make them buy the product. Therefore, packaging is considered as a very essential part of the product. It is becoming such an indispensable part that it is being referred to as the fifth 'P' of the marketing-mix. But before we go into the reasons as to why packaging is becoming so important, it is essential to first understand the concept of packaging and differentiate it from the term packing. In simple terms, *packing* refers to the protection of goods from breakage, spoilage, leakage or pilferage when transported and stored, while *packaging* is a broader term, and is concerned with designing and producing of appropriate packages for a product.

Successful brands are improving and enhancing the quality of their packaging. Most of us have vivid memories of talcum powders, baby foods and malted beverages in staid tin containers. Those were the days when packaging was not taken very seriously and its basic function was to ensure the delivery of the products. Then came an era when plastics like polyethylene, polypropylene, PET, etc., started replacing most metallic packaging by virtue of their easy availability, low cost and better design flexibility.

But these days nobody uses rigid containers and polyethylene. Different types of materials are used these days for packaging goods, such as paper, fiberboard, jute, plastic, glass, steel, aluminum, cork, ceramics, wood, etc. New shapes, designs, colours and forms are also being instituted. It's mainly because of the effective packaging that the consumer goods have moved ahead to evolve as fast moving consumer goods (FMCG). FMCGs are attractively packaged, branded, labelled and distributed all over the world. Their packages are effective enough to generate a self appeal and there is a ready demand for them in the market. A well-designed package will always be able to hold the attention and interest of the target audience for long in the product, and their chances of being purchased increase.

Apart from functional design and format of the package, packaging has also improved tremendously in terms of its appearance, attractiveness, quality and utility. From all this discussion, it can be easily inferred that *Packaging is often referred to as a silent salesman* due to its ability to influence consumers at the point of purchase. It also acts as a form of brand communication, imparting personality, positioning, values and benefits to the brand. Some of the important functions performed by packaging are listed below.

6.6.1 Importance/Functions of Packaging

- Packaging makes goods catchy, colourful, informative, and facilitate the sale of the product.

- It also protects the goods from breakerage, pilferage, spoilage or contamination.
- It also retains the moisture of the goods and keeps them fresh for long.
- Packaging can also add functional utility to the product as it becomes easy to handle and store.
- Rising consumer affluence means that consumers are willing to pay a little more for the convenience, appearance, dependability and prestige of better packages.
- It helps in preventing adulteration of the goods.
- With increasing competition in the market place, attractive packaging helps in catching the attention of the target audience.
- It is of immense importance in big departmental stores where there is widespread use of self-service and all the brands lie parallel on the same counter.
- Aesthetic factors are essential to make a brand stand out, to entice new shoppers and ensure that existing users can find it.
- Packaging increases the utility of branding a product. The brand name and mark can be printed on the packages and it may be used for advertising the product.
- The package advertising copy lasts for as long as the product is being used in its packaged form. Whenever the user uses the product, he is exposed to the message on the label every time.
- Finally, Packaging gives individuality or identification to a product.

Developing effective packaging may involve a huge monetary investment and take several months to complete. Companies may pay attention to growing environmental and safety concerns about packaging. The concept of going green and resorting to eco-friendly and recyclable packaging materials is being followed by most of the companies these days. Low-volume, low-priced packages are also being designed for rural and urban areas. Sachets of detergents and shampoos priced at ₹1, 2, or 5 are being introduced in the markets. Coke introduced its small bottle for ₹5 in rural markets. Most of the FMCGs are also resorting to such small, economical packaging of their goods and positioning them accordingly.

Power of Innovative Packaging

Companies are even trying to come up with innovative packaging. According to a report submitted in "The Brand Equity" from *The Economic Times*, dated 9th September, 2011, "designers like, Manish Malhotra, designed special cans for PepsiCo for Diwali 2011; Goa-based designer, Wendell Rodericks designed the confectionary brand Polo of Nestle and limited edition bottle of Himalayan Natural Mineral water for Nourisheo, a joint venture between PepsiCo and Tata Global Beverages, during Lakme Fashion Week in July 2011; Tarun Tahliani designed the ATM for Citibank India at DLF Emporio Mall in 2010".

Source: The Brand Equity, the Economic Times, 9th September, 2011.

All these facts clearly highlight the growing importance of packaging in today's market scenario.

6.6.2 Requisites of a Good Package

In order to realise all the benefits listed and perform all its functions properly, it is very important for every package to keep certain requisites into account as illustrated in Figure 6.9.

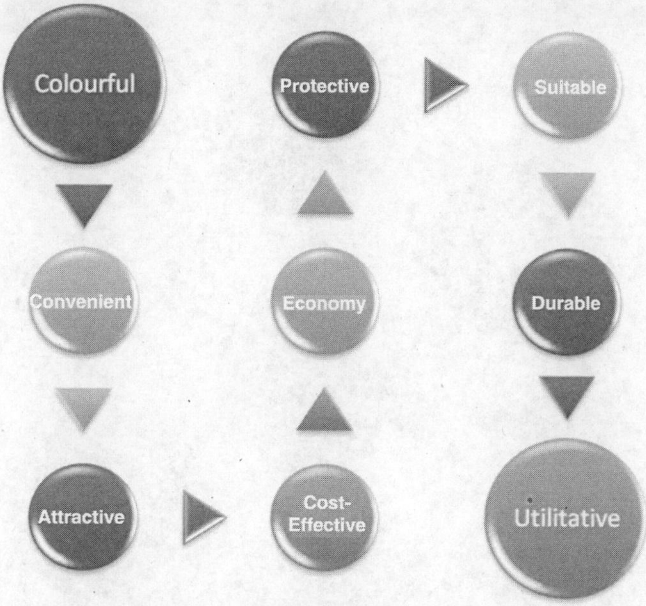

Figure 6.9 Requisites of a good package.

The focus on package development and branding will see a growing importance in the years to come, as this is one essential step to be taken by marketers to ensure growth of their brand amidst tough competition in the market.

6.7 BRANDING

Branding is a key concept in marketing circles. A well-defined brand drives sales, builds customer loyalty, creates brand value, and most of all, it can be the catalyst for business growth as consumers will be motivated to buy that product. The most distinctive skill of professional marketers is their ability to create, maintain, protect and enhance brands. Marketers say that "branding is the art and cornerstone of marketing". The term *branding* has been defined by the American Marketing Association (1995) as—

> *A name, term, symbol, design or a combination of them which is intended to identify the goods or services of one seller or group of sellers, and to differentiate them from those of competitors.*

A brand name consists of words, letters and/or numbers which may be vocalized, while a brand mark is the part of the brand which appears in the form of a symbol, design, or distinctive colouring or lettering. It is recognised by sight but cannot be expressed by pronouncing. A *Trade Mark* is a legal term and refers to a brand which is registered under the Trade and Merchandise Marks Act, 1958.

6.7.1 Features of Branding

A brand is essentially a seller's promise to deliver a specific set of features, benefits and services consistently to the buyer. It can convey up to six levels of meanings as depicted nicely in Figure 6.10.

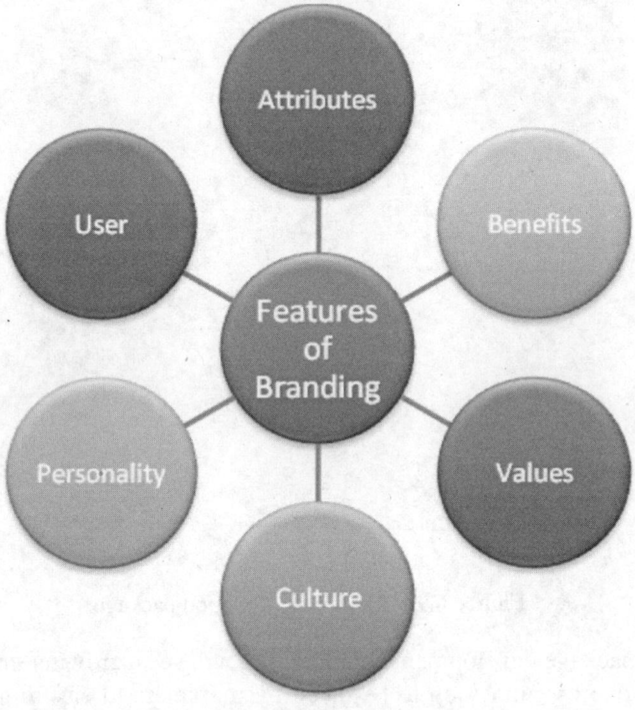

Figure 6.10 Features of branding.

Attributes

A brand brings to mind certain attributes. For example, Mercedes suggests an expensive, well-built, well-engineered, durable and a high-prestige automobile.

Benefits

Attributes must be translated into functional and emotional benefits. For example, quality, durability, comfort, prestige, etc.

Values

Indicates something about the producer's values. Mercedes stands for high performance, safety and prestige.

Culture

Band may represent a certain culture. Mercedes represents German culture—organised, efficient and high quality.

Personality

Brand can project certain personality. Mercedes may suggest a no-nonsense boss (person) or a lion (animal), a power symbol.

User

The brand suggests the kind of consumer who buys or uses the product. One can expect to see a 55-year old executive behind the wheel of a Mercedes, not a 20-year old secretary.

Therefore, the branding challenge is to develop a set of positive associations for the brand.

6.7.2 Characteristics of a Good Brand

- Short and simple
- Easy to spell and read
- Easy to recognise and remember
- Easy to pronounce
- Can be pronounced in only one way
- Can be pronounced in all languages
- Suggestive of product benefits
- Adaptable to packaging and labeling
- Always timely
- Legally available for use

6.7.3 Functions of Branding

Product Differentiation

Branding helps in differentiating a brand from its competitors and gives the product a distinctive identity.

Advertising

A brand name is used to advertise the product and establish an image in the minds of the prospective consumers.

Better Quality of Goods

Standardization in brands ensures better quality of goods and genuineness of the product to the consumers.

Competitive Advantage

Consumers are always willing to buy products they know and trust. A strong, well-defined brand, gives a competitive advantage to the product in the market. It might allow companies to charge more for their product, knowing that consumers will remain loyal, and buy it at the higher cost.

Consumer Protection

Prices of branded product are fixed by manufacturers and are printed on the cover itself. This protects the consumers because middlemen cannot charge more than the printed price.

Adds to the Prestige or the Goodwill of the Firm

Once established, the brand prestige remains for years and results in a high degree of brand loyalty amongst consumers.

Brand Loyalty

Strategic branding leads to a strong brand equity, which means the added value brought to a company's products or services, that allows them to charge more for their brand than what identical, unbranded products command.

6.7.4 Brand Equity

Brands vary in the amount of power and value they have in the marketplace. They can be broadly divided into five categories as displayed in Figure 6.11. At one extreme are brands that are not known by most buyers. Then there are brands for which buyers have a fairly high degree of brand awareness. Beyond this are brands with a high degree of brand acceptability, followed by brands that enjoy a high degree of brand preference. Finally, there are brands that enjoy brand loyalty to the maximum.

Brand equity is build around a high degree of brand acceptability, preference and loyalty. It is a result of high degree of brand-name recognition, perceived brand quality, and strong mental and emotional associations. Brands which enjoy a high degree of acceptability, are preferred over others, and have a committed and loyal clientele are considered to be enjoying brand equity, such as brands like Raymond's, Mercedes, BMW, Sony, etc.

6.7.5 High Brand Equity Provides a Number of Competitive Advantages

- The customer will enjoy reduced marketing costs because of less expenditure on advertising as the consumer already have brand awareness and loyalty.
- The brand is so popular amongst the consumer that the company can enjoy more trade leverage in bargaining with distributors and retailers.

Figure 6.11 Brand equity.

- The company can charge a higher price than its competitors because the brand has high perceived quality.
- The company can more easily launch extensions because the brand name is already popular and has loyal clientele.
- The brand loyalty gives the company an advantage over their competitors.

6.7.6 Brand-Strategy Decisions

The company can introduce:

Line extensions: Existing brand name extended to new sizes or flavours in the existing product category, such as—Tropicana juice in orange, apple litchi, mixed fruit, etc.

Brand extensions: Brand name extended to new product category, such as—Amul milk, Amul cheese, Amul butter, Amul cream, etc.

Multibrands: New brand names introduced in the same product category, for example, Hindustan Lever's different brands of bathing soaps, such as: Dove, Liril, Pears, Rexsona, Lifebuoy, Hamam, Breeze, Jai, etc.

New brands: New brand name for a new category product, such as—Hindustan Levers' Dove in bathing soaps, Surf Excel in fabric detergents and Brook Bond Red Label in tea.

Co brands: Products bearing two or more well-known brand names, such as—LG colour TV, Samsung colour TV, Sony colour TV, etc.

Finally, it can be safely concluded that in a world of consumers making choices in short spans. At the point of purchase, the development of Packaging and Branding is becoming one of the essential requisite to realise their maximum potential.

6.8 LABELING

A label is a part of the product which provides information to the customers that describes the product, its content, the manufacturing date and time of manufacture, when to use it, how to use it and where to keep it, etc. Labeling can be done on the package itself or it can be done by attaching an extra sheet inside the product. The label is used to communicate brand, grade and other information about the product. Various agricultural and food products are grade labeled as A, B, C depending on various quality parameters. Labeling has promotional and informational uses to customers. It might promote the product through its attractive graphics.

LET US SUM UP

- A product can be more than a physical thing—it may be a service, a feeling, a pleasure, a reputation or an experience. In reality, the consumer obtains a bundle of satisfactions as a result of buying a product.
- A product is a set of tangible and intangible attributes, including packaging, colour, price, manufacturer's prestige, retailer's prestige, and manufacturer's and retailer's services, which the buyer may accept as offering want-satisfaction.

- A product is compared to an onion, which has various layers. As we peel the top layer, the next layer comes out. The same way a product has five layers—Core, basic, expected, augmented and potential.
- Based on the tangibility and durability, the product can be classified into three main groups—non-durable, durable and services.
- The vast array of consumer goods can be classified on the basis of their shopping habits—namely convenience goods, shopping goods, specialty goods and unsought goods.
- Industrial goods fall into two categories—raw materials, and fabricated materials and parts.
- The development of a new product can proceed through a series of seven stages, such as idea generation, idea screening, concept development and testing, business analysis, product and marketing mix development, market testing and commercialization. During each stage, management must decide carefully whether to move on to the next stage, abandon the product or seek additional information.
- A new product progresses through a sequence of stages from introduction to growth, maturity and decline. Each stage is associated with changes in the marketing situation, thus impacting the marketing strategy and the marketing mix.
- Product mix and product line are two expressions used in connection with the range and variety of the products of a firm.
- Packaging is often referred to as a silent salesman due to its ability to influence consumers at the point of purchase.
- A brand is essentially a seller's promise to deliver a specific set of features, benefits and services consistently to the buyers.
- A label is a part of the product which provides information to the customers which describes the product, its content, the manufacturer date and time of manufacture, when to use it, how to use it and where to keep it, etc.

QUESTIONS TO CHECK YOUR PROGRESS

Short Answer Questions

1. Define the concept of product.
2. Draw a neatly labeled diagram of the composition of a product.
3. Who are called laggards?
4. Name the first step in the new product development process.
5. What is go-error and drop-error?
6. What is test marketing?
7. Name the stage of the life cycle characterized by low sales, heavy promotion, low profit and minimal competition.
8. What is the longest stage in the product's life cycle called?
9. Price reductions, promotion cutbacks, and competitor dropout are characteristics of which stage of the Product Life Cycle?
10. List out three qualities of effective package.
11. What are the various features of an effective brand name?
12. Name the act under which the brand name gets registered.

13. Explain the concept of brand equity.

14. Select the most appropriate answer from the given options—

(i) Branding becomes very important for the following reasons:
   (a) it helps in differentiating a brand from its competitors
   (b) standardized brands ensure better quality of goods and genuineness of the product
   (c) a strong well-defined brand gives a competitive advantage to the product
   (d) all of the above

(ii) A product can be successfully branded, provided—
   (a) it leads to economies of scale
   (b) the potential demand is going to be small
   (c) products can be easily identifiable afterwards
   (d) product quality will be inconsistent

Long Answer Questions

1. Visit the nearby market and gather information regarding the various products available there and classify them in various categories on the basis of their level of composition.

2. Why is it said that the competition takes place at the augmentation stage?

3. Why is it important to convert a product into potential product?

4. Differentiate between the following—
   (a) Consumer goods vs Industrial goods
   (b) Convenience goods vs Specialty goods
   (c) Unsought goods vs Shopping goods

5. Explain in brief—
   (a) Why is it important for producers to go through all the stages carefully for developing a new product idea?
   (b) Why is it that despite taking all the precautions, some of the new products meet with failure in the markets? Give examples.

6. Differentiate between concept testing and test marketing.

7. Define early majority, late majority, laggards or non-adopters, and opinion leaders.

8. Draw a neatly labelled diagram of the Product Life Cycle and explain the level of sales and profits during the various stages.

9. Explain the significance of diffusion and adaptation of innovations theory in the life of a product.

10. Why are after sale and other product related services included in an organisation's marketing decisions?

11. Examine the salient factors that ought to be taken into account while introducing a new product. Illustrate your answer.

12. Explain the difference in the marketing strategies followed by marketers in the introduction stage and growth stage.

13. How might a company's advertising strategies differ, depending on whether its product is in the introduction stage or the maturity stage of its life cycle?

14. Why maturity stage is considered as the longest stage in the life of a product?

15. Explain the various strategies used by marketers at the decline stage.

16. "A package is considered as a silent salesman". Do you agree with the statement? Explain.

17. Examine the role of packaging in the overall marketing strategy. What factors account for the growing importance of packaging as a tool of product promotion? Briefly explain each of them.
18. Explain the significance of branding and labeling in the success of a product in the market.
19. Is there any difference between a brand name and trademark? If so, why is this difference important?
20. "Branding is a useful tool both for consumers and manufacturers". Discuss the statement and highlight the considerations when giving a brand name.
21. Define the concept of brand equity. Why is it important for companies to build strong brand equity in the market?
22. What is the "Battle of the Brands"? Who do you think will win and why?
23. Select a familiar company and assume that you are an idea manager responsible for generating new product ideas. How would you structure the new product development process? What sources of new ideas would be most valuable?

CHAPTER 7

Pricing Decisions

Learning Outcomes

After studying this chapter, you will be able to:

- ❖ Understand the concept and objectives of pricing
- ❖ Identify the significance of costs and demand in setting the price
- ❖ Explain various cost and market based pricing methods
- ❖ Develop a pricing structure
- ❖ Compare the various geographical pricing methods
- ❖ Express the price discounts and allowances

Price is all around us, and is one of the most important 'P' in the marketing mix of an organisation. Despite the fact that most of the products have been designed very well, distributed to every nook and corner and promoted very aggressively, are still not able to meet with success only because of one reason, that is, they have not been priced appropriately. Indian consumers are considered to be highly price sensitive, therefore, pricing decisions become very important decisions for any organisation, if they want to achieve success in the Indian market.

In simple terms, *price* is defined as a numerical statement of what a customer must pay for a product or service. One of the leading causes of new product failures is—either under or over pricing. People are not going to buy the product in both the circumstances. If a product is overpriced, it is considered as too expensive, beyond the pocket of many people who are not going to buy it. If it is underpriced, like in the case of clothing, watches, perfumes, etc., it is directly assumed that the company must have compromised on the quality of the product and it is treated as an inferior product, and again in that case, people are not willing to purchase it. Therefore, it is very important for the marketers to price the product ideally at a level where it is neither overpriced nor underpriced.

One of the problems with effective pricing is the tendency of the marketers in India to fix price at a level which helps them recover the cost. Their only focus is on recovering cost, and they do not give any importance to delivering value to the consumers. Customer considerations, especially value to the user, are virtually ignored, while in the real sense, if a business has to be successful in today's competitive scenario, the concept of value should always be taken into consideration while arriving at important pricing decisions.

These days, consumers are highly value driven. "Value for money", "Best value", are fairly common. The concept of value can be explained as a buyer's overall evaluation of the product or service based on his or her perceptions of the benefits received, compared to what must be given up. It includes not only the monetary price, but also the time and effort that are involved in the purchase of the product. Superior value results from either offering customers lower prices for equivalent benefits, or providing unique product benefits that more than compensate the customers for paying a higher price. Creating and sustaining superior value is crucial for establishing competitive advantage. Thus, we would like to conclude our general introduction about pricing that the time has come when the Indian marketers should change their pricing decisions from being cost driven to value driven. Pricing should be done in such a manner that the customers are able to get the value for money and justify their purchase. The following example of Aircel tries to highlight the value-driven pricing policy of the company.

Aircel—Joy of a Little Extra

In one of the very interesting observations, we could notice that these are tough times for most mobile operators. Amidst the cut throat competition prevailing in the market, all mobile operators are trying to come up with unique marketing strategies.

While Airtel tries to connect with the consumers by using its catchy music and the charm of college students, Vodafone seeks to 'Delight' its consumers with its tailor-made offers and Idea tries to spread the 'Honey Bunny' virus to the entire nation. But Aircel, the fifth largest player in the market, has opted to go the route of selling extra benefits to the customers. They are trying to target the value-driven consumers by offering them little bit extra in their recent campaign.

The campaign titled 'Joy of a Little Extra' consists of three 30 second commercials depicting various 'slices of life' situations that range from grown-up men jumping with joy on getting an extra run in a friendly neighbourhood match, to a classroom of kids feeling elated when their teacher gives them a few more minutes to complete an exam. The third ad shows the joy felt by a housewife on getting an unexpected bonus while shopping for vegetables.

According to Prasoon Joshi, Chairman, McCann World Group India, "*Simple joys of life are the most precious ones to cherish and the brands that deliver are the ones that the consumers will love. Hence there is a conscious attempt to dial up the 'human connect' of the brand*".

In their earlier campaigns also, Aircel has been trying to provide value-driven services to their customers, who mainly comprise students and young working professionals. It's only because of their value-based marketing strategies that Aircel has managed to show positive net additions during the last six months of 2012. This clearly highlights one fact that the time has come when marketers have to shift their focus from cost-based pricing to value-based pricing strategies.

Source: An article by Amit Bapna, ET Bureau, "Aircel striving to establish a human connect with its new brand campaign 'Joy of a Little Extra', in Brand Equity, The Economics Times, 13th February 2013.

Questions for Discussion

1. Aircel, the fifth largest mobile operator has been able to give tough competition to the leaders in the category with their various pricing initiatives. Do you approve of their decisions?
2. "Value-driven pricing is the call of the hour". Do you agree? Explain in the light of the Aircel's pricing policies.
3. Can you suggest some better pricing strategies to Airtel and Vodafone to match the competition?

7.1 FACTORS AFFECTING THE PRICE

A firm must set a price for the first time when it develops a new product, or when it introduces its regular product into a new distribution channel or geographical area. While setting a price there are many factors which are to be taken into consideration. Some of the important factors, as depicted in Figure 7.1, are:

- Selecting the pricing objectives
- Determining the demand of the goods
- Estimating costs
- Analysing competitor's costs, prices and offers
- Other environmental factors
- Selecting a pricing method
- Selecting the final price

- **Selecting the Pricing Objectives**
- **Determining the Demand of the Goods**
- **Estimating Costs**
- **Analysing Competitors Costs, Prices, and Offers**
- **Other Environmental Factors**
- **Selecting a Pricing Method**
- **Selecting the Final Price**

Figure 7.1 Factors affecting the price.

7.1.1 Selecting the Pricing Objectives

Pricing policy of a company gets strongly affected by its marketing and other objectives. The clearer a firm's objectives are, the easier it will be to set the price. There can be various pricing objectives followed by different companies at different timings, such as:

Survival

This pricing objective becomes important for organisations suffering from the problem of overcapacity in production, intensified competition and low demand for the goods in the market. This objective is generally followed in the short run to ensure the survival of the organisation. Prices are kept at a level where they are able to cover the variable cost and some part of the fixed cost so that the company is able to stay in business. But this is only a short-term objective, because it generally does not result in much profitability. In such cases, companies expect their situation to improve in future so that they are able to make profits in the longer run.

Maximising Current Profits

Marketers estimate the demand and costs associated with alternative prices and choose the price that produces maximum current profits, cash flow, or rate of return on investment. Thinking only in terms of current financial performance results in a short term vision as the organisation is ignoring effects of all other variables on prices, such as competitors pricing, middleman's considerations, legal restrictions, changing consumer preferences, etc.

Maximising Market Share

For some organisations, maximising market share is their sole objective. They believe that higher sales volume will lead to lower unit costs, increased market share and higher long-term profit. In order to increase their market share and make the goods available to each and every consumer, they willingly keep the price low. But this strategy can work only in such markets which are highly price sensitive where low price can stimulate demand and result in increased market share. Organisations following this pricing objective believe in ensuring the profitability in the long run by enjoying the benefits of 'Economies of Scale' due to mass production and distribution.

Market Skimming Pricing

Some companies set high prices to skim the market. They believe that there are sufficient numbers of buyers and there is a high current demand for the product. Moreover, the high price communicates the image of a superior product and gives the company a leverage in the long run to reduce the price as price cuts are always welcome in the Indian scenario.

Price Quality Leadership

Some of the companies boost up on the quality front and price their products at a higher level than that of their competitors to convey an image of high quality product to the consumers.

Achieve a Target Level of Return on Investment

For some companies, achieving a minimum target level of Return on Investment (ROI) is an objective which guides them while pricing the product.

Be a Price Leader

Some companies believe in being the price leader in the market, so they purposely set the price at a level where all the new entrants have no choice but to follow them. This strategy helps in cutting down unnecessary competition in the market.

Discourage Entry by New Competitors

For some companies, especially in the short run, the main objective is to keep the competitors out of that market area. For this purpose they set the price at such a low level where it is not feasible for the new entrants to survive.

Use Price of One Product to Sell Other Products in Line

At times, companies set the price of one product at a low level in order to push the sale of an otherwise slow moving product, or a new product for which there is low demand.

Success Mantra for Parle-G

Parle-G has been a leader in the biscuit segment for last 75 years. Despite the tough competition given to them by Britannia and ITC, Parle-G's has been able to hold their distinction as the largest selling biscuit brand mainly because of its strong distribution network that covers over six million retail stores in the country. Along with reach, another big reason for Parle-G being a winner is its adoption across the socio-economic strata. "*One pack of Parle-G gives 400 gm calories to a person and is equivalent to one meal*", says Pravin Kulkarnii, Marketing head, Parle Products. The pricing strategy has also taken the price-sensitiveness of these consumers into account. From 1994 to 2008, Parle-G was priced at ₹4 a pack. In 2008, the price was increased marginally to ₹4.50, but as there was an immediate impact on volumes, the company went back to ₹4. In the last three years, the company has reduced the weight of the packs but has not changed the price. Today Parle-G is available at ₹1, ₹2, ₹3, ₹4, ₹5, ₹10, ₹20 and ₹55. The ₹1 to ₹4 packs are available only in Tier 2 and 3 cities and the rural markets.

Source: Preeti Chamikutty, "Will Parle-G be relevant to the next generation", Brand Equity, The Economic Times, 16th January' 2013.

Questions for Discussion

1. Do you support Parle G's decision to stick to a constant price of ₹4 for the 400 gm pack?
2. Targeting the product in rural markets calls for low unit pricing. Explain this view point in the light of various such initiatives by FMCG organisation.

Another good example of an effective pricing strategy has been the success of Parle-G Company, a pioneer in the biscuit segment. They have been able to capture a substantial share of the market and remain at the top for so many years, mainly because of their appropriate pricing strategy which they have designed keeping the Indian consumer into account.

7.1.2 Determining the Demand of Goods

After deciding about the specific objectives to follow, determining the demand for the product is another very important factor in setting the price of a product. In normal course, the relationship between the price and the demand is an inverse relationship—the higher the price, the lower the demand. But in the case of certain luxury products, or prestigious products, the demand curve sometimes rises upwards. A perfume company might raise its prices and be able to sell more perfumes rather than at low prices.

Thus, it becomes very important for any marketer to first estimate their likely demand. It can be estimated with the help of statistically analysing the past prices and quantities sold. Another factor to estimate their relationship is by asking buyers to state how many units they would buy at different proposed prices, or by conducting market research, keeping the provision for competitors' price policy, or changes in the other elements of marketing mix, or changes in other environmental variables.

It is not only important to estimate the demand, but even more important is to estimate the price elasticity of demand in order to know how to adjust the price with the changing demand. How responsive or elastic the demand would be to a change in the price is a very important factor determining the change. For example, if demand is hardly going to change with a small change in price, we say that demand is *inelastic* and there is no point in bringing any change in the price. While if demand varies considerably with a change in price, we say that demand is *elastic* and it is worth bringing in the change in price.

Demand is likely to be less elastic in cases:

- When the product is high in demand
- Where there are few or no substitutes or competitors in the market
- Where buyers are indifferent towards higher price
- Where the buyers are not willing to put in an effort of changing their buying habits or searching for lower prices
- Where buyers think that the higher prices are justified by quality, prestige or exclusiveness
- Where buyers are less price sensitive when they cannot store the product

If demand is elastic, the seller will consider lowering the price because a low price will produce more Total Revenue. This makes sense as long as the cost of producing and selling more units does not increase disproportionately.

7.1.3 Estimating the Costs of the Product

Another very important factor determining the price is the recovery of Total Cost incurred on setting up of business. As has already been explained, in India most of the pricing decisions are highly cost-driven rather than value-driven. The focus of most of the companies is on recovering the total cost of setting up the business including the production, distribution, promotion and all other types of marketing costs along with ensuring a fair rate of return on investment.

Types of Cost

The various types of costs incurred by an organisation in setting up and running of their business can be explained as under:

Fixed Cost: These are costs that do not vary with the level of production or sales volume, rather these are the basic infrastructural costs that are incurred in order to bring the business into existence, such as the cost of land, machinery, building, etc.

Variable/Marginal Cost: It varies directly with the level of production. In other words, *Variable Cost* is defined as the cost of producing one extra unit of product.

Total Cost (TC) = Fixed Cost (FC) + Variable Cost (VC) , for any given level of production.

Average cost: It is the cost per unit at a level of production. It is equal to TC/total number of units produced.

Given the choice, companies would like to charge a price that will help them recover the Total Cost (TC) at the earliest. But at times, when a company is facing stiff competition in the market, and the demand is reducing, it have no choice but to price its goods at a level where at least the Variable Cost (VC) or the Marginal Cost (MC) is recovered and it is able to survive in the market.

Figure 7.2 clearly depicts the setting up of a price. Given a choice, the firm would like to set the price at p_m, but this is possible only when it is expecting a high demand in the market. The firm might like to set the price at p_2, because at this point, it will be able to recover the Average Total Cost (ATC). But in case the firm is facing stiff competition and is not able to recover the total cost, it may have to set the price at p_1 where at least the Marginal Cost (MC) is recovered.

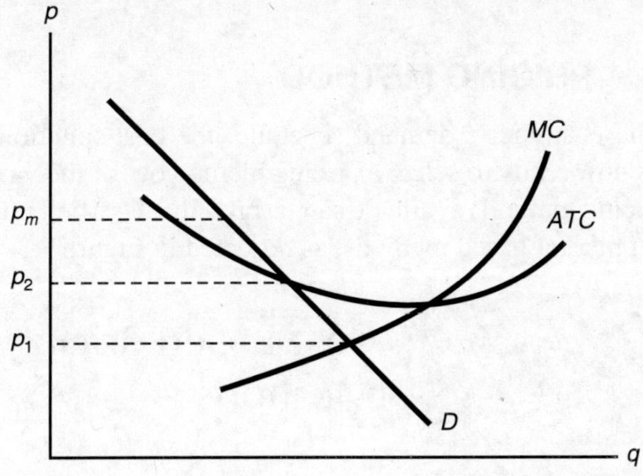

Figure 7.2 Diagram representing cost-based pricing.

7.1.4 Analysing Competitor's Costs, Prices and Offers

While fixing the price of the product keeping into account the market demand and the cost structure of the firm, the firm must take into consideration the competitor's costs, prices and possible price reactions. If the firm's offer is similar to a major competitor's offer, then the firm will have to price the product close to the competitor, or they will lose their sales. If the firm's offer is superior, the firm can charge more and if the offer is inferior, the firm will not be able to charge more than the competitor.

7.1.5 Other Environmental Factors

Besides considering the demand and cost of the product and the competitor's costs and prices it is important for the marketers to keep various environmental factors discussed as under into account while arriving at the price of a product.

Economic Conditions do play an important role in price fixation. Prices of products get strongly influenced by the fact that, whether the economy is going through inflation or recession. During the recession period, prices of most of the commodities are reduced to maintain their level of sales because of the declining purchasing power of the people. While in inflation, the prices of all the commodities increase putting great burden on the common man.

Resellers' Margins are also important in price determination. If resellers increase their margins, it directly affects the final price being paid by the consumers. For instance, petrol pump dealers went on strike a number of times recently, and finally the oil marketing companies had to agree to increase the margin for the resellers resulting in increased price of petrol for the consumers.

Government's Concern about pricing gets reflected in various laws and regulations formulated by them with regards to price controls, import duties, quotas, taxes etc. The recent decline in the value of the Rupee, vis-à-vis the Dollar, in the international markets has also affected the price of imported products or products using imported parts. The increase in the oil prices internationally left no alternatives for the oil companies but to increase the price of the petrol in India.

Hence, all the above mentioned factors are to be taken into consideration by marketers for fixing the price of a product.

7.2 SELECTING A PRICING METHOD

Given the three Cs—the customer's demand schedule, the cost function, and the competitor's prices—the company is now ready to select a pricing method out of the various methods available to them. The various pricing methods available can be broadly classified into two major categories, cost-based methods and market based methods, as reflected in Figure 7.3.

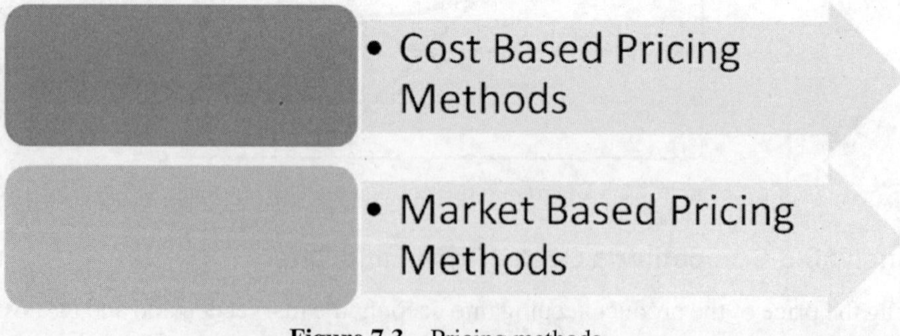

Figure 7.3 Pricing methods.

7.2.1 Cost-Based Pricing Methods

These are the pricing methods where the focus of the manufacturer is on recovering their costs as soon as possible and make some profit. Some of the important cost-based methods are discussed as under:

Mark-Up-Pricing

It is one of the basic pricing methods in which a standard mark-up is added to the cost of the product to ensure some return to the marketer for their effort and the risk taken by them. The mark-up is calculated either as a percentage of Sales or Costs.

Suppose a manufacturer has the following costs and sales expectations:

Variable costs per unit = ₹10

Fixed cost = ₹3,00,000

Expected unit sales = 50,000 Units

In this case, the manufacturing unit cost is calculated with the help of a formula that states—

Unit cost = Variable cost + Fixed cost/Expected unit sales

Unit cost = 10 + (3,00,000/50,000)

= 10 + 6 = ₹16

Now, if the manufacturer wants to earn a 20 per cent mark-up on sales, the mark-up price is calculated by—

Mark-up price = Unit cost/ (1 – desired return on sales)

= 16/(1 – 0.20)

= 16/0.80 = ₹20

The manufacturer would charge dealers ₹20 per product and make a profit of ₹4 per unit. The dealers in turn will mark-up the product. If the dealers want to earn 50 per cent on their selling price, they will mark-up the product to ₹40. This is equivalent to a cost mark-up of 100 per cent.

Mark-up pricing method is generally used by organisations which are selling seasonal goods, speciality items, or slow-moving goods, in order to cover the risk of not selling during the off-season. This method cannot be considered as a highly logical method because it completely ignores the current demand, perceived value to the consumer, the competitive forces prevailing in the market and impact of other environmental variables on pricing.

Target-Return Pricing

In target-return pricing, the organisation would like to set the price at a level which helps them recover the cost and ensure some minimum targeted rate of return on investment. This pricing method is used by public utilities, which need to make a rate of return on their investment. In this method, variable and fixed costs per unit are estimated. A rate of return is then taken, which is a certain percentage of the capital invested in the product, and the result is divided by the estimated sales. The resulting return per unit is added to the unit cost to arrive at a price.

Suppose the same product manufacturer has invested ₹10,00,000 in business and wants to set a price to earn 20 per cent ROI, specifically ₹2,00,000. The target-return price is given by the following formula:

Target return price = Unit cost + (Desired return × Capital invested)/Unit Sales

= 16 + (0.20 × 10,00,000)/50,000 = 16 + 4 = ₹20

The manufacturer will realize this 20 per cent ROI, provided its costs and estimated sales turn out to be accurate.

The Cost-plus Pricing Method

This method remains popular because of the following reasons:

1. These methods are logical and comparatively easier to follow.
2. It is easier for marketers to determine cost rather than estimating demand.
3. These pricing methods reduce unnecessary price competition in the market where all firms in the Industry follows them.
4. Cost-plus pricing is also considered fair to both buyers and sellers as it brings stability in the prices and ensures some fair rate of return on investment to the sellers.

7.2.2 Market-Based Pricing Method

In this case the pricing methods are governed by the market forces—the demand and supply situations in the market, the competitive pressures, legal constraints and the environmental factors. Various market-based pricing methods are discussed as under:

Floor Pricing

In this pricing method, a very low price is charged—a price that just covers cost. This method is usually followed in order to maintain a presence in the market in a highly competitive environment. This policy is followed only for a short span of time in order to ensure the survival of the business in tough conditions.

Competitors' Parity Method or Parity Pricing or Going Rate Pricing

This is charging a price that is roughly equivalent to the average price charged by the major competitors'. In this case, practically all the firms in the Industry charge similar prices for their goods and will try to manage an equal market share. This pricing policy has an advantage that it minimises the cut-throat competition in the market and ensures an overall price stability. The profits and revenues of all the firms are also likely to be somewhat similar, keeping their costs into account. This pricing policy aims at the 'live and let live' philosophy. This is illustrated in Figure 7.4.

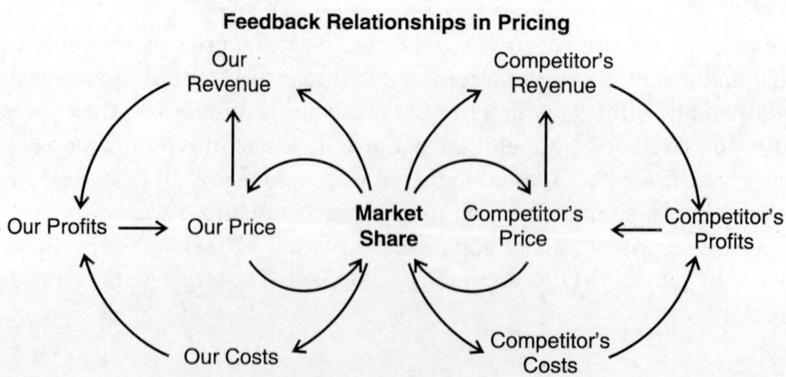

Figure 7.4 Competitors' parity method.

Price Leadership Pricing

In this method, a leading firm in the industry sets the price at a level which is followed by all other firms which join the industry subsequently. This pricing strategy helps in minimizing price wars and results in a fairly stable market share for all the firms.

Stay-Out-Pricing

In this pricing method, the leading firm, which is there in the business for quite some time, purposely charges a price lower than what the demand conditions require in order to discourage market entry by new competitors. The moment the competitor is out of the market arena, the firm might revert back to high pricing. This pricing strategy is unethical to some extent as it is followed by successful companies to keep the new entrants away from the Industry.

Differential Pricing

In this case, different prices are charged for different versions of the same product on the basis of the quality and value delivered to the consumers. For example, the basic model with a very plain and simple packaging may be priced at a lower level than the superior model of the product with one or two added features and better packaging priced at a higher level. The basic formula for using this method of pricing is to charge a price at par with the value delivered to the consumers.

Perceived Value Pricing

The practice of pricing the product in accordance with what customers perceive the product to be worth is known as '*perceived value pricing*'. It is a customer-centric pricing approach that gives first priority to customer's product valuation above the cost, competition and other considerations. Customers will remain loyal to such firms because they think that they are getting value for money.

Sealed-Bid Pricing

In this case, the firm bases its price on expectations of how competitors will quote the price rather than the firm's costs or demand to win a contract. The final contract is won by the firm which quotes the minimum price (Lowest Bid). The basic objective in this pricing strategy is to win the contract by quoting lesser than the competitor, while an effort is made to recover the cost.

Psychological Pricing

Generally, high priced products are perceived as high quality in India. Buyers carry in their mind a reference price formed by noticing current prices, past prices or the buying context. Sellers often manipulate these reference prices and play with the psyche of consumers by resorting to psychological pricing. They believe that the price should end in an odd number, such as, Bata Shoe Company pricing their shoes at ₹699 rather than ₹700 or ₹999 rather than ₹1,000.

Bundle Pricing

This pricing policy is followed to give a push to the sale of some of the slow moving products. In this case, a bundle of products or services are combined and a consolidated price is kept for them which is lower than the sum total of the price of all the assembled goods individually. For example, a cosmetic company may plan to sell its talcum powder, cream, lipstick and nail paint together at a low price for the bundle than the sum of the price for all the individual items in order to push their sale. Another example can be that of the camera companies, trying to sell the camera and films in one pack at an overall reduced price.

Cross Benefit Pricing

In this case, the price of one product in a product line is set at or below the cost, but the price of its related complements is set at a relatively high level to recover the cost. This strategy is purposely followed to increase the sale of a product and recover the cost by selling the related complements at a higher price. For example, Playstation 3 is purposely sold by the company at a lesser price to increase its demand, while each CD for the playstation is priced at a high level to recover the overall cost. Another example is that the price of a computer is kept low but the price of various computer softwares is generally kept very high.

Penetration Pricing

It involves the charging of a price that is relatively lower than the average price of major competitors and what customers are accustomed to paying. In this case, the organisation sets a very low price for the product. This pricing strategy is generally followed in case of launching a new product and where the firm is initially targeting on a larger market share. They intend to make profits by a huge turnover. This pricing strategy works best in case of convenience goods or other goods which are of day-to-day consumption and are meant for the masses. This strategy also helps in giving a tough competition to the marketers because at times it becomes very difficult for them to adjust to such low prices. This strategy should be followed under the following situations:

1. When the product is basic in nature and is meant for the masses, such as salt, sugar, pulses, etc.;
2. A large market exists for the product, examples include fruits, vegetables, etc.;
3. Customers are highly price sensitive;
4. Product is highly price elastic, i.e. a small decrease in the price of the product is capable of attracting a huge crowd;
5. There is intense competition in the market, for example, low end mobile phones;
6. Company intends to make profit in the long run by huge turnover; and
7. Long product life cycles.

This kind of pricing works best with products which are in demand and there is a huge market for them. One of the biggest problems which come in the way of this pricing policy is that it becomes difficult for the organisations to increase the price at a later date because of the resulting hue and cry even though the cost have increased. Moreover, in some cases, people treat such goods as inferior because they might think that the producer must have compromised on the quality only then are they able to sell the product at such low prices. But despite these facts, this strategy is being successfully followed by most of the companies especially in case of consumer packaged goods market.

Premium Pricing or Skimming Pricing or Skim-the-Cream Pricing

In this case, the price charged is intended to be high relative to the average price of major competitors and what customers are a accustomed to paying. The company follows the policy of setting a high price in the market. By following this strategy the marketer wants to project their product as a premium product or a quality product to the consumer. This strategy works best for luxurious goods, such as designer clothes, expensive mobile phones, wrist watches, etc., where the consumer is ready to pay a high price for better quality. The higher initial price also gives the company a leverage of reducing the price at a later stage and involving the next layer of price sensitive consumers as depicted in Figure 7.5.

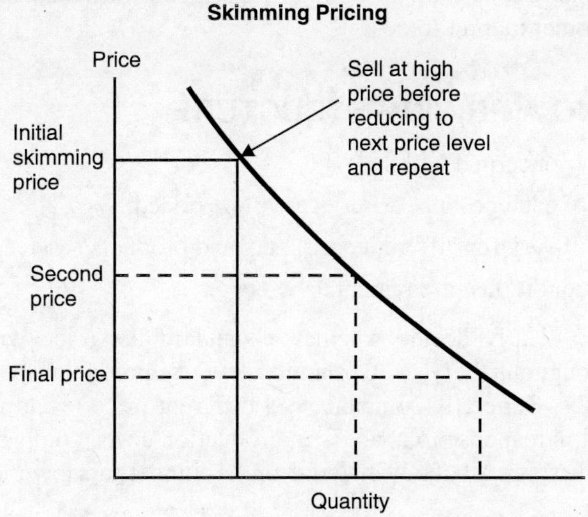

Figure 7.5 Illustration of skimming pricing.

'Skim the cream' pricing involves setting a high initial price and targeting it to those who are willing to pay before aiming at the product at more price-sensitive consumers. This expression has been borrowed from the farming practice of milking cows—the cream rises to the top and you skim it off. Skimming strategy is generally used in the following situations:

1. High entry barriers;
2. Product is luxurious in nature;
3. The company has designed an exclusive product for the target audience;
4. People don't mind paying a premium price for better quality;
5. Short product life cycles; and
6. Demand is highly price inelastic.

The advantage of using a skimming price policy is that it immediately confers the prestige of a quality product, as people in India strongly believe that when it is expensive, it must be good. The company can also benefit by recovering their costs faster and making huge profits. Moreover, this price policy can give the leverage to the manufacturer to reduce the price at a later date and attract the next layer of price-sensitive consumers as a price cut is always a welcome move in our country. It is suitable for the products that have shorter life cycles or which may face competition at some point in the future, such as play station, jewellery, digital technology, new DVDs, etc.

7.3 SELECTING THE FINAL PRICING METHOD

After going through the various pricing methods available to them, the manufacturers have to finally make a choice of an appropriate pricing method. Generally the Cost-based methods are very popular because they are easy to implement and manage, but unfortunately this often leads to a situation that fails to take advantage of the market opportunities confronting the firm. These days' markets are full of competition and marketers at times have no choice but to go by any of the market-based pricing strategy if they want to stand the intensified competition. In that case, the choice of a pricing method depends on the other marketing mix variables, the stage of their product life cycle and various other market forces.

7.4 DEVELOPING A PRICING STRUCTURE

The pricing structure is concerned with:

- What aspects of each product or service will be priced;
- How prices will vary for different customers and products/services; and
- The time and conditions of payment.

Manufacturers have to clearly decide whether a standard list price will be charged for the product or service throughout the year, or should they be introducing certain discounts for the buyers at different times. Generally companies set different price levels which require frequent modifications in prices in response to changes in production costs, competitor's tactics, evolving market conditions, increasing cost of raw material, or the competitors lowering their product prices.

7.5 GEOGRAPHICAL PRICING POLICIES

Geographical pricing involves the company's decisions about pricing its products for different customers at different locations and countries. When products are to be dispatched by ship, train or truck, the management has to decide as to who is going to pay the freight charges. This may either be paid by the seller, or by the buyer, or both may share it. Geographical pricing policies significantly affect the manufacturer's decision about the warehousing facilities and the distribution of products in various markets. Other things such as price, quality and terms of sale being the same, a customer will prefer to buy from a manufacturer who is either closest to him, or absorbs the whole or part of the freight cost himself. Some of the geographical pricing policies are displayed as under in Figure 7.6.

FOB pricing: *Free on Board* pricing implies that the entire freight cost will be borne by the buyer. The cost of handling and loading is borne by the seller. Hence it is called Free on Board (FOB). Calcutta price is higher than the FOB. Factory price as the former includes freight charges to the place of destination. The term *FOB Calcutta* means that the price quoted includes shipment to Calcutta. The seller is responsible for shipment charges to Calcutta.

Home delivered pricing: The delivery charges are built into the price paid by the customer.

Zone pricing: This denotes same price of the product in the same zone. A product may be sold at different prices in different zones because of differences in transportation costs, local taxes, etc., but in a particular zone it is sold at the same price irrespective of differences in distance between two places inside the zone.

Uniform delivered pricing: A company that views the entire country as its delivery zone and charges the same price, its pricing policy is called *uniform delivered pricing*. The same price is quoted to all buyers regardless of their location. This strategy is also used by many retailers who believe that 'free' delivery is an additional service that strengthens their market position.

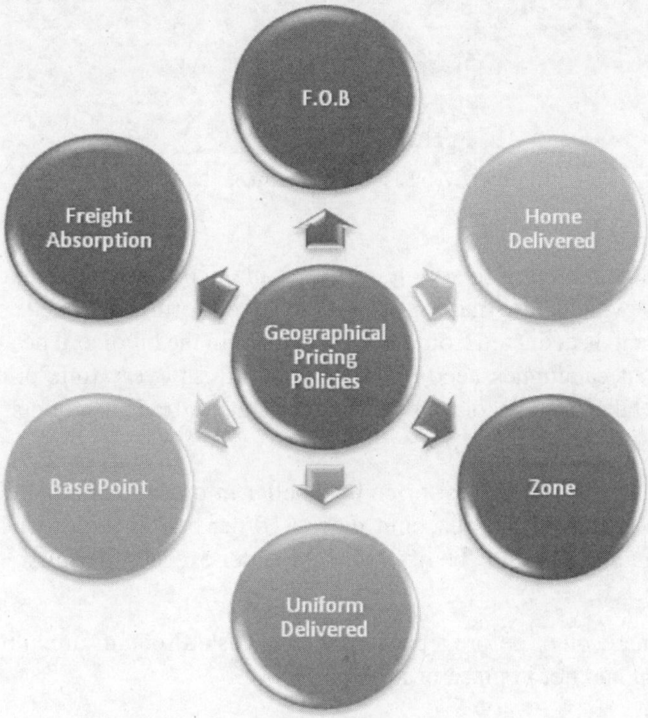

Figure 7.6 Geographical pricing policies.

Base-point pricing: This involves the selection of one or more locations to serve as base points. Customers are charged prices and delivery expenses as if their orders were executed from these points.

Freight absorption pricing: In this case, the manufacturer will set a price for the customer which is equal to its factory price plus the freight costs at par with the amount being charged by their competitive seller located near that customer. This is adopted to offset the competitive disadvantages of FOB factory pricing, as a nearby supplier has an advantage over more distant suppliers—at least with respect to freight costs. Freight absorption policy will facilitate a supplier to compete in distant markets.

7.6 PRICE DISCOUNTS AND ALLOWANCES

In order to attract the customers from the competitors or at times to clear the stock, companies announce discounts and allowances to their customers. Most companies will adjust their list price and give discounts and allowances for early payments, volume purchases and off-season buying. Companies must do this carefully or they might find their profits being eroded by undue discounts. Some of the commonly offered discounts and allowances are listed below in Figure 7.7.

Figure 7.7 List of discounts and allowances.

Trade Discount

It is given to the buyers buying for resale, for example, wholesalers or retailers, in payment for marketing functions which these traders are expected to perform. It is stated as a certain percentage of the quoted price and is deducted from the quoted price in the invoice. The advantage of allowing trade discount is that catalogues need not be printed afresh every time prices fluctuate, for the fluctuations can be taken into account by varying the rate of trade discounts.

Quantity Discounts

It is a deduction offered from the list price by a seller in order to stimulate the customer to buy in larger quantities. For example, discount maybe 10 per cent if the order is up to 10 units and additional 5 per cent discount may be offered if the order exceeds 10 units.

Cash Discount

When payment is made on or before a particular date, cash discounts are allowed. It is in addition to the trade discount and not in place of it.

Seasonal Discount

A seasonal discount is a price reduction to buyers who buy merchandise or services out of season. Air conditioner manufacturers will offer seasonal discounts to customers in the winter season to encourage early ordering.

Allowances

These are extra payments designed to gain reseller participation in special programme. The manufacturer may offer allowances to distributors for promotional activities, advertising allowances, window display allowance, free samples, etc. It amounts to a price reduction of an amount spent by the distributor in performing promotional services.

Thus, to conclude, pricing decisions involve the management in deciding about the basic pricing policies and to work out the decisions regarding the geographical pricing and price discounts.

LET US SUM UP

- Price is one of the most significant factors in achieving marketing success. It is the amount of money or money's worth needed to acquire a product.
- Before setting up the price of the product, management should identify its pricing goals, such as, earning a targeted Return On Investment, maximize Profits, increasing Sales, increase Market Share, stabilise Prices and meet Competition.

- Other key factors influencing the price setting are demand for the product, competitors' reactions, marketing-mix strategies, cost of the product and other environmental variables.
- The various pricing methods are divided mainly into two categories—Cost-based and Market-based pricing methods.
- In Cost-based pricing method, a producer usually sets the price to cover Total Cost (TC). In some cases, however, the best policy may be to set a price that covers Marginal Cost only.
- In actual business situations, price setting is influenced by market conditions. The demand and supply situations and the competitive forces play an important role in price setting.
- When a firm is launching a new product, it must choose a market skimming or a market penetration pricing strategy. Market skimming involves setting high initial price, while in market penetration a low initial price is set.
- Strategies also have to be worked out for giving discounts and allowances-deductions from the list price to consumers from time to time.
- Freight costs must be considered in pricing. A producer can require the buyer to pay all freight cost (FOB factory pricing), or they can absorb all freight costs (uniform delivered pricing).

QUESTIONS TO CHECK YOUR PROGRESS

Short Answer Questions

1. Whether the price will be set at a high level or lower level in the following situations:

(i) When the company is aiming to maximise their current profits ....

(ii) When survival becomes the main focus..

(iii) In order to increase the market share of the product......................................

(iv) In a highly competitive market..

(v) When the firm is introducing a new luxurious product......................................

(vi) When a company is marketing a perishable product.......................................

2. Name the pricing method used:

(i) The practice of pricing the product in accordance with what customers perceive the product to be worth is called...

(ii) Charging a price that just covers cost usually in order to maintain a presence in the market in highly competitive environment is ....

(iii) Charging a price that is roughly equivalent to the average price charged by the major competitors...

(iv) The prices are set for different market segments based on the value each segment receives from the product or service..

(v) The firm determines the price that would yield its target rate of return on investment...

(vi) Charging a price that is low relative to the average price of major competitors and what customers are accustomed to paying..

(vii) Pricing method, in which a standard mark-up is added to the products cost.......................... ....

(viii) A set of products or services are combined and a lower single price is charged for the bundle...

3. A market segment has a large number of buyers. High initial price does not attract competitors to the market, but it does communicate superior product image. Which pricing strategy is it?
4. Southwest Airlines has set its ticket prices lower than anyone else's price. It operates in a market that is highly price sensitive and one in which low prices stimulate market growth. Its costs have fallen as it has become more efficient at providing air plane service to its customers. Name the pricing strategy being followed by Southwest Airline.
5. A watch manufacturer incurs a variable cost of ₹10 per watch and fixed cost of ₹4,00,000. What should be the price to reach a 25 per cent of mark-up on selling price for each of the 50,000 watches it decides to sell?

Long Answer Questions

1. "Pricing should be value-driven not cost-driven". Do you agree with the statement?
2. What factors are taken into consideration while determining the price of a consumer product? Explain.
3. Describe the various internal and external forces that influence the pricing strategy of a firm.
4. What do you understand by psychological pricing and premium pricing? Based on your personal experience, give an example of both.
5. "When a firm considers initiating a price change, it must carefully consider its customers and competitors reaction". Elaborate.
6. How is price related to demand?
7. How do competitor's pricing affect an organisation's pricing strategy?
8. List out the various pricing objectives clearly. Which of these objectives do you believe (a) is the most commonly used; (b) is the most difficult to achieve; and (c) has the greatest potential for long-term growth of the organisation. Explain.
9. Explain the process of price determination.
10. Explain the various cost-based pricing methods with examples.
11. What are the limitations and merits of the cost-plus methods of setting up base price?
12. Distinguish between cost oriented pricing, demand oriented pricing and competition oriented pricing.
13. What are the alternate pricing strategies available to a marketer who wants to introduce a new product in a highly competitive market?
14. What are the pricing strategies followed at different stages of the Product Life Cycle?
15. What pricing objectives would a skimming pricing policy most likely implement? Could the same be true for a penetration pricing policy?
16. Which of the pricing strategies—penetration or skimming—would be recommended in case of the following products and why?
    (i) A new safety lock
    (ii) An automatic dishwasher
    (iii) A new improved computer
17. Write short notes on the following:
    (i) Bundle pricing
    (ii) Perceived value pricing
    (iii) Stay-out pricing
    (iv) Competitor's parity pricing
    (v) Psychological pricing
    (vi) Return on investment pricing
18. How do you define geographical pricing? Is it possible for a company to charge the same price all over the country?
19. Visit a nearby market and gather information regarding the products offering various types of discounts and allowances.

CHAPTER 8

Promotion Strategy

Learning Outcomes

After studying this chapter, you will be able to:

- Understand the concept, need, functions and importance of promotion
- Define the various promotional tools
- Discuss the unique features of various promotional tools
- Explain the factors affecting the promotional mix
- Describe the concept of integrated promotion management
- Identify the reasons for the importance of integrated promotion management

Promotion, the third 'P' in the marketing-mix, plays a very important role in the marketing programme of any organisation. After producing an excellent product and pricing it appropriately, it becomes essential for a marketer to inform the target audience about the availability of the product. In the first two P's the firm was interacting and taking decisions within the organisation with their employees and suppliers. But now, at this stage, the firm has to communicate with their target audience—their present and potential customers, because nothing will sell unless and until the company beats the drum and inform the masses about the availability of the new product and its unique features. Hence, by now this thing is very clear that the company might have produced the best product, priced it very appropriately and with the help of physical distribution decisions, might have taken the pain of ensuring that goods are made available to the consumers' right next door. Despite all this there is no guarantee that the product will sell. The most important thing required at this stage is to inform the people about the product, because people are not going to dream of that product.

Ruth Kassinger (2002) was found quoting in his book, *Build a Better Mousetrap,* that Emerson once said that, *you make the best mousetrap, and the world will beat a path to your door.* But, in today's scenario, this has resulted in the mousetrap fallacy because even if you make the best mousetrap, nobody will ever come to your door unless and until you go and inform people about your mousetrap and you'll have to impress upon them as to how it is best and why it is better than that of the others. Therefore, informing people is the most important activity which a marketer has to undertake very seriously in today's environment to ensure their survival and success, and this is nothing but in simple words called *Promotion*. Henceforth, a marketer has to perform the various promotional activities with utmost care and precaution. Before we go into the details of discussing the various promotional tools and their significance, it is very important for us to understand at this stage as to what is basically the concept of promotion and why is it becoming an indispensable activity for the business today.

According to Philip Kotler (1999)—

> *Promotion may be defined as the coordination of all seller initiated efforts to set up channels of information and persuasion to facilitate the sale of the product or service or the acceptance of an idea.*

In the words of William J Stanton (1994)—

> *Promotion is the element in an organisation's marketing mix that serves to inform, persuade and remind the market of a product and/or the organisation selling it, in hopes of influencing the recipients' feelings, beliefs or behaviour.*

After going through the perceptions of both the authors, it is very clear that the job of promotion is basically to inform the people about the availability of products, change their attitude and belief about the product, and persuade them to try or buy that new product by impressing upon them about the unique features of the product.

8.1 NEED/FUNCTION/IMPORTANCE OF PROMOTION

There are three basic functions of promotion—informing, persuading, and reminding the prospective customers about a company and its products. The companies might have designed the best products, but they will not be able to sell unless and until people know about them. Therefore, it becomes very important for companies to rely on various promotional tools, but the relative importance of these tools varies according to the circumstances being faced by them. Before we go on to the discussion of the various promotional tools which are available to the marketers, it is very important for us to first understand the reasons as to why promotion is becoming such an indispensable activity in today's marketing scenario. Some of the reasons emphasising the need, function, or the importance of promotion are listed as under:

8.1.1 Increasing Distance between the Place of Production and Place of Consumption

These days firms are able to distribute their products to far-off places with the help of various channels of distribution available as discussed in the next unit. Because distribution channels are often too long, a product may pass through various levels before it finally reaches to the consumers. Therefore, a producer must inform all their middlemen, as well as the ultimate consumers or business users about the product using various promotional tools.

8.1.2 Promotion Affects the Demand and Demand Elasticity of the Product

A firm hopes that promotion will help to increase the demand for the products and affect their demand elasticity. The intent is to make the demand more inelastic, i.e. the management wants promotion to increase the attractiveness of a product, so that the quantity demanded will decline very little, even if the price goes up (inelastic demand), and sales will increase considerably if the price goes down (elastic demand).

8.1.3 Persuasion Function

The intense competition among different industries, as well as among firms within the industry, puts tremendous pressure on the promotional programme of sellers. As more and more variety is being provided to the consumer to choose from, the need for an equal amount of promotion is being felt. Marketers have to constantly make efforts and impress upon the present and potential customers that they should prefer their brands over that of the competitors because of the product's unique features.

8.1.4 Reminder Function

Consumers must also be reminded about the constant availability of the product and its potential to satisfy.

8.1.5 During the Period of Product Shortages as Well

Promotion is an activity which is carried out successfully even during the time of product scarcity or shortages, to hold on to the interest of the consumers. It is used to reduce the demand temporarily or permanently, with the aim of not destroying the demand but simply to reduce it, shift it or postpone it.

8.1.6 Improve the Overall Standard of Living of People

Various promotional tools have resulted in an increase in the overall standard of living of people by making them purchase the various goods or services.

8.1.7 To Overcome the Problem of Economic Recession

Promotion as a tool has helped a lot in fighting out the overall recession which is prevailing in the economy. In order to come out off the recession, one of the most important decisions is to increase the demand of goods. At the time when the economy is into deep recession, the demand can be increased only by cutting down the price and advertising heavily, and informing the consumer about the reduced prices. Therefore, the promotional tools of persuasive advertising, convincing personal selling, lucrative sales promotion incentives and positive publicity can help an economy increase the demand of the goods and come out of the recession.

8.2 PROMOTIONAL TOOLS

There are four basic tools of promotion—advertising, personal selling, sales promotion, publicity and public relations. However, these days some of the organisations have started relying on Direct

Marketing and Internet Marketing as the other major promotional tools to communicate with their target audience. Each has distinct features that determine in what situations it will be most effective. We are going to explain the various promotional tools as depicted in Figure 8.1 along with their unique features in the next paragraphs.

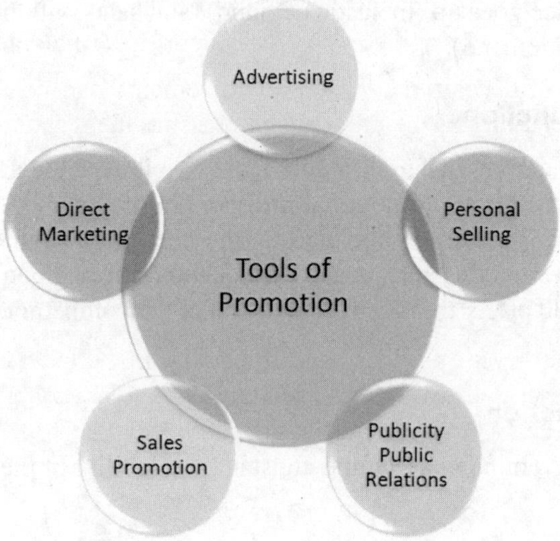

Figure 8.1 Tools of promotion.

8.2.1 Advertising

According to the American Marketing Association (1995)—

> *Advertising is any paid form of non-personal presentation and promotion of ideas, goods or services by an identified sponsor.*

Unique Features of Advertising

1. Paid form of promotion: Advertising is a paid form of promotion; anything which is not paid for cannot be called advertising. For example, when heroes and heroines come and perform on various reality shows before the release of their movies, can be only called a publicity event and cannot be called advertising because they are not being paid for their performances.

2. Non-personal presentation: Messages through advertisements are made available to the target audience with the help of various mediums. This results in a monologue and not a dialogue with the target audience. Here the sponsor is not in front of the audience to answer their doubts or queries. Therefore, the audience does not feel obligated to pay attention or respond to advertisements.

3. Public presentation: Advertising is a mode of public presentation where the message can get transmitted to millions of people at one time.

4. Persuasiveness: Advertisements generally proves to be very persuasive with the artful use of colour, sound, and celebrities.

5. Pervasiveness: Advertising is the only tool with the help of which a message can be repeated many times without irritating the target audience. The more the frequency of the message, the better are the chances of the message being retained.

6. Amplified expressiveness: It is the only tool where the companies can resort to dramatise the situation and promote their products with the help of colour and sound. Lots of glamour can be added in the advertisements by bringing in popular celebrities from cinema, sports or television.

7. Constant reminder and reassurance: Advertisements can constantly remind customers about the availability and utility of the product and reassure them about their purchase.

8. Strengthens other promotional mix elements: Advertising is the basic promotional tool, as it strengthens the application of other promotional tools at large. Personal selling can never be a success without first introducing the products through advertisements in general mediums, and at the same time there is no point introducing the various sales promotion incentives, unless and until the incentives are brought to the notice of the consumers with the help of the advertisements.

9. Unconvincing at times: This is one of the major limitations of advertising, that advertisements at times can prove to be unconvincing and cannot force the customer to purchase the goods at once. As most of the advertisements are viewed and noticed by customers at their own will, the chances of their getting unnoticed and unconvincing are high.

8.2.2 Personal Selling

According to the American Marketing Association (1995)—

> *Personal selling is a face-to-face interaction with one or more prospective purchasers for the purpose of making presentations, answering questions and procuring order.*

Unique Features of Personal Selling

1. Face-to-face interaction: This is one of the most important features of personal selling as it ensures face-to-face interaction between the salesperson and the customers. It results in a dialogue between them and the customers can get all their doubts cleared by the salesperson, and are finally convinced about the quality of the product.

2. Highly convincing: If a salesperson is smart and persuasive, he/she can convince his/her customers into buying the product by making excellent presentations. Generally, the chances of a sale being materialised in personal selling are more in comparison to simply showing advertisements.

3. Response generation: As the salesperson is right in front and is able to take good care of the customer, the customer generally feels obligated to buy the product from him/her.

4. Cultivation of formal as well as informal relationship: Most of the time the relationship between the salesperson and the customer turns out to be very strong and healthy because of the cultivation of a formal, as well as an informal relationship between them.

5. Immediate feedback: As the salesperson is right across the customer, he is in a position to get an immediate feedback. He/she can obviously make note of the comments being given by the customer, and at the same time is in a position to judge even the inherent feelings and emotions of the customers, by simply noticing their body language. Therefore, the salesperson is in a position to understand the obvious, as well as the non-obvious reasons for the purchase or non-purchase of the goods.

6. Lack of dramatisation and glamorization: Sales presentations are generally kept simple by making use of short simple sentences. Use of flowery expressions and exaggerated claims is not advisable for the salespeople. Thus, there are not many opportunities available to the salespeople to add glamour into their presentations and create hype for the product.

7. No repetition: Salespeople do not get an opportunity to repeat the message again and again, so it is expected of them to put forward their point of view assertively and impressively in one shot. It is generally the first few minutes of their presentation which can make or mar their conversation with the customers.

8.2.3 Sales Promotion

According to the American Marketing Association (1995)—

> *Sales promotion is defined as a variety of short-term incentives used to encourage a trial or purchase of a product or service which is designed to supplement and coordinate personal selling and advertisement.*

Unique Features of Sales Promotion

1. Attention catching device: Sales promotion incentives are introduced to catch the attention of the target audience and communicate with them the idea of buying the product immediately by offering something catchy and attractive along with the product.

2. Additional incentive: The sales promotion incentives introduced should genuinely be attractive and worthy enough, so that the customer feels like buying the product immediately because of them.

3. Short term effect: The incentives should always be introduced for a short span of time and should finally be withdrawn after the expiry of the period. The incentives will lose their charm if they are made to continue for long, because then the customer will start taking them for granted and will not rush to make the purchase of the product.

4. Legitimacy: The incentives offered should always be legitimate and if the company is offering something free with the product, in that case, it should genuinely be free and its cost should not be added to the price of the product.

5. Complementary: Sales promotion complements advertising and personal selling and adds to their effectiveness. A good advertisement, along with effective sales promotion incentives, can give a push to the sales and at the same time it also facilitates the job of the sales person to motivate the consumer to buy the product immediately.

8.2.4 Public Relations and Publicity

Both of these are a variety of programmes designed to promote or protect, a company's image or its individual products. According to the American Marketing Association (1995)—

Publicity is a non personnel stimulation of demand for a product, service or business unit by planting commercially significant news about it in the published medium or obtaining a favorable presentation of it on radio, television, or a stage that is not paid for by the sponsor.

Publicity is done through mass media such as newspapers, magazines or television, but it usually comes in the form of a news story, an editorial, or an announcement about the organisation or its products and services. Like advertising, publicity involves non-personal communication to a mass audience, but unlike advertising, publicity is not directly paid for by the company. It takes place when an independent person gives his or her opinion about the product through any medium. At times, the company attempts to intentionally plant a news story or request the media to cover a campaign on their product, service or idea. The purpose of publicity is to catch the attention of those people who do not believe in the genuineness or authenticity of advertising and pass on the information regarding their product to them in the form of a news story. It is important to recognise the distinction between publicity and public relations.

Canfield and Moore (1973) have defined *Public Relations* as—

The management function which evaluates public attitudes, identifies the policies and procedures of an individual or organisation with the public interest, and executes a program of action to earn public understanding and acceptance.

Public relations uses publicity and a variety of other tools—including special publications, participation in community activities, fund raising, sponsorship of events and various public affair activities—to enhance an organisation's image.

Unique Features of Publicity and Public Relations

1. Non personal presentation: Publicity is always done by third parties, who have no personal interest in the organisation, with the help of certain media. Public Relations, on the other hand, is handled by an employee of the organisation whose job is to ensure coordination between the company and its customers, suppliers, government and general public.

2. Non-paid: Publicity is a non-paid presentation of information about a product, service, idea or a business unit by a third party. It is generally considered as an honest submission by an independent person.

3. High credibility and legitimacy: As it is being done by an independent person, who has no personal interest in the organisation, publicity is always considered more credible and legitimate than advertisements, which are purposely designed by the sponsor.

4. Ability to catch people off guard: Both publicity and public relations have the capability to catch people off guard and pass on the information regarding the product or service to them easily. In this case, people who are otherwise not very comfortable with the idea of advertisements, and generally tend to ignore advertisements, are able to get the information about the product through publicity and public relations campaigns.

5. Dramatisation: These days even publicity is planned to a certain extent by planting commercially significant news about a product or service in various mediums. The launch of a new product is purposely done in a big way by inviting various celebrities and organising big shows.

6. It can be both positive as well as negative: Publicity is an honest submission by a third party; it can be both positive as well as negative. It can go in favour of the company, or it can go against the image of the company, therefore the companies have to take care of publicity with utmost care.

8.2.5 Direct Marketing

According to the American Marketing Association (1995)—

> *Direct marketing involves the use of mail, telephone, fax, e-mail or Internet to communicate directly with or solicit a direct response from specific customers and prospects.*

In Direct Marketing, organisations communicate directly with the target customers to generate a response or a transaction. It involves a variety of mediums through which selling takes place, such as through mail, tele-marketing, direct response advertisements, the Internet and various broadband and print media. One of the major tools for Direct Marketing is direct response advertising, wherein a product is promoted through an advertisement that encourages the customer to purchase directly from the manufacturer. The availability of Credit Cards and toll-free phone numbers has also facilitated the purchase of products from direct response advertisements. Very recently, the rapid growth of the Internet is fuelling the growth of Direct Marketing; Tele-marketing is also being used for the purpose. Some of the examples of successful Direct Marketing are Reader's Digest magazine, Amway, Tupperware, etc.

Unique Features of Direct Marketing

1. Personal messages: Generally, the direct mail messages, which are designed for a specific audience, are addressed personally to the person concerned and have a bit of a personal touch to them as compared to all other promotional tools, where a general expression is used.

2. Customised: As explained earlier, most of the Direct Marketing messages are customised keeping the target audience into account. They are delivered directly to the concerned person and a direct response is sought from them.

3. Up-to-date-direct: Marketing messages are designed frequently and are sent at short intervals. Thus, as and when there is a change in the product, or a new feature has been added, or a new scheme is introduced, it is brought to the notice of the target audience with revised messages.

4. Interactive and instant feedback: Direct Marketing turns out to be a highly interactive medium, especially in tele-marketing, with the help of the toll-free number and Internet, where customers log on to the websites and they can call or ask for additional information besides the one being delivered directly from the manufacturer, instantly. Customers can also provide their feedback immediately to the company.

5. Secrecy is maintained: Direct Marketing tools provide the manufacturers an exclusive advantage of keeping their advertising campaign secret from the competitors, as they address their messages directly and personally to the target audience. In most of the cases the competitors do not get to know about the promises being made by the manufacturer to the customers giving the manufacturer a competitive advantage.

6. Economical pricing: Direct Marketing also provides the advantage of economical pricing to the customers, as the manufacturer in this case can do away with the middleman. The middleman's commission is saved, which is passed on to the customers in the form of reduced prices.

7. Sales promotion incentives: In addition to advertising on the web, marketers offer various sales promotion incentives, such as coupons, contests and sweepstakes offers to conduct Direct Marketing activities more effectively and efficiently.

8.3 DETERMINING THE PROMOTION MIX

Till now we have discussed the various promotional tools at length and we can say this with a guarantee that none of the promotional tool is complete in itself. Each and every promotional tool enjoys a number of strengths, but at the same time, they suffer from certain limitations as well. It is not possible for any company to rely completely on any single promotional tool, thus, they have no choice but to work out a promotional mix. In order to arrive at the best promotional campaign, it is very important for the company to combine all the promotional mix elements, balancing their strengths and weaknesses effectively.

According to William J Stanton (1994)—

> *An organisation's combination of personal selling, advertising, sales promotion, public relations and publicity to help in achieving its marketing objectives is its promotional mix.*

Deciding about the promotional mix is a very difficult marketing decision, because there is no tailor-made formula for working out an appropriate promotional mix. To add to the problem, there is another important feature which makes this decision very difficult, that is, the cross substitutability of all the promotional tools. All these tools are quite capable of performing similar functions of creating awareness, arousing interest, cultivating desire and directing the consumer to the purchase action. Therefore, when it comes to deciding about the allocation of money on each and every promotional tool, the company has to be very careful and take into consideration a number of factors.

8.3.1 Factors Affecting Promotional Mix

Some of the important factors are being discussed as under and are nicely depicted in Figure 8.2.

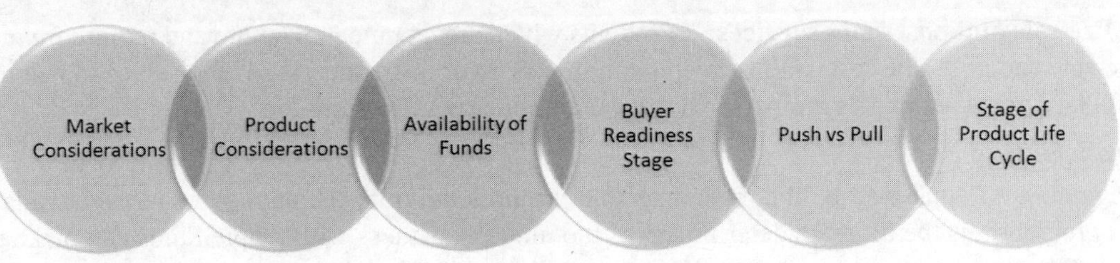

Figure 8.2 Factors affecting promotion mix.

Market Considerations

1. Type of product market: Promotional allocations depend on the fact that whether the product is consumer or industrial in nature. In case of consumer goods, as the number of consumers is large, companies prefer spending heavily on advertising, sales promotion, personal selling and public relations, in that order. While in case of industrial or business markets, there are few consumers and the order placed by them is generally in bulk. They need to be addressed and taken care of personally. Therefore, companies spend heavily on personal selling, sales promotion, advertising and public relations, in that order.

2. Geographic scope of the market: Personal selling may be adequate in a small local market, but as the market broadens geographically, greater emphasis must be placed on advertising because it is only with the help of advertisements that a message can be spread to millions of people, spread across various geographical territories, in one go.

3. Concentration of the market: The total number of prospective buyers is another consideration. If the potential buyers are few, personal selling will be more effective than advertising and vice versa. For example, a firm selling vacuum cleaners would definitely like to approach all their prospective customers personally and try selling the product by explaining the various product features to them. As against this, a firm selling a tooth paste would like to advertise it heavily through various mediums possible and will sell it to a large number of people through various retail outlets.

4. Level of competition in the market: If there is intensified competition in the market, the marketers will resort to heavy advertising and aggressive sales promotion incentives in order to carve a place for themselves. The advertising will be comparative in nature, where the focus will be more on proving the superiority of the advertised brand over that of the competitors. Sales promotion will be able to provide extra incentives to the consumers to prefer their product.

Product Considerations

Several product attributes influence promotional strategy. The most important are:

1. The unit value of the product: A product with low unit value is relatively uncomplicated, involves little risk for the buyer, and must appeal to a mass market to survive. As a result, advertising would be the primary promotional tool.

2. Degree of customisation: If a product must be adapted to the individual customer needs, personal selling is a necessity as the sales person will explain the exclusive features to the consumer in detail. However, the benefits of most standardised products can be effectively communicated in advertising.

3. Pre-sale and post-sales services: Products which are technical in nature and require frequent pre-sale and post-sale servicing to keep them in good working order, lend themselves to personal selling. Typical examples are personal computers, microwave ovens, etc.

Availability of Funds

Regardless of what may be the most desirable promotional mix, the amount of money available for promotion is the ultimate determinant of the mix. A business with ample funds can make use of advertising much effectively, than a firm with limited financial resources. Small or financially weak companies are likely to rely on personal selling, dealer displays or joint manufacturer-retailer promotions. Lack of money may limit the options a firm has for its promotional effort. For example, television advertising can carry a particular promotional message to a larger number of people at a lower cost per person, than can most other media. Yet a firm may have to rely on a less expensive media, such as point-of-purchase displays, because it lacks the funds to take advantage of television's efficiency.

Buyer-Readiness Stage

Promotional tools vary in effectiveness at different stages of a buyer readiness as depicted in Figure 8.3. Advertising along with publicity, plays the most important role in the *awareness stage* more than what is played by 'cold calls' from sales representatives. Customer *comprehension and knowledge* is primarily affected by education, with advertising and personal selling playing a secondary role. *Liking* refers to how the market feels about the product or brand. Persuasive advertising and personal selling can be used to move a knowledgeable audience from being indifferent to liking a brand. Creating *preference* involves distinguishing among brands such that the market prefers the advertised brand. At this stage also, the focus is more on using advertising and personal selling, but advertisements are now comparative in nature where the focus is on comparing the product with the competitors' product and proving the superiority of the brand over them. The sales force also makes an effort to meet the customers and convince them as to why their brand should be purchased, as it is better than the competitors.

Conviction entails the actual decision or commitment to purchase. Customer conviction is influenced by personal selling, followed closely by advertising, where both the tools try to finally convince the consumers about the utility of the product and arouse a strong desire to purchase it. *Purchase* can be delayed or postponed indefinitely, even for customers who are convinced that they should buy a product. Therefore, action may be triggered with the help of various sales promotion incentives, such as price discounts or offering additional incentives. Closing the sales is influenced mostly by personal selling and sales promotion.

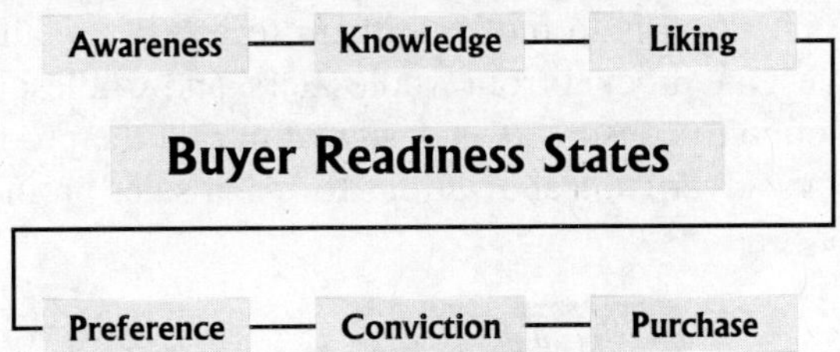

Figure 8.3 Buyer readiness stage.

Push vs Pull Strategy

The promotional mix is greatly influenced by whether the company chooses a push or a pull strategy to create sales. As we have seen already, producers aim their promotional mix at both middlemen and end users. A promotional programme aimed primarily at middlemen is called a *push strategy*, and a promotional programme directed primarily at end users is called a *pull strategy*.

Push strategy as illustrated in Figure 8.4 involves the manufacturer using sales force and trade promotion to induce intermediaries to carry, promote and sell the product to end users. Therefore, when a manufacturer uses a push strategy, the main focus for promoting the goods relies on the middlemen and it's through them that the goods are brought to the notice of the consumers and the sales are generated. Defined in other terms the product is *pushed* through the channel. The producer will promote heavily to the wholesalers, who in turn will also use a push strategy to the retailers. In turn, the retailers promote to consumers. A push strategy usually involves a lot of personal selling and sales promotion, including contests for salespeople and displays at trade shows. Push strategy is especially appropriate where there is low brand loyalty in a category, brand choice is made in the store, the product is an impulse item, and product benefits are well understood.

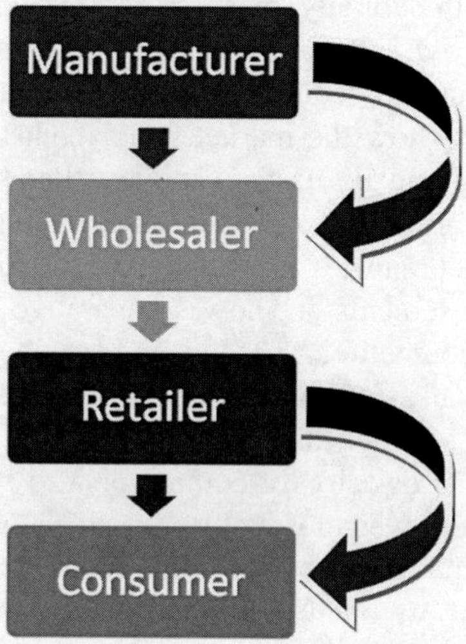

Figure 8.4 Push strategy.

With a *pull strategy*, as illustrated in Figure 8.5, promotion is directed at end users—usually the ultimate consumers. The intention is to motivate them to ask the retailers for the product. The retailers, in turn, will request the product from wholesalers, and wholesalers will order it from the producer. In effect, promotion to consumers is designed to *pull* the product through the channel. This strategy relies on heavy advertising and various forms of sales promotion, such as premiums, samples or in-store demonstrations.

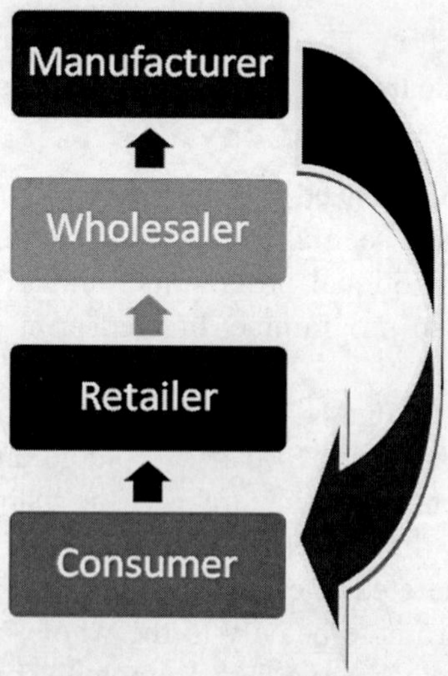

Figure 8.5 Pull strategy.

Companies in the same industry may differ in their emphasis on push or pull. For example, Hindustan Unilever relies more on push, while Procter & Gamble more on pull strategy.

Product Life Cycle Stage

The choice of the promotional tools also varies according to the Life Cycle Stage of the product. Different combinations of promotional tools are used during the four stages of a product's life cycle.

1. In the introduction stage: As the product is new and people do not know about it, a lot of emphasis is placed on advertising the product heavily and creating positive publicity. Advertising and publicity have the highest cost effectiveness at this stage, followed by personal selling, to gain distribution coverage and sales promotion to induce trial.

2. In the growth stage: When the sales start picking up and people are in a mood to buy the product, a lot of emphasis is placed on personal selling, where the salesperson takes care of the last minute doubts and queries of the customers and realises the sales. At this stage, companies deploy a huge sales force to increase their sales turnover, followed by advertising which continues to build up the demand for the product. Very little reliance is placed on the sales promotion incentives, because demand has its own momentum through word of mouth.

3. In the maturity stage: Where sales practically become stagnant and remain at one level, it is very important for the company to sustain sales at that level. For that reason various sales promotion incentives are introduced at this stage to retain the loyal customers, followed by advertising which serves to send constant reminders to customers that the product is still the best product. Third in importance comes personal selling as salesmen try to retain their contacts with their loyal customers and continue generating sales from them.

4. In the decline stage: Where the sales start declining at a rapid pace, sales promotion incentives are continued to be used to lure the customers, advertising and publicity are reduced and salespeople give the product only minimal attention.

After discussing the various factors which are to be taken into consideration for arriving at the best promotional mix we can conclude that in order to survive in today's environment it is very essential for all the companies to strike a balance between the various promotional tools in such a manner, that they are able to realise their marketing goals successfully.

8.4 INTEGRATED MARKETING PROMOTION

As discussed above, we observed that the promotion can be carried out with the help of a variety of promotional tools. As most of the companies are using various promotional tools, it becomes essential to ensure integration amongst them. It is important to integrate and coordinate the advertising claims with what is being communicated by the sales-force. The variety of other communication techniques, such as websites on the Internet, Direct Marketing, sales promotion, and publicity and public relations need to be coordinated with advertising and personal selling so that a consolidated picture of the product emerges in front of the consumer. All this has led to an evaluation of the concept, called *Integrated Marketing Communications* (*IMC*).

George E. Belch and Michael A. Belch (2003) have been found quoting the definition of Integrated Marketing Communications given by the American Association of Advertising Agencies (the 4 "As")—

> *The concept of marketing communications planning that recognizes the added value of a comprehensive plan, that evaluates the strategic roles of a variety of communication disciplines—for example, general advertising, direct response, sales promotion and public relations—and combines these disciplines to provide clarity, consistency and maximum communications impact.*

4A'S

The 4A's definition focuses on the process of using all forms of promotion in a coordinated manner to achieve maximum communication impact. A consumer is able to form an opinion about the company or its brands on the basis of the information they receive from packaging, advertisements, direct-marketing efforts, publicity, sales promotions, websites, point-of-purchase displays and even the type of store where a product or service is sold. The integrated marketing communications approach seeks to coordinate all the marketing and promotional activities and project a consistent and unified image to the consumer.

8.4.1 Reasons for Growing Importance of Integrated Marketing Promotion

The concept of Integrated Marketing Promotion has been one of the most significant developments in the field of marketing that occurred during the 1990s. This approach has become popular amongst all types of firms, whether they are large or small, or whether they are into consumer products, or services, or business-to-business (B2B) marketing. There are a number of reasons as to why marketers are adapting this approach. Some of the important ones are listed as under:

Synergetic Effect

A fundamental reason, as to why companies are strategically integrating the various promotional tools rather than having them operate autonomously, is that by coordinating their marketing communications efforts, companies can avoid duplication and take advantage of synergy among various promotional tools, and develop more efficient and effective marketing communications programmes.

Environmental Adaptation

Consumers profile has changed over the years with regard to their demographics, lifestyles, media usage, and buying and shopping patterns. Hence, it has become essential for marketers to integrate their marketing promotions to convey the messages effectively to such dynamic consumers.

Emergence of New Media Options

As marketers are experimenting with new media options, it is very important for them to ensure coordination amongst all of them.

Growing Importance of Various Sales Promotion Incentives

These days, marketers are shifting their focus towards introducing more and more of sales promotion incentives to the consumers. But simply introducing the sales promotion incentives will not be effective unless and until the consumers are informed about them through advertisements. Therefore, coordination between advertising and sales promotion becomes a necessity.

The Rapid Growth of the Internet

The Internet revolution is well underway and the Internet audience is growing rapidly. It is changing the very nature of how companies do business and the ways they communicate and interact with the consumers. It is because of Internet that it is now possible for the companies to ensure integration amongst all their promotional tools.

Because of all the reasons listed above it has been possible for the marketers these days to ensure the integration, or in other words, the coordination between all promotional tools used by them. Promotion is an expensive affair, so if companies want to realise the worth of the money spent on promotion, it is very important for them to ensure that the messages which are passed on through all the mediums should be properly coordinated and that the consumer gets a consolidated and cohesive picture of the product. Ensuring integration is also becoming important because of an emerging development in the field of marketing—the concept of Relationship Marketing or Customer Relationship Management (CRM). The focus of the marketer is more on retaining the customers, besides creating more and more of new customers, because one loyal customer results in bringing more customers for the company by spreading a positive word-of-mouth message. We would like to conclude the entire discussion about the significance of information being provided to consumers, through various promotional activities with the help of the findings of a study mentioned as under:

New Informed Consumer

In 2012, IPG Network conducted a study titled 'New Realities' across the US, China and Germany. For the 'New Realities 2012' study, IPG collaborated with Draftfcb Ulka's Cogito Consulting for the India leg of the study and recently released the findings. The study has revealed the information processing, involvement and source preferences of Indian consumers. Some of the highlights of the study are as follows:

Does Information Confuse or Enable?

When it comes to information and the consumer, words and phrases like 'information explosion', 'information overload' and 'over-informed society' have become pretty regular in the media. The 'New Realities 2012' study reveals an interesting finding. According to them, contrary to the fears expressed earlier, the consumers feel empowered as information helps them in being smarter and more in command. In fact, this feeling is more dominant amongst the consumers in India than in other countries.

Surprisingly, it is not just the younger age groups that feel that way. This feeling is prevalent more in the older age groups—the 40 plus age group welcomes information and believes that it gives them more confidence to make the right choices and puts them in control. Interestingly, there is very little difference between genders as men and women depict near identical mindset.

Is the Indian Consumer More Sceptical?

Not all information is useful, not all information sources are credible and not all information can be credible. The Indian consumer seems to echo this in a more significant manner than consumers in other countries. In India, twice as many consumers seem to question the credibility of information as in the US. Print and TV are still important sources. Universally, word-of-mouth emerges as the most important medium. Opinion, whether sought or not, from friends and relatives scores significantly higher than any other medium. Despite being an on-line study, which is naturally biased towards the digital media, the 'New Realities 2012' study, seems to indicate that the significant gains made by digital media has not dented the value of traditional media in a major way.

In fact, in countries like Brazil and India, print and TV are still valued more than social media or Internet search or reviews, while in China, the digital media scores much better than TV or print, perhaps a reflection of the maturity/credibility of TV and print media in that country.

Information is Valuable even After the Purchase

An overwhelming majority of the respondents eagerly access information on brands and products, even after their purchase. Consumers justify or re-assure themselves on having made a correct purchase decision by seeking out more information from various sources.

Information has Social Currency

In a country where everyone has an opinion and an argument for everything, knowledge about brands and products is social currency. The Indian consumers are well ahead of their international counterparts when it comes to using knowledge as a social currency.

The sense of self esteem and pride of knowledge is evident with the scores for India being significantly higher than other countries. It is this social currency that also fuels the word-of-mouth and creates a whole new cycle of information transmission, and translation as well.

In an environment where information seems to be overflowing, the consumers seem to have devised their own ways to prioritise information, value it and use it. Whether it is pre-purchase, post-purchase, whether it is for self or others, the Indian consumer is happy to swim in the sea of information and soak in the benefits.

Source: Kinjal Medh, "New informed consumer", Brand Equity, The Economic Times, December 31st 2012.

Questions for Discussion

1. Today's consumers are more informed and look for information from various sources. Do you agree with this perception, give your views.
2. If you have to buy a consumer product, such as, an expensive mobile or a laptop computer, you will rely on information from which sources, before finalising your purchase decision.

LET US SUM UP

- Promotion may be defined as the coordination of all seller initiated efforts to set up channels of information and persuasion to facilitate the sale of the product or service or the acceptance of an idea.
- Promotion serves three essential roles—it informs, persuades and reminds the prospective customers about a company and its products.
- There are four basic tools of promotion—advertising, personal selling, sales promotion, publicity and public relations. However Direct Marketing and Internet Marketing are also being used by marketers to communicate with their target audiences.
- Advertising is any paid form of non-personal presentation and promotion of ideas, goods or services by an identified sponsor.

- Personal selling is a face-to-face interaction with one or more prospective purchasers, for the purpose of making presentations, answering questions and procuring orders.
- Sales Promotion is defined as a variety of short-term incentives used to encourage a trial or purchase of a product or service which is designed to supplement and coordinate personal selling and advertisement.
- In publicity, the company attempts to get the media to cover or run a favourite story on a product, service, cause or event to affect awareness, knowledge, opinions, or behaviour.
- Direct Marketing is a promotional tool in which organisations communicate directly with target customers to generate a response or a transaction.
- In order to arrive at the best promotional campaign, it is very important for the company to combine all the promotional mix elements, balancing their strengths and weaknesses effectively.
- Promotional mix is heavily influenced by the choice of the push or pull strategy. A promotional programme aimed primarily at middlemen, is called a push strategy and a promotional programme directed primarily at end users is called a pull strategy.
- Different combinations of promotional tools are used during the four stages of a product's life cycle.
- As most of the companies are using various promotional tools, it becomes essential to ensure integration amongst them.

QUESTIONS TO CHECK YOUR PROGRESS

Short Answer Questions

1. What is promotion?
2. What are the important objectives of promotion?
3. What is "better mousetrap fallacy"? Explain with examples.
4. Differentiate between the concept of advertising and publicity.
5. List out three unique benefits of sales promotion incentives.
6. Explain the AIDA model of setting advertising objectives.
7. Name the strategy used in the following cases:
   (i) The Malaysian Tourism Board is advertising heavily in television and other consumer magazines and offering consumer discounts on hotels and airfares. The Malaysian Tourism Board wants travellers to ask their travel agents to make all the arrangements to send them to Malaysia for a holiday.
   (ii) The Malaysian Tourism Board would be using the strategy of advertising heavily to travel agents to get the agents to sell the benefits of a vacation to Malaysia to its clients. With this strategy, it could also provide total discounts and free guided tours as incentives to the travel agents.

   What promotional tools are most important when the buyer is in the awareness stage of the product life cycle?
8. What promotional tools are most important when the buyer is in the awareness stage of the product life cycle?
9. Select the most appropriate option to the following statements—
   (i) The cost per person comes out to be the minimum in case of:
   (a) personal selling (b) trade promotion
   (c) advertising (d) consumer promotion

(ii) If the company's focus is short-term, it will concentrate on:
 (a) advertising (b) sales promotion
 (c) personal selling (d) publicity

(iii) Posters and leaflets received along with your morning newspaper relates to:
 (a) sales promotion (b) public relations
 (c) personal selling (d) advertising

(iv) Which of the following can give positive as well as negative information about the product:
 (a) advertising (b) personal selling
 (c) publicity (d) sales promotion

10. Fill in the blanks—

(i) An organisation's combination of personal selling, advertising, sales promotion, public relations and publicity, to help in achieving its marketing objectives is called____________.

(ii) Personal selling may be adequate in a small local market, but as the market broadens geographically, greater emphasis must be placed on____________.

(iii) Products which are technical in nature and require frequent servicing to keep them in good working order, rely more on________________.

(iv) In order to ensure the purchase of the product, companies use____________.

(v) The manufacturer using sales force and trade promotion to induce intermediaries to carry, promote and sell the product to end users, call for ______________strategy.

(vi) ______________ is the longest stage in the life of a product.

(vii) Sales promotion incentives are used aggressively at the __________ stage of the PLC.

Long Answer Questions

1. "Effective communication is the essence of promotion". Discuss the statement in the light of the importance of promotion in marketing.
2. The marketing communicator can use one or more types of appeals or themes to produce a desired response—(a) What are these types of appeals? (b) When should each be used? (c) Provide an example of each type of appeal using three different advertisements.
3. Explain the unique characteristics of all promotional tools. Why is it important for marketers to understand these characteristics in selecting these tools?
4. Define the role of advertising, sales promotion and publicity in the promotion mix.
5. "Advertising costs too much. The billions of dollars spent annually on advertising could be put to better use". Do you agree or disagree? Why?
6. "Advertising is the most visible element of the promotion". Comment, highlighting the importance of advertising in modern marketing.
7. Critics charge that advertising seeks to manipulate its audience, whereas, supporters claim that it merely seeks to persuade. Which interpretation do you agree with? Why?
8. Why is personal selling generally a more important promotional tool than advertising for a marketer? Under what conditions might advertising be the dominant element in the promotion mix?
9. How does sales promotion complement advertising and personal selling?
10. Enumerate the various promotional tools used by business organisations to boost the sales and explain any four methods of sales promotion.
11. List out the various factors affecting the choice of an appropriate promotion mix.

12. Discuss the following for their role in determining the promotion mix—(a) product considerations; (b) pricing policies; (c) distribution strategies; and (d) target market characteristics.
13. Suggest appropriate promotional strategies at different stages of the product life cycle.
14. "Push strategy is better than pull strategy for FMCGs and vice versa is true for industrial products". Do you agree?
15. Explain how integrated marketing communication is a powerful and cost-effective promotional strategy.
16. What promotional strategy should be used for marketing the following products—(a) designer furniture; (b) books; (c) bathroom fittings; (d) exhaust fans; and (e) a new breakfast cereal.

CHAPTER 9

Channels of Distribution

Learning Outcomes

After studying this chapter, you will be able to:

- ❖ Understand the concept and functions of distribution channels
- ❖ Explain the types, importance and functions of the middlemen
- ❖ Classify the factors affecting the choice of channels
- ❖ Discuss various channel management decisions
- ❖ Define the concept of channel dynamics
- ❖ State the procedure for market logistics

After producing a good product, pricing it appropriately and promoting it aggressively, it is important for marketers to decide as to how to make the goods available right next door to the consumers. Most producers do not sell their goods directly to the final users. They take the help of a set of intermediaries performing a variety of functions. These intermediaries constitute a *Marketing Channel*, also called a *Trade Channel* or the *Distribution Channel*.

According to the American Marketing Association (1995)—

> *Distribution channels are the set of firms and individuals that take title or assist in transferring title of the particular goods or services as it moves from the producer to the consumer. A channel always includes both the producer and the final customer for the product, as well as all middlemen involved in the title transfer.*

Some intermediaries, such as wholesalers and retailers are called *merchants* because they buy goods, take title to them and resell the merchandise to the consumers at a profit. While others, such as dealers, brokers, and distributors are called *agents*. Their job is to simply search for customers and negotiate on the producer's behalf, but they do not take title to the goods and bear the risk.

Still there are others, such as transportation companies, independent warehouses, banks, and advertising agencies whose job is to assist in the distribution process, but they neither take title to goods, nor negotiate purchases or sales; they are simply called *facilitators*.

Generally companies employ middlemen to take advantage of their contacts, experience, specialization and scale of operations.

9.1 CHANNEL LEVELS

The producers and the final customers are part of every channel, while the number and the nature of intermediaries decide the length of the channel.

9.1.1 A Zero-Level Channel

A zero-level channel is also called a *Direct Marketing Channel.* It consists of manufacturer's selling directly to the final customers as depicted in Figure 9.1. Important examples are door-to-door sales, mail-order selling, tele-marketing, Internet selling, and manufacturer-owned stores. Amway is an example of Direct Marketing, Tupperware representatives sell kitchen goods through home parties, Reader's Digest is selling through Direct Marketing, and some manufacturers are selling their products through Tele shopping, such as home shopping, with the help of hour-long commercials called 'infomercials'. These days, a number of companies selling through the Internet are also growing rapidly thereby adding to the success of zero-level channels.

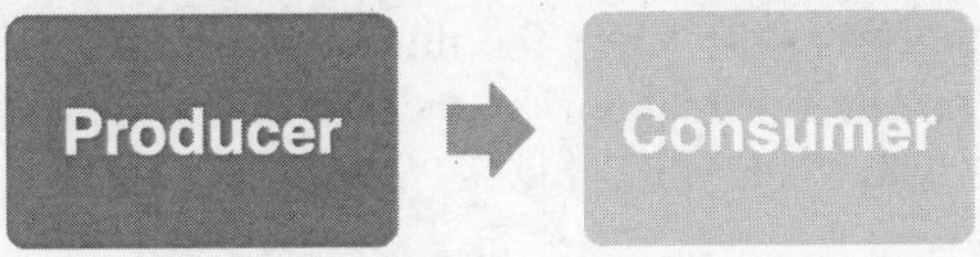

Figure 9.1 Zero-level channel.

9.1.2 A One-Level Channel

Contains one selling intermediary, such as a wholesaler or retailer (Figure 9.2).

Figure 9.2 One-level channel.

9.1.3 A Two-Level Channel

Contains two intermediaries, generally found in consumer markets, as depicted in Figure 9.3. A wholesaler and retailer are the typical intermediaries in such a channel.

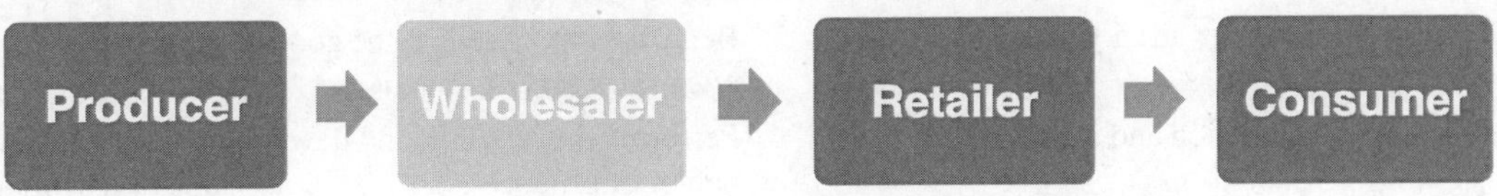

Figure 9.3 Two-level channel.

9.1.4 A Three-Level or Multilevel Channel

A three-level or multilevel channel is made up of three or more intermediaries. In some industries wholesalers sell to jobbers, who sell to small retailers, who finally sell it to the consumers. The channel is depicted in Figure 9.4.

Figure 9.4 Multi-level channel.

Thus, a channel can have various levels of distribution depending on various factors which will be discussed later in the chapter.

9.2 IMPORTANCE OF MIDDLEMAN

Middlemen are criticised severely by various people on various fronts. Some people have even gone to the extent of treating them as *parasites that suck the blood of both the manufacturers as well as the consumers.* However, in reality, a middleman is a very important link between the manufacturer and the consumer. This intermediary is important to both as it performs a number of services for them. There is an old saying in marketing that *you can eliminate the middleman, but you cannot eliminate their functions (activities),* someone has to perform those activities. It is because of its importance that over the years the number of intermediaries have been increasing rather than decreasing. Some of the reasons as to why a middleman is important to both the consumers and the producers are listed in Table 9.1.

Table 9.1 Importance of Middlemen to Consumers and Producers

For Consumers	For Producers
Anticipate the needs and wants of consumers and feed the information back to the producers	Disseminates the information regarding the products and services to the consumers and acts as a sales specialist for producers
Does bulk-breaking, i.e. dividing large shipments into smaller quantities	Acts as a buffer by keeping stock of the goods and sometimes does bulk-breaking by breaking the bulk into small lots and selling it to the consumers in small lots
Perform storage and warehousing in order to ensure a smooth supply of goods all the year	Maintains the warehouses on behalf of the producers and bears the storage costs
Transports goods from the place of production to the place of consumption	Transports goods from the place of production to the warehouses
Provides credit facility to consumers	Provides funds in advance to producers
Gives guarantee and warranty on the products	Bears the risk of selling the goods and renders all the after-sales service functions
Provide free installation and repair facility	Performs the research and development services on behalf of producers

9.3 FUNCTIONS OF CHANNELS OF DISTRIBUTION

A distribution channel performs the work of moving goods from producers to consumers. It overcomes the time, place and possession gaps that separate goods and services from those who have them, to those who want them. Members of the marketing channel perform a number of key functions as depicted in Figure 9.5:

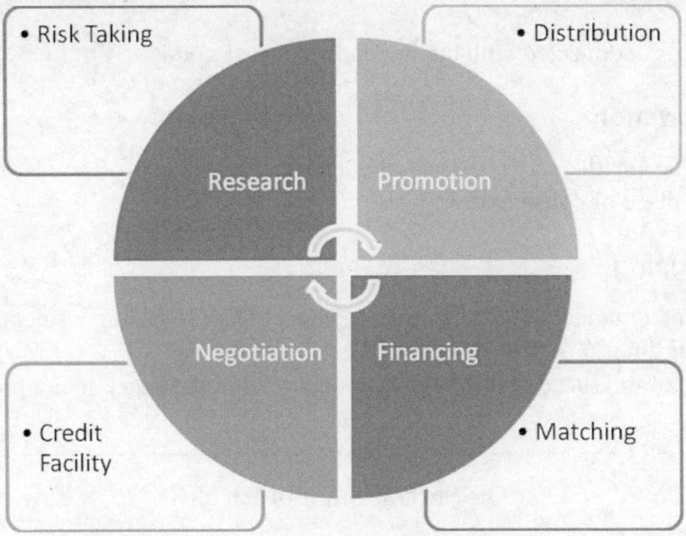

Figure 9.5 Functions of channel of distribution.

9.3.1 Research

Intermediaries gather information about the current and the potential customers, competitors and other forces in the marketing environment as they are able to observe them closely, and feed all the information back to the organisation to help them in designing their product and marketing strategy.

9.3.2 Promotion

They perform the job of informing, persuading and motivating people to buy the product.

9.3.3 Negotiation

Their job is to negotiate and reach on agreements on price and other terms and conditions with the customers on behalf of the manufacturers.

9.3.4 Contact

Middlemen work as a contact between the customer and the manufacturers. Their job is to pass on the information regarding the goods and services from the producer to the consumers, and convey the consumer's feedback with regard to their needs and wants to the manufacturers.

9.3.5 Financing

At times, middlemen render financial support to manufacturers by lending them money in advance to ensure the timely delivery of goods and at the same time they might extend credit facility to the consumers.

9.3.6 Risk-Taking

They assume the risk connected with buying and selling of goods.

9.3.7 Transportation

Middlemen provide for the successive storage and the movement of goods from their place of production to the place of consumption.

9.3.8 Warehousing

At times, middlemen maintain warehouses and keep a buffer to ensure a smooth supply of goods to the market at all times.

An example of the success of distribution networks in the success of a product is quoted as under:

The Success Story of Parle-G

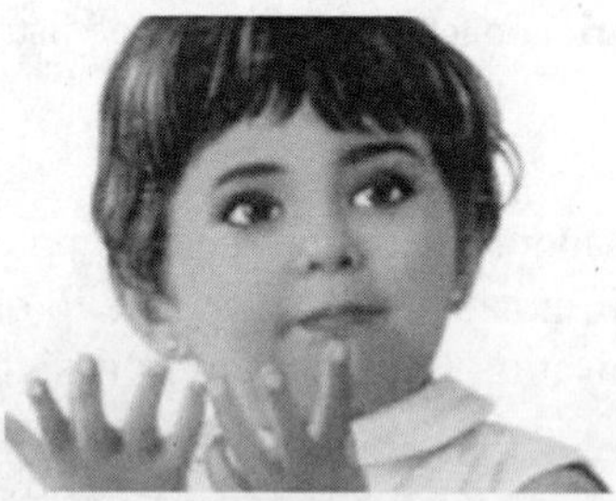

Parle-G has been a leader in the biscuit segment for the last 75 years. Despite the tough competition given to them by Britannia and ITC, Parle-G has been able to hold its distinction as the largest selling biscuit brand mainly because of its strong distribution network that covers over six million retail stores in the country. The brand is available even in villages with a population of 500. *A lot of non-biscuit consuming customers start eating Parle-G when they first enter into this product category*, says Pravin Kulkarnii, Marketing Head, Parle Products. According to a recent report in ET, the glucose category grew at a slower rate than cream biscuits and cookies during the April to September 2012 period. However, Mayank Shah, Group Product Manager, Parle Products, challenges the numbers. *Neilsen only tracks 25,000 urban, Tier 1 and Class 1 towns retail outlets, whereas, Parle-G has a reach even in villages with a population of 500. The numbers reported are not accurate and far from the truth.* Shah says that Neilsen doesn't include hotels, canteen store departments and railways or factory canteens, which are also among the many places that Parle-G is available.

Source: Preeti Chamikutty, "Will Parle-G be relevant to the next generation", Brand Equity, The Economic Times, January 16th 2013.

Questions for Discussion

1. Do you think that an intensive distribution policy has been the success mantra for Parle G?
2. Can you suggest some more marketing strategies to Parle G to attract new customers towards their product?

9.4 FACTORS AFFECTING THE CHOICE OF DISTRIBUTION CHANNELS

A company should follow the criteria of three C's—Channel control, Coverage and Cost, as shown in Figure 9.6, that are consistent with the desired level of customer service. While following these three criteria a company has to take into consideration various factors, some of the important ones are listed as under:

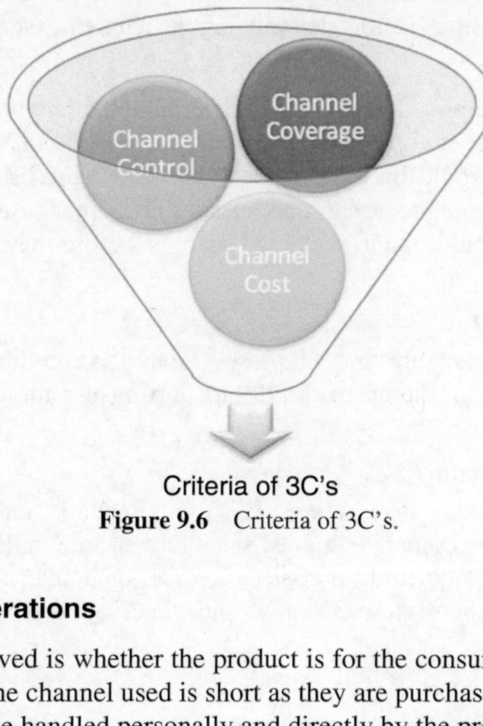

Figure 9.6 Criteria of 3C's.

9.4.1 Market Considerations

The first thing to be observed is whether the product is for the consumer or industrial market. In case of Industrial goods, the channel used is short as they are purchased by some of the buyers in bulk, so the orders are to be handled personally and directly by the producer himself.

In case of Consumer goods, the channel is generally long because the numbers of consumers is large who are generally distributed far and wide, so they can be served by the middleman.

Geographic Concentration of the Market

The geographic dispersal of the consumer determines the length of the channel—the wider the distribution, the longer is going to be the channel, and vice-versa.

Order Size of the Consumer

In case the consumers prefer to buy in bulk and place large orders, they need to be attended personally by the manufacturer. Therefore, the channel will be short. In contrast, the consumers who buy frequently and in small lots are generally entertained by the middlemen and the channel in that case will be long.

Buying Habits of the Consumer

In case the consumers are very specific about the purchases, take very little time and make the entire payment in one go, the channel is going to be short because the manufacturer can personally attend them. As against this, if the consumers wants credit, seek variety, ask for lots of detail and personal attention, the channel is going to be long because the manufacturer will not be able to attend them personally and will seek the services of the middleman who can perform all these functions very well.

9.4.2 Product Considerations

The basic nature of the product determines the length of the channel and the type of middlemen brought into the picture. Various factors determining the nature of the product are listed as under:

Unit Value of the Product

Whether the product is cheap or luxurious, will determine the length of the channel. If the unit value of the product is less, it's going to be purchased more frequently by a large number of consumer so the channel would be long, while if the unit value is large and it's a luxurious commodity, the channel is going to be short because the consumer will seek the personal attention of the manufacturer and would like to seek clarifications before they finally decide to purchase the product.

Perishability of the Product

If the product is perishable in nature, and if it passes through various hands before finally reaching the consumer, and vice versa, the channel will be short or else the quality of the product will deteriorate.

Technical Nature of the Product

If the product is highly technical in nature, its various features and composition needs to be explained personally by the company's trained sales-force or the middlemen. Moreover, in such cases, a consumer will seek numerous after-sales services, guarantees and warranties, which can be delivered personally by their sales staff only. Thus, in case of more technical goods there will be a shorter channel, and vice versa.

Size and Weight of the Product

If the size of the product is bigger, its shape is large and it is a heavy product then the channel will be short because it is difficult to transport and move such goods through various middlemen, while if the product is small, compact and light weighted, it can be easily transported and transferred from one middleman to another, and the channel can be long.

Standardization and Grading of the Product

The goods which are standardized in nature, their labelling, packaging and grading takes place in the factory itself, in such cases the channel can be long because it is convenient to transport such goods to far off places and promote them aggressively through national or international media while, in comparison, if the goods are loose and unpacked, they cannot be easily transported and promoted to far off places, therefore the channel will be short.

9.4.3 Middlemen Considerations

The choice of a particular channel and the types of middlemen involved depends to a large extent on the availability of the right kind of middlemen and the right set of services being provided by them. Some of the factors taken into consideration are listed below:

Services Provided by Middlemen

If the product is technical in nature or is something which requires numerous services to be performed by the middlemen, in that case the willingness and the capability of the middlemen to provide such services will determine the length of the channel. If more services are required, the channel will be short, and vice versa.

Availability of the Desired Middlemen

Availability of the middleman is determined by first identifying whether they are willing to deal in the manufacture's goods, and secondly ensuring that they are not dealing in any competitor's product, or may not be willing to add another product line.

Attitude of the Middlemen Towards the Manufacturer's Policies

Whether the middleman is willing to agree to the manufacturer's policies and provide them with all the services asked for also determines the choice of middlemen.

Financial Capability of the Middlemen

The middlemen should be financially sound so that they should be in a position to pay back all the money to the producers in time and if the need arises, they may be in a position to give advance money to the producers.

Legal Constraints

In certain cases there are few legal requirements which need to be fulfilled before someone can be appointed as the middlemen. For example, medicines can be sold only through pharmaceutical shops being handled by persons who are qualified pharmacists.

9.4.4 Company Considerations

Finally, the decision about the length of the channel and the number of intermediaries involved is taken by the manufacturer keeping into account the following factors:

Financial Capability of the Company

Managing channels of distribution personally involves a huge monetary investment. If an organisation is financially sound, and can afford to maintain and manage a large network of shops, they might opt for Direct Marketing. While in comparison, if an organisation is running short of funds they might hand over the responsibility of marketing and selling activities to their middlemen.

Ability of the Top Management

If the Top Management has marketing and selling skills they might like to handle their marketing and distribution activities themselves, the channel will be short in that case, or otherwise they might take the services of a large number of middlemen and the channel will be long.

Desire for the Channel Control

If the management wants to retain a strong control over the channel members, and wants to personally supervise each and every activity, the channel will be short, or vice versa.

Services Provided by the Seller

If the manufacturer is ready to provide additional services such as—packaging, grading, labeling, promotion, etc. to the middleman, the channel can be long, or vice versa.

Thus, to conclude, it can be said that all the factors listed above determine the length of the channel.

9.5 INTENSITY OF MARKET COVERAGE

After deciding about the length of the channel, manufacturers have to decide about the number of intermediaries they are going to use at each channel level. Three strategies, as explained by Philip Kotler (1999), are available as depicted in Figure 9.7—Exclusive Distribution, Selective Distribution and Intensive Distribution.

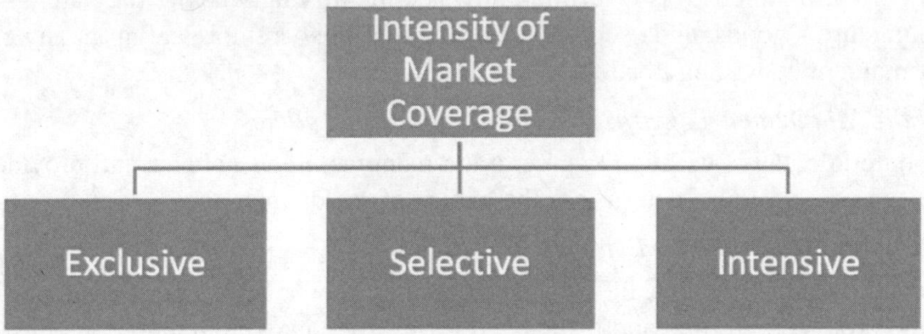

Figure 9.7 Intensity of market coverage.

9.5.1 Exclusive Distribution

It means limiting the number of intermediaries to a bare minimum. It is used when the producer wants to maintain control over the service level and service outputs offered by the resellers. Often it involves exclusive dealing arrangements in which the resellers agree not to carry competing brands. By granting Exclusive Distribution, the producer hopes to obtain more dedicated and committed service from the intermediaries. This channel arrangement is generally found in case of the distribution of new automobiles, some major appliances and some women apparel brands.

9.5.2 Selective Distribution

It involves the use of more than a few but less than all of the intermediaries who are willing to carry a particular product. It is used by established companies, and by new companies seeking distributors. The company does not have to put its efforts into too many outlets; it enables the producers to gain adequate market coverage with more control and less cost than Intensive Distribution. Nike, the world's largest athletic shoe maker, is a good example of Selective Distribution. Consumer shopping, specialty goods and industrial accessory equipments are included in this category.

9.5.3 Intensive Distribution

It means selling the products though every outlet where the final consumer will reasonably look for it. It involves the process of the manufacturer placing the goods or services in as many outlets as possible. This strategy is generally used for consumer convenience goods where the consumer demands immediate satisfaction and prefers buying products that are conveniently available to them right next door.

Finally, whether the company would like to go in for Exclusive, Selective or Intensive Distribution depends to a large extent on their economic viability, control criteria and the adaptability of the channel to the product. Therefore, designing a channel system calls for analyzing customer needs, establishing channel objectives, and identifying and evaluating the major channel alternatives.

9.6 CHANNEL MANAGEMENT DECISIONS

Once the decisions about the type of middleman involved are made, it is important to treat them respectfully and give them the opportunity to be profitable. There are certain important elements which are to be taken into consideration, such as:

Distributors' territorial rights: It is very important to define the distributors' territories and the terms and conditions clearly so that there should not be any overlapping and any confusion between them.

Conditions of sales: There should be clarity about the payment terms and the producer guarantee. Most producers grant cash discounts to distributors for early payment. They might also guarantee distributors against defective merchandise or price declines, or take the goods back if they are not sold.

Price policy: It calls for the producer to establish a price list and schedule of discounts and allowances that the middleman can see as equitable and sufficient.

Mutual services and responsibilities: These are conditions that must be carefully spelt out, especially in franchised and exclusive agency channels. Terms and conditions should be clearly laid out regarding physical facility being provided by the producer, promotional policies and buyback supplies from specified vendors.

9.6.1 Selecting the Channel Members

Selection of channel members is done very carefully by the producer. Before selecting any middlemen the producer would want to evaluate the number of years they have been in business, the other product lines that have been dealt with, growth and profit record, solvency, cooperativeness, and their reputation.

If the middlemen are sales agents, producers will want to evaluate the number and character of various other product lines carried by them, and the size and quantity of their sales force. If the intermediaries are departmental stores that want exclusive distribution, the producer will want to evaluate locations, future growth potential and the type of clientele.

9.6.2 Motivating Channel Members

The company needs to determine intermediaries' needs and arrive at an arrangement where they are able to deliver superior value to them. It is very important to keep the channel members highly motivated to ensure their best performance and commitment towards the organisation. The task of motivating channel members starts with understanding their basic needs and wants, and trying to provide them with some incentive to work efficiently with the producer. The producer can make use of various types of powers to elicit cooperation, as depicted in Figure 9.8.

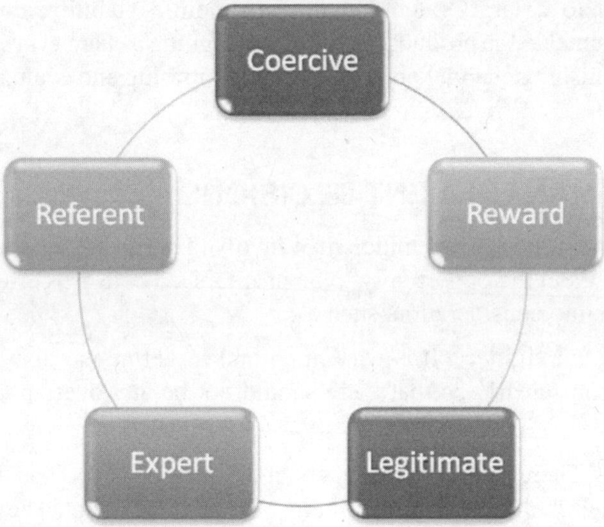

Figure 9.8 Sources of power for middlemen.

Coercive Power

Occurs when a manufacturer threatens to withdraw a contract or terminate a relationship if intermediaries fail to cooperate.

Reward Power

Occurs when the manufacturer offers intermediaries an extra benefit for performing certain specific functions. Reward power typically produces better results than coercive power.

Legitimate Power

Legitimate power is used when the manufacturer requires a behaviour from the middlemen that is warranted under the contract. As long as the intermediaries view the manufacturer as a legitimate leader they always follow him.

Expert Power

Expert power can be applied when the manufacturer has special knowledge that the intermediary values. A manufacturer may have a sophisticated system of distributor sales training.

Referent Power

Occurs when the manufacturer is so highly respected that intermediaries feel proud to be associated with them. Companies like Sony, IBM, Mercedes and BMW have high reverence power.

9.6.3 Evaluating and Modifying Channel Arrangements

Producers must periodically evaluate intermediaries' performance against standards such as sales quota attainment, average inventory levels, customer delivery time, treatment of damaged and lost goods, and cooperation in promotional and training programmes. They might have to modify channel arrangements if the middleman's performance is not found satisfactory or up to the mark.

9.7 TYPES OF MIDDLEMEN

After discussing about the need for middlemen, let's now discuss about the various types of middlemen available. The various types of middlemen can be broadly divided into two categories—Agent middlemen and Merchant middlemen.

9.7.1 Agent Middlemen

Agent middlemen are also known as a *Functional middlemen* and *Mercantile agents*. These are those marketing institutions that assist in the transfer of the title of goods without taking any title to them, and act as agents of the owner of goods, accepting remuneration in the form of brokerage or commission. They serve the interests of both, the buyers and the sellers, as shown in Figure 9.9.

Figure 9.9 Types of agent middlemen.

Commission Agent

Commission agents work on commission basis and try to sell goods on behalf of the producer to the consumer without taking any title to goods. Their job is simply to bring the buyers and sellers together on a common platform, and initiate discussions amongst them for finalizing the transaction. For example, property dealers.

Broker

Brokers generally deal in buying and selling of shares, bonds or debentures on behalf of the buyers or sellers. They charge a brokerage for their services. For example, share brokers, etc.

Forwarding and Clearing Agents

Forwarding agents are those who help in the export of goods by picking up the goods from the place of production, carrying them to the nearest port, fulfilling all the custom requirements and finally ensuring the shipment of goods on behalf of the producer. The Clearing agent, on the other hand, receive the consignment coming from abroad at the port, performs all the custom formalities and ensures that goods reach their destination. For the services performed, these brokers/agents charge a pre-decided commission.

Auctioneer

An Auctioneer agent is the one who helps in the sales of property or any other goods by conducting an auction and selling the goods to the highest bidder.

9.7.2 Merchant Middlemen

According to the American Marketing Association (1995)—*merchant middlemen are those intermediaries who take the title to goods, bear the risks, perform various marketing functions and hope to gain by making profits on transactions.* The types of Merchant Middlemen are shown in Figure 9.10.

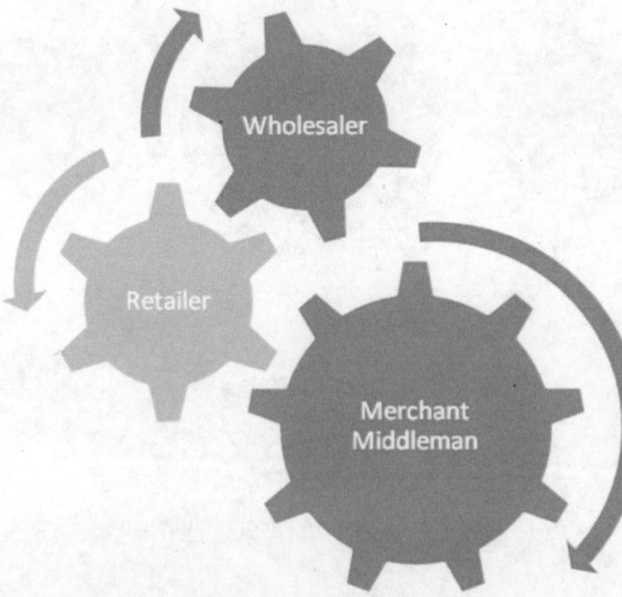

Figure 9.10 Types of merchant middlemen.

Wholesaler

According to the American Marketing Association (1995)—

> *A wholesaler is a business unit which buys and resells merchandise to retailers and other industrial users and/or commercial users but doesn't sell a significant amount of goods to the ultimate consumer.*

Retailer

According to the American Marketing Association (1995)—

> *A retailer is a merchant or occasionally an agent or a business unit whose main business is selling the goods directly to the ultimate consumer for non-business use.*

Although both, wholesalers and retailers are the important types of merchant middleman, yet their exits differences in their basic nature as highlighted in Table 9.2 and the functions performed by them as explained in Table 9.3 as under:

Table 9.2 Difference between Retailers and Wholesalers

Wholesalers	Retailers
Buy in bulk	Buy in small lots
Do not sell goods to the ultimate consumers	Sell the goods to the ultimate consumers
Might sell in bulk for business use	Get goods from wholesaler and sell for personal consumption
Promote the product	Never promote, just pass the information through word-of-mouth
Concentrated at small places	Widely distributed
Provide goods on credit to the retailers	They generally do not sell goods on credit

Table 9.3 Functions Performed by Merchant Middleman

Wholesalers	Retailers
Bulk buying from manufacturers	Assembling from various sources and keeping wide assortment of goods under one roof
Bulk breaking for customers	Grading and packing for customers
Selling to other channel members	Selling to ultimate consumers
Promoting products	Undertake sales promotion activities through window displays and point-of-purchase display materials
Warehousing and storage function to ensure the smooth supply of goods all year round	Keep buffer–sell in convenient lots at convenient places and time intervals to consumers
Risk-taking	Risk bearing
Transportation	Maintain personal contact with the customers
Financing producers	Give credit facility to customers
Disseminating marketing information	Give consumer feedback to the producer or whole-salers

9.8 CHANNEL DYNAMICS

Distribution channels do not stand still. New wholesaling and retailing institutions emerge and new channel systems develop. We will look at the recent growth of Vertical, Horizontal and Multichannel Marketing Systems and the how these systems cooperate, conflict and compete. Figure 9.11 depicts the three types of distribution systems as under:

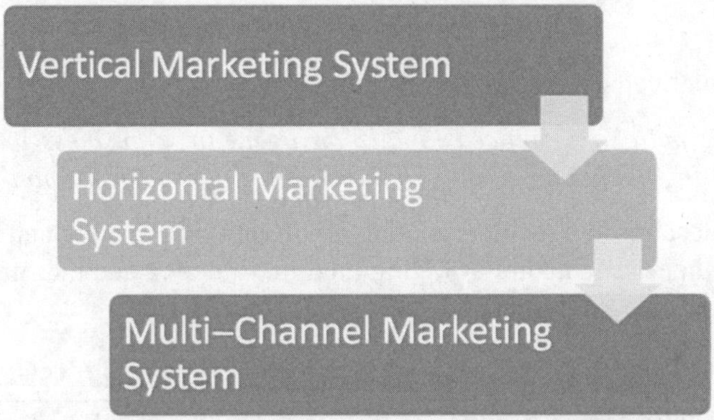

Figure 9.11 Types of distribution systems.

9.8.1 Vertical Marketing System (VMS)

A conventional marketing channel comprises an independent producer, wholesaler(s) and retailer(s). In such cases each channel member operates independently and tries to maximize their profits. No channel member tries to exercise any control over other members.

A Vertical Marketing System, by contrast, comprises the producer, wholesaler(s) and retailer(s) acting as a unified system out of which one of them emerges to be the channel captain and others agree to follow him. This system has the advantage of ensuring a close coordination and cooperation between all channel members. When all of them work together, they are generally able to generate more sales and a loyal clientele. They achieve economies through size, bargaining power and elimination of duplicated services. For example, manufacturers of a dominant brand are able to secure strong trade cooperation and support from resellers. Procter and Gamble is able to command high levels of cooperation from their intermediaries in connection with displays, shelf space, promotions and price policies.

9.8.2 Horizontal Marketing System (HMS)

In this channel development, two or more unrelated companies put together resources or programmes to exploit an emerging marketing opportunity. Each company lacks the capital, know-how, production and marketing resources to venture alone, or it is afraid of the risk. The companies might work with each other on temporary or permanent bases or create a joint venture company. For example, car companies enter into a contract with various banks and provide zero per cent financing on easy terms and conditions to customers to facilitate the purchase of the cars. This brings business both to car companies as well as to banks.

9.8.3 Multichannel Marketing System (MMS)

This occurs when a single firm uses two or more marketing channels to reach one or more customer segments. It gives three benefits to the company—first, *increased market coverage*—as companies can further add channels to reach consumer segments currently not reachable. Secondly, *lower channel cost*—companies may add a new channel to lower the cost of selling to an existing customer group, for example, selling by phone rather than personally visiting small customers. Third, *more customized selling*—companies may add channels whose selling features fit the requirements of customers more adequately, for example adding technical sales force to sell more complex equipment.

The multichannel marketing system may suffer from the problems of coordination and cooperation between the various marketing channels resulting into conflict between their members as they might end up competing between themselves for the same set of consumers.

9.9 MARKET LOGISTICS

Physical distribution starts at the factory level. This is where the managers decide about the location of warehouses (stocking points) and the transportation system which delivers the goods to the final destinations in the desired time or at the lowest total cost. Physical distribution has now been expanded into the broader concept of Supply Chain Management (SCM). Supply Chain Management starts before the products have been produced—it involves procuring the right inputs (raw materials, components and capital equipment), converting them efficiently into finished products and dispatching them to the final destinations. The supply chain perspective can help a company identify efficient and sincere suppliers and distributors who always deliver the raw materials in time and at the right price so that the manufacturer can have timely production and delivery of goods at low costs.

Market Logistics involves planning the infrastructure in order to implement and control the physical flow of materials and final goods from point-of-origin to points-of-use, to meet customer requirements at a profit. It calls for Integrated Logistics System (ILS), involving material management, material flow systems and physical distribution regulated by Information Technology (IT).

9.9.1 Market Logistics Planning has Four Steps

- To decide about the best way to deliver quality products to consumers at low cost.
- To decide about the best channel options available for reaching the customers.
- To develop an efficient system for conducting sales forecasts and handling warehouses, transportation and material management.
- Implementing the solutions with the help of various information systems, equipment, policies, and procedures in order to ensure efficiency and an effective timeline.

Market Logistics involves a process of ensuring a smooth assembly line production, efficient upkeep of goods in warehouses and an excellent transportation system to ensure smooth and timely delivery of goods to the consumers throughout the year. The first step is sales forecasting, where with the help of various forecasting techniques, the organisation would like to project the likely demand for the next year or so, and on the basis of the forecast they can schedule production, distribution and inventory levels. Production plans indicate the raw materials to be purchased by the purchasing department to ensure smooth production. These materials arrive through inbound transportation, enter the receiving area and are stored in a raw material inventory. Raw materials are converted into finished goods. Finished goods are kept in warehouses as inventory to ensure the smooth supply of goods in the market with the help of efficient transportation systems.

9.9.2 Market Logistics Objectives

Many companies state their Market Logistics objectives as getting the right goods to the right places at the right time for the least cost. However, it is difficult for the organisations to ensure everything and maintain low cost because if they want to deliver quality goods to their customers with the best of services throughout the year, they do have to spend a huge amount on keeping multiple warehouses, efficient packaging and quick transportation system, all of which raises the Market Logistics cost.

Given the Market Logistics objectives, the company must design a system that should help them to achieve those objectives efficiently and with minimum cost and loss of customers. According to Philip Kotler (1999), an efficient Market Logistics system will have the following cost:

$$M = T + FW + VW + S$$

where

M = Total Market Logistics cost of proposed system

T = Total freight cost of proposed system

FW = Total fixed warehouse cost of proposed system

VW = Total variable warehousing cost (including inventory) of proposed system

S = Total cost of lost sales due to average delivery delay under proposed system

Choosing a right market logistics system calls for working out the various possible combinations of the proposed systems and selecting the system which helps in reducing the overall cost and minimizing the lost sales.

9.9.3 Market Logistics Decisions

According to Philip Kotler (1999), four major decisions must be made in regard to market logistics, as depicted in Figure 9.12.

- How should orders be handled? (Order processing)
- Where should stocks be located? (Warehousing)
- How much stock should be held? (Inventory)
- How should goods be shipped? (Transportation)

Order Processing

Most of the companies today are trying to shorten the order-to-payment-cycle, that is, the time between an order's receipt, delivery and payment. This cycle involves many steps, including receiving the order from customers, making an entry, scheduling the production accordingly, arranging for transportation and delivery, and collecting the payment. Therefore, the organisation should make an effort to ensure a smooth process and give the customers maximum satisfaction and increase the company's profitability.

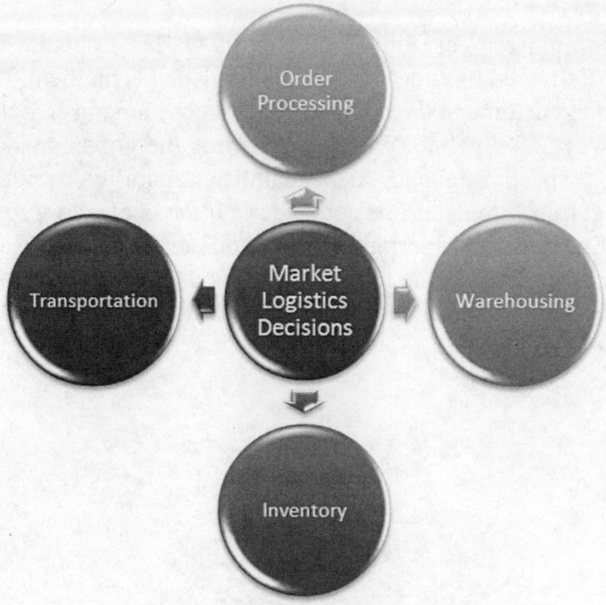

Figure 9.12 Market logistics decisions.

Warehousing

Every company has to maintain warehouses so that they are able to store finished goods and ensure a balance between production and consumption. Another important decision regarding warehousing is to decide about the number and location of the warehouse, i.e. whether it should be located near the market or near the production plant. Maintaining more stocking locations and that too near the market can mean that goods can be delivered to customers more quickly, but it will also result in higher warehousing and inventory costs. Thus, it becomes essential for the organisation to carefully decide about the inventory levels which are to be kept at or near the plant, and those to be located in warehouses in other locations. The company might own private warehouses and also rent space in the public warehouses.

Inventory

Inventory levels represent a major cost. Salespeople would like their company to carry enough stock to handle all customer orders immediately. However, this is not cost-effective as maintaining higher levels of inventory will add to blocked investment. Maintaining the quality of goods in the warehouses with the help of refrigeration and other means will further add to the cost. Therefore, the management needs to know as to how much their sales and profits would increase as a result of carrying larger inventories and promising faster deliveries to their customers, and accordingly make a decision. Inventory decision making further involves knowing about the order-reorder cycle of the consumers. If they are into the habit of placing larger orders, the frequency of order placed will be less and the organisation will be able to manage with low inventory levels. The company needs to balance order-processing costs and inventory-carrying costs. If the suppliers are dependable, then the manufacturer can carry much lower levels of inventory and still meet customer's expectations by delivering orders in time. The basic idea is to arrange for well-timed flows, not stocks.

Transportation

Transportation decision plays a very important role in Market Logistics because the efficiency with which goods are delivered on time and the quality depends on them. In shipping goods to its warehouses, dealers and customers, the company can choose among five transportation modes—rail, air, truck, waterway and pipeline. While transporting the goods, marketers have to consider various criteria, such as speed, frequency, dependability, capability, availability, traceability, and cost. For speed, air and truck are the prime contenders. If the goal is low cost, then it is waterways and pipeline. In deciding on its transportation modes, marketers can choose from private, contract and common carriers. They can decide to send their goods through airlines, the Indian railways, waterways or various road transport organisations. The various combinations available to marketers are depicted in Figure 9.13 as under:

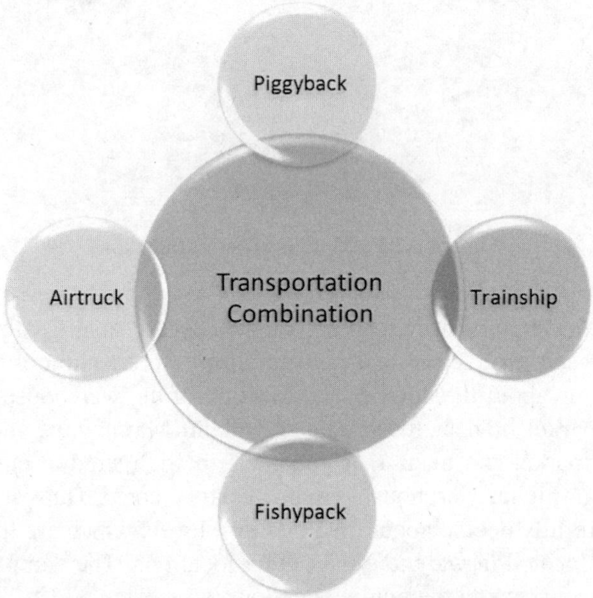

Figure 9.13 Various transportation combinations.

- **Piggyback** describes the use of rail and truck.
- **Fishypack** describes the use of water and truck.
- **Trainship** describes the use of water and rail.
- **Airtruck** describes the use of air and truck.

To conclude, it can be said that producers of physical products and services must decide on Market Logistics—the best way to store and move their goods and services to market destination. The logistics task is to coordinate the activities of suppliers, purchasing agents, manufacturers, marketers, channel members and customers. Major gains in logistical efficiency have come from advances in Information Technology. The ultimate goal of Market Logistics is to meet customer's requirements in an efficient and profitable way.

LET US SUM UP

- Most producers do not sell their goods directly to the final users. Channels of distribution are used to distribute goods from the place of production to the place of consumption.
- A distribution channel overcomes the time, place, and possession gaps that separate goods and services from those who make them, to those who need or want them. Members of the marketing channel perform a number of key functions—research, promotion, contact, negotiation, financing, risk-taking, matching, credit-facility, transportation and warehousing.
- In case of Industrial goods, the channel used is generally short as these goods are purchased by some of the buyers in bulk so the orders are to be handled personally and directly by the producer himself.
- In case of Consumer goods, the channel is generally long because the number of consumers is large and are generally widely spread, therefore they can be served better by the middleman.
- The choice of a particular channel and the types of middlemen involved depends to a large extent on the availability of the right kind of middlemen and the right set of services being provided by them.
- Manufacturers also have to decide about the number and intensity of intermediaries they are going to use at each channel level. For this three strategies are available to them— exclusive distribution, selective distribution and intensive distribution.
- The various types of middleman can be broadly divided into two categories—agent middleman and merchant middleman.
- Agent middlemen are also known as *functional middlemen* and *mercantile agents*. These are those marketing institutions that assist in the transfer of the title of goods without taking any title to them, and act as an agent of the owner of goods and take his remuneration in the form of brokerage or commission.
- Merchant middlemen are those intermediaries who take the title to goods, bear the risks, perform various marketing functions and hope to gain by making profits on transactions.
- A wholesaler is a business unit which buys and resells merchandise to retailers and other industrial users and/or commercial users, but doesn't sell a significant amount of goods to the ultimate consumer.
- A retailer is a merchant or occasionally an agent or a business unit whose main business is to sell the goods directly to the ultimate consumer for non-business use.
- Distribution channels do not stand still. New wholesaling and retailing institutions emerge and new channel systems develop, such as Vertical Marketing Systems, Horizontal Marketing Systems and Multiple Marketing Systems.
- Market Logistics involves planning the infrastructure in order to meet the demand effectively and profitably. In other words, it is implementing and controlling the physical flow of materials and final goods from point of origin to point of use, to meet customer requirements at a profit.
- There are four major Market Logistics decisions taken by marketers regarding the order—processing, warehousing, inventory-levels and transportation combinations.
- The ultimate goal of market logistics is to meet customer's requirements in an efficient and profitable way.

QUESTIONS TO CHECK YOUR PROGRESS

Short Answer Questions

1. Define channels of distribution.
2. Name the distribution system where two or more unrelated companies put together resources or programmes to exploit an emerging marketing opportunity.
3. Define the three Cs criteria for the selection of channels.
4. "The choice of channel gets affected by the availability and willingness of middlemen". Do you agree?
5. State whether the following statements are true or false:
   (i) Middlemen design the product for the consumers and produce them accordingly. (............)
   (ii) They anticipate the needs and wants of the consumers and feed the information back to the producers. (..........)
   (iii) They perform aggressive promotional activities on behalf of the producer. (...........)
   (iv) They provide for buyer's payment of their bills through banks and other financial institutions. (............)
   (v) A middleman does not bear any risk regarding the sale of the product. (............)
   (vi) Performs the research and development services on behalf of producers. (............)
   (vii) Acts as a buffer by keeping stock of the goods and sometimes does bulk-breaking. (.............)
   (viii) Provide free installation and repair facility to the consumers. (..........)

Long Answer Questions

1. Visit a nearby market and gather information regarding the various types of middlemen in the area.
2. "You can eliminate the middleman, but you cannot eliminate their essential distribution activities". Discuss how this statement is supported or refuted by a Vertical Marketing System.
3. Discuss the strategy of direct distribution to the customers and the advantages there off.
4. Examine the role of a middleman in the present-day business. Is it desirable and feasible to eliminate them?
5. From a producer's viewpoint what are the competitive advantages of exclusive distribution?
6. Discuss the various factors you would like to consider for selecting the channels of distribution for a consumer product which is sold all over India.
7. "While deciding about the intensity of distribution, the manufacturer has three choices, namely, Intensive Distribution, Selective Distribution and Exclusive Distribution". Explain.
8. Is a policy of Intensive Distribution consistent with consumer buying habits for convenience goods? For shopping goods? Or in case of business goods?
9. Is Intensive Distribution a prerequisite for expanding the market territory? Discuss.
10. It is said that, "middleman always grows fat at the expense of both producers and consumers". Do you agree with this statement? Give reasons for your answer.
11. What you mean by channels of distribution? What channels of distribution would you institute for marketing the following products— (a) a soft drink; (b) an industrial chemical; (c) a computer software; and (d) a vacuum cleaner. State reasons in support of your answer.
12. "Selection of distribution channels requires a compromise between cost and control". Discuss.

13. "Middlemen must be continuously motivated to do their job". What approach would you use to motivate channel members so that they put in their best performance?
14. "The Physical Distribution System in a company depends upon costs involved and the level of customer service". Comment.
15. "The objective of a modern physical distribution system in a company should be to operate at the lowest possible total cost". Do you agree with the statement? Elaborate your answer.
16. Differentiate between an agent middleman and merchant middleman. Describe the guidelines for their proper functioning in Indian markets.
17. "Market Logistics is an area of potentially high cost savings and improved customer satisfaction". Comment in the light of major logistics decisions.
18. Explain with an example the Vertical and Horizontal Marketing Systems.
19. How are retailers benefited from e-commerce?
20. Write short notes on—(a) marketing logistics (b) intensity of distribution (c) channel conflicts (d) direct marketing (e) multilevel marketing (f) Vertical Marketing System (g) channel dynamics.
21. A new ready-made garment company is planning to launch its new garments in the market and wishes to appoint retail outlets in all the major towns. What should be the criteria for selecting retail outlets?
22. "The wholesaler as an intermediary between the manufacturer and the retailers rendering service to both of them". Explain.
23. Differentiate between—(a) Agent middlemen and merchant middlemen; (b) the VMS, HMS, MMS; (c) Wholesalers and retailers.

CHAPTER 10

Retailing

Learning Outcomes

After studying this chapter, you will be able to:

- Define the concept of small-scale retailers
- Discuss the types of mobile and large-scale retailers
- Explain about the departmental stores and multiple chain stores
- Describe about the mail order houses and consumer cooperative stores
- Express the details about the hire purchase trading houses
- Understand the emerging retail scenario in India and the role of FDI in retail

Indian retail industry is one of the emerging sectors with huge growth potential. According to the Investment Commission of India, the retail sector is expected to grow almost three times than its current levels to USD 660 billion by 2015. However, in spite of the tremendous growth opportunities in the retail scenario in India, this sector has been the most neglected and has been surrounded by numerous controversies and criticism. The growth of organised retailing has been very slow in comparison to the rest of the world. The current retail scenario in India can be broadly classified into major categories—small-scale retailers and large-scale retailers.

10.1 SMALL SCALE RETAILERS

Small-scale retailing can be divided into two types—one, where retailers move from one place to another called *mobile* or *itinerant* retailing; second, where retailers operate from a small fixed premise called *fixed shop retailing*. The capital invested in small-scale retailing is generally very small and turnout of goods is comparatively low. The various types of small-scale retailers can be classified as depicted in Figure 10.1.

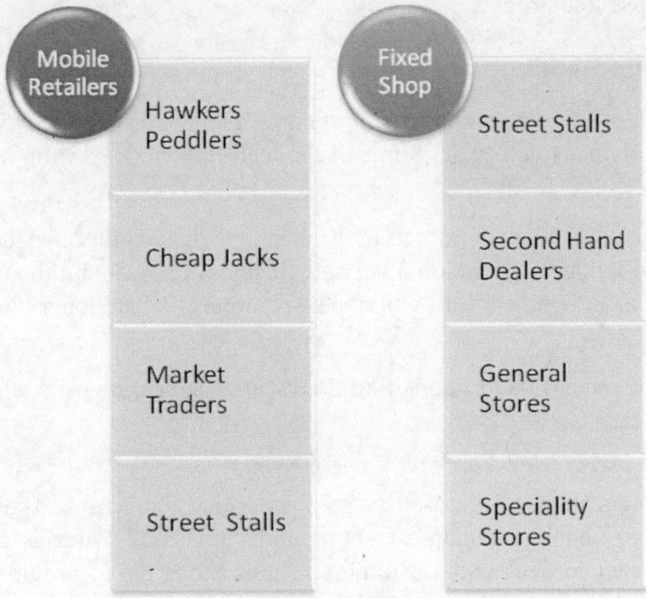

Figure 10.1 Types of small scale retailers.

10.1.1 Mobile Retailers

The important characteristic of mobile retailers is that they move from place to place to sell their goods to the ultimate consumers. They generally carry very little stock, operate with a very small amount of capital, change from one line of activity to another, and operate with minimum or no establishment expenses. Mobile retailers are generally found dealing in perishable products like fruits, vegetables, eggs, bread, etc., or non-perishable low unit value products like household articles. Some of the well-known mobile retailers include:

Hawkers and Paddlers

They sell goods from door to door carrying goods in carts, on animals, or on their heads. This type of retailing is called house-to-house retailing and is one of the oldest methods of retailing.

Cheap Jacks

They generally hire small shops in residential localities for selling the goods. They shift from one locality to another depending upon the prospects of getting profitable business.

Market Traders

These retailers sell their goods at periodical markets which can be weekly, monthly or annual. Therefore, they move from one place to another in search of appropriate markets.

Street Sellers or Pavement Shops

They generally display their goods in busy street corners or simply on the pavements of the roads that have frequent traffic. Such retailers are generally seen selling books, pens, handbags, key holders, or other household articles.

10.1.2 Fixed Shop Retailers

These retailers operate their business from a properly established shop, but with a relatively small amount of capital and on a small scale. Some of the well-known fixed shop retailers include:

Street Stalls

These are small shops situated on the streets and crossings. These stalls have limited space capacity and naturally the stallholders operate on a very small scale. They obtain their supplies from local dealers or wholesalers and prefer dealing in expensive items like stationery items, cosmetics, etc.

Second-Hand Dealers

They deal in used or second-hand goods like books, magazines, utensils, clothes, furniture and other household articles.

General Stores or General Merchants or Variety Stores

These retail establishments are organised as sole proprietary concerns. These are generally set up in localities with a wide assortment of goods under one roof. Sales assistants are generally employed by the owner to deal with customers. These shops try to provide all the day-to-day requirements of the consumers to the nearest point of purchase.

Speciality Stores

These stores carry a narrow product line with deep assortment within that line under one roof, such as children's clothes, ladies' garments, shoe shop, or pharmacy, etc. Such stores are generally located in central shopping places.

Difference between speciality stores and general stores: Speciality stores should be distinguished from general stores in at least three respects—

- Speciality stores are generally located in central shopping places and not in residential localities where general stores are generally found.
- Speciality stores deal in single-line items, whereas, general stores deal in a wide assortment of goods.
- The prices charged by speciality stores are comparatively higher than those charged by general stores.

10.2 LARGE SCALE RETAILING

Large scale retailing is involved in selling of goods by large retailers in small quantities to the ultimate consumers. It is done by large organisations managed generally by big joint-stock companies. Some of the popularly found large-scale retail establishments can be classified as depicted in Figure 10.2.

Figure 10.2 Large scale retail outlets.

10.2.1 Departmental Stores

These are large retailing institutions that carry a very wide assortment of product lines under one roof, such as clothing, home furnishings and household goods. These stores are highly organised business enterprises. Goods are handled by well-defined, centrally organised departments, which make an attempt to cater to most of the needs of customers at one place. 'From pin to plane' is the range of goods which may be dealt in by the different departments of a big Departmental Store. Each department of the Departmental Store is established as an independent unit, dealing in a particular product line, with the objective of earning profit as a unit. Generally, these stores are located in central places in big cities and cater to the customers seeking shopping goods as opposed to convenience goods, and are often considered to be the retailing leaders in a community.

Organisation and Management

Departmental Stores are mostly organised as a joint-stock company. The board of directors is the topmost decision-making authority and policy formulating organ. However, the actual supervision and implementation is in the hands of the Managing Director or the General Manager. Under the General Manager are sectional managers, each in-charge of a particular section. A departmental store usually consists of seven sections as depicted in Figure 10.3.

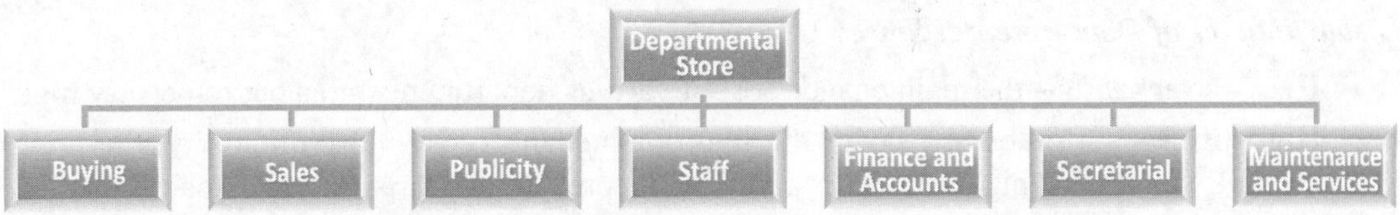

Figure 10.3 Organisation of departmental store.

1. **Buying section** is responsible for the collective buying for the entire store.
2. **Sales section** is accountable for selling various products organised under different departments.
3. **Publicity section** is held responsible for advertising, store displays and sales promotion.
4. **Staff section** is in charge for the recruitment, selection, training and compensation of employees.
5. **Finance and accounts section** is liable for handling the finances of the Departmental Store.
6. **Secretarial section** is responsible for conducting office correspondence, filing and other secretarial work.
7. **Maintenance and service section** holds the responsibility of carrying out repairs and providing various services to the customers.

Origin of Departmental Stores

The Departmental Store is a European innovation. France is said to be the home of departmental stores where 'Bon Marche', the first departmental store, is said to have been founded in 1852 in Paris. The world famous store 'Sears Roebuck' of USA was established in 1886. Departmental Stores were not very popular in India earlier, where most retailing is done on a small scale. 'Spencer's' in Madras (Chennai) was the first department store of India, but over the years the scenario saw a change and we now have various departmental stores in India, for example, Big Bazaar, Reliance Fresh, etc. However, these stand in no comparison to the giant stores of the US, UK and other European countries.

Advantages of Departmental Stores

1. **Convenience of shopping**.
2. **Central location**.
3. **Services to customers**—such as free home delivery, recreation, postal services, banking facilities, etc.
4. **Economies of scale**—enjoyed by the owners, as well as the consumers.
5. **Effective advertising**—Departmental Stores can afford to spend huge amounts of money on advertising and other promotional tools.
6. **Specialisation**—being a large organisation, a Departmental Store can take full advantage of division of labour. Skilled and trained staff can be employed in every department to increase the efficiency of operations.
7. **Financial strength**—Departmental Stores enjoy large financial resources and good credit standing.

Disadvantages of Departmental Stores

1. **Heavy overheads**—the maintenance cost of various departments turns out to be very high.
2. **High prices**—in order to recover the high maintenance cost and profitability, the prices generally tend to be higher in the departmental stores in comparison to the small shops.
3. **Inconvenient location**—people have to generally travel long distances to visit these departmental stores which are centrally located.

4. **Lack of personal attention**—as the sales staff is generally salaried, they may at times lose the motivation to attend the consumer properly.
5. **Heavy investment**—as the Departmental Store tries to meet all the requirements of the consumers under one roof, the amount of capital invested turns out to be very high.
6. **High risk**—as companies are making huge financial investment at one place, there is high risk involved in their decision. The Departmental Store can turn out to be highly popular and profitable, but at the same time it can turn out to be a highly loss-making unit because of its inconvenient location.

10.2.2 Multiple Shops or Chain Stores

The Chain Stores are one of the most important retail developments of the twentieth century. These are defined as two or more outlets that are commonly owned and controlled, sell similar lines of products, have a central buying system, and operate in different localities of a particular area and/or in different parts of the country. The Bata Shoe Company can be said to be maintaining the largest network of multiple stores in India.

Unique Characteristics of Multiple Stores

1. **Central Ownership** is the key factor that differentiates corporate chains from voluntary associations of independent wholesalers or retailers.
2. **Individual Units** in a chain have very little autonomy.
3. **Centralised Buying** results in considerable standardisation in the operating policies of the units in a chain.
4. **Similar Goods** are sold at similar terms and conditions all over.

Ownership and Management

Multiple shops or chain stores are owned and controlled by joint-stock companies. The board of directors is the highest decision-making and policy formulating organ. Overall supervision is entrusted to the Managing director and General Manager. Under them are state or district managers responsible for the efficient management of stores in the district or state. Branch or local shop managers come under the district managers who are concerned with the efficient working of the respective shops. Every important policy relating to purchases, store displays, pricing or sales is decided in the head office without any measure of delegation of authority to local managers.

Origin

The concept of chain stores developed in the USA and the first chain 'The Great Atlantic and Pacific Tea Company' was set up in 1859 in New York followed by their expansion in England and other countries. The concept of retail organisation made its appearance on the marketing scene of India quite late. *Bata Shoe Company* was the first example of a chain store in India, after that Usha Sales Ltd., DCM, Mafatlal Textile Shops, etc., are another examples of chain stores in our country.

Advantages of Chain Stores

1. **Price advantage**—They have the ability to achieve a price advantage over independents by moving towards high volume and lower margins because their size allows them to buy large quantities to take maximum advantage of quantity discounts and lower transportation costs.

2. **Efficient management—**Chains are able to hire good managers and develop scientific procedures in the areas of sales forecasting, inventory control, pricing and promotion.
3. **Elimination of middleman—**The chain can integrate wholesaling and retailing functions.
4. **Promotional economies—**Chains can achieve promotional economies by advertising on a large scale that can benefit all of their stores and spreading the cost over a large volume.
5. **Flexibility—**Chains permit their units some freedom to meet variations in consumer preferences and competition in local markets.
6. **Diversified risk**—Chain stores do not have all their eggs in one basket and are able to diversify their risk at various locations. Losses in one store can be offset by profits in other units.

Disadvantages of Multiple Chain Stores

1. **Standardisation:**—The hallmark of a chain store system and a major factor in its success is a mixed blessing. It also means inflexibility as often a chain cannot adjust rapidly to its local market situation.
2. **Lack of personal drive**—Personal drive, creativity, interest and the will to serve is found to be absent or present in less than the necessary degree in the management of various stores.
3. **Low rate of employee's morale**—Management has to work hard to motivate their employees to put in their best, as the majority of them are salaried employees.

Departmental Stores versus Multiple Shops

1. **Variety**—Departmental Stores offer a variety of products, while multiple shops specialise in one product line.
2. **Location**—Departmental Stores are located at one central location, while multiple shops are located in each and every nook and corner of the area.
3. **Personal service**—Departmental Stores cater to different needs and conveniences of the customers and give maximum importance to personal service, while multiple shops do not pay much attention to personal services aspect, as they accord highest priority to uniformity of layout and decentralised selling.
4. **Grant of facilities**—Departmental Stores provide more facilities like—free home delivery, repairs and maintenance in comparison to multiple chain stores.
5. **Prices charged**—Departmental Stores generally charge relatively high prices in comparison to the multiple chain stores.
6. **Risk involved**—There is more risk involved in case of department stores.

10.2.3 Mail Order Houses

Mail and telephone order retailing includes placing of an order by mail or telephone selecting products from an advertisement or from a direct-mail appeal, and delivery of products by means of parcel post. Thus, it involves selling through post for the retailers and shopping by post for the consumers. Goods are dispatched through the Value Payable Post (VPP) or a courier service, and sometimes the seller may insist on advance payment of a certain percentage of the price. There is no direct contact between the seller and the buyer.

Direct marketers runs an advertisement in a newspaper or a magazine or on radio or television describing some product, and the customer can write or phone for it. The marketer can even send mail pieces like letters, folders, etc., to prospective customers whose names are on the mailing list of high potential buyers of the product category. The mailing list of names and addresses of prospects is most important in this case. This method has proved very successful in promoting books, magazine subscriptions and food products.

Origin

The mail order business grew in the USA in the last decade of the nineteenth century. One noted mail order house of word is the 'Sears Roebuck' Company of the USA. In India this concept was introduced recently. The success of *Reader's Digest* magazine is a live example of this method.

Advantages of Mail Order Houses

1. Countrywide market
2. Lower overhead expenditures
3. Convenience for customers living in far-off places
4. Small capital investment
5. Low risk
6. No risk of bad debts
7. Customers can shop at leisure from catalogues
8. Saves the inconvenience of going to stores

Disadvantages of Mail Order Houses

1. Lack of personal contact between the seller and the buyer
2. No opportunity for customers to inspect goods
3. No facility of credit purchasing
4. Time taking in executing order
5. Little flexibility
6. Outdated catalogues as they are prepared long before they are issued, therefore it is very difficult to inform the consumers about the price changes and new product offerings.

10.2.4 Consumers' Cooperative Stores

These are retail firms owned by its customers. Consumers' cooperatives are started by community residents who felt that local retailers are not serving them well, or are either charging too high a price or providing poor quality products. The residents contribute money to open their own store, and they vote on its policies and elect a group to manage it. The store may set its prices low or set normal prices, with members receiving a patronage dividend based on the individual level of purchases. The 'Super Bazaar' in India was a famous example of the consumers' cooperative.

Advantages of Consumers' Cooperative

1. Reduction in cost of retailing—results in more savings and a higher standard of living for its members that contribute to the economic stability of its members.
2. Provision of better quality products

3. Promotion of economic security
4. Better citizenship
5. Check on monopoly—and profiteering by a producer's monopoly or middlemen.

Disadvantages of Consumers' Cooperatives

1. No or low attention—to store displays and external appearance of the store, because of which the regular customers do not feel attracted towards them.
2. Lack of professional management
3. Huge losses

Because of these reasons, consumers' cooperatives have not come up in a big way in India.

10.2.5 Hire Purchase Trading Houses

This is a form of trade in which credit is granted to the buyers on the security of a lien on the goods sold. The purchaser enters into an agreement with the seller for paying the price of the goods purchased on instalments basis. The buyer is given the possession of the goods immediately, but ownership of the goods is transferred in their name only when the final instalment is paid by them. Generally, the seller reserves the right to take back the articles sold on hire purchase if there is default by the buyer, and in that event the total amount paid by the buyer is treated as higher charge for making use of the article.

Hire Purchase versus Instalment Selling

1. Under the instalment system, the buyer becomes the legal owner of the goods at the time of agreement, but in case of hire purchases the buyer does not get ownership right on goods.
2. In an instalment system, the seller has no right to recover the goods but can only sue for payment, while under hire purchase the seller is entitled to take back the goods in case of default in payment by the buyer and forfeit the amount already paid by the buyer.
3. Articles sold can be returned by the hire purchaser by terminating the contract. He cannot be compelled to pay further instalments. But the buyer under the instalment system cannot terminate the contract or return the article. He is bound to pay all the instalments.
4. Hire purchase is a conditional sale and becomes a full-fledged transaction only after full payment. On the other hand, the instalment system is an outright sale in which only the payment is deferred.

Advantages of Hire Purchase Trading Houses

1. People with limited means can purchase and enjoy costly articles.
2. Push up sales of costly articles—Hire Purchase System is a useful device to push up the sales of costly articles giving the organisation the advantage of mass production as mass selling encourages mass production.
3. Hire Purchase System is a boon to small-scale industries and farmers as they can purchase machinery and equipment on instalments and need not delay operations for want of money.
4. It integrates the habit of saving in people because they are under an obligation to pay fixed instalments periodically.

Disadvantages of Hire Purchase Trading Houses

1. People go beyond their pockets as with small means they are tempted to purchase luxury products which they cannot afford.
2. Prices under hire purchase are high as the seller charges interest on the unpaid amount. He also adds some margin for bad debt risk and collection charges.
3. Sellers have to bear the high risk and in case of default in payment they have the right to take back the goods, but the recovered second-hand goods may not fetch them sufficient prices. Legal action involves wastage of time, money and efforts.
4. Large amount of capital investment is required to carry on a hire purchase business as a large part of the investment remains blocked in book debts.

10.3 RETAILING IN INDIA—AN EMERGING ISSUE FDI IN RETAIL—PROS AND CONS

A severe Balance of Payment problem pushed India on its journey towards economic reforms in 1991. To be competent in the International Economy, we needed a policy shift to privatization. Some baby steps in this direction were taken by India in the 1980s, but it was not until 1991 that the government indicated an organised shift to a more open economy with more dependence on market forces, an increased role for the private sector including foreign investment, and a restructuring of the role of the government. Indian retail industry has a huge growth potential in the years to come. After remaining under protection for years, this sector has been opened up to external competition. According to the Investment Commission of India, the retail sector is expected to grow almost three times than its current levels to USD 660 billion by 2015. Various factors have been responsible for the growth in the retailing sector. Some of the important ones are listed as under:

10.3.1 Reasons for the Growth of Retailing

- Expansion of consumer class
- Rise in income and purchasing power
- Growing number of working women
- Rising discretionary income

- Changing lifestyle
- Change in the consumer mindset—consumers are becoming more brand conscious
- Access to easy and cheap consumer credit
- Rising use of plastic money

However, in spite of the tremendous growth opportunities in the retail scenario in India, this sector has been neglected the most, and has been surrounded by numerous controversies and criticism. The growth of organised retailing has been very slow in comparison to the rest of the world. It was only in December 2011 that the Indian government removed the 51 per cent cap on Foreign Direct Investment (FDI) into single-brand retail outlets and opened the market fully to foreign investors by permitting 100 per cent foreign investment in this area.

Easing Foreign Direct Investment was an important part of India's economic reforms because it was believed that it would lead to an increase in the total volume of investment in the economy, enhance production technology, and boost entry to world markets. Earlier in 1993, foreign institutional investors were allowed to purchase shares of listed Indian companies in the stock market. The policy now allows 100 per cent foreign ownership in a large number of industries and majority ownership in all except banks, insurance companies, telecommunications and airlines.

10.3.2 Conditions for FDI in Retail

There are many conditions attached with the 51 per cent FDI in retail—

- FDI is allowed only after the approval from Foreign Investment Promotion Board (FIPB). They will give approval after judging the various parameters from case to case.
- There is a criterion of minimum investment of USD100 million.
- Out of the total investment, 50 per cent should be done on improving the back end infrastructure.
- Of all the requirements, 30 per cent of all the raw materials have to be procured from the small and medium enterprises in India.
- Permission to set retail stores will be given only in cities with a minimum population of 10 lakh.
- Moreover, retailers had to seek a No Objection Certificate (NOC) from each state. Till date, nine states and two union territories lave allowed FDI to invest in their state/UTs.

10.3.3 Debate on FDI in Retail

These reforms will create a very different environment for India's retail sector. Recently, a great debate has cropped up against the government plans to bring in FDI in the Indian retail sector. There are many positive factors in favour of FDI in the Indian retail service though many groups are protesting against its introduction. Therefore, it becomes important for us to look at both the aspects and understand the benefits which our country can reap, along with the expected problems. We will look at the major issues for, as well as against the movement, as given in Figure 10.4.

The decision of permitting FDI in retail was criticized in the political circles and appreciated in the economic circle. The Prime Minister of India, in his address to the nation, called the decision a need of the economy. Foreign Direct Investment in Indian retail is greatly welcomed by most of the leading retailers of the US and European countries, including Wal-Mart (USA), Tesco (UK), Metro (Germany) and Carrefour (France).

Figure 10.4 Issues for and against the FDI in retail.

The Policy of FDI in retail is being criticised by many political parties on the grounds that it will affect the employment scenario in India adversely since the unorganized retail sector is able to provide employment opportunities to many people in the country. But if the problem is true to a certain extent, it is expected of the government to take adequate measures to protect the unorganized retailers. Moreover, it will be better if a comparison is made between the advantages and the disadvantages of allowing unrestrained FDI in the retail sector. We have with us the success stories from countries like Indonesia and China. In both the countries, the issue of allowing FDI in the retail sector first met with severe protests, but later they realised that allowing FDI led to the growth of the Gross Domestic Product (GDP) and a sharp rise in the level of employment in their country. Thus, it will be better if we learn certain lessons from their experiences.

Political parties are also opposing the FDI in retail on the grounds that it will negatively affect the farming community. While on the other hand, farmers are likely to be benefited by the foreign investment. Farmers in India get only 10 per cent to 12 per cent of the price the consumer pays for the agro-products. With organized retailing it will benefit farmers in a big way, as big retailers sell their product at very competitive prices therefore they prefer buying it directly from farmers. This will result in the elimination of the middlemen which can benefit both the farmers as they will get better price for their produce and the consumers as it will help them in getting the food products at cheaper prices. This can also help in checking the food inflation.

The government has added another dimension of social benefit to its plan for allowing Foreign Direct Investment (FDI) in retail. It has been made compulsory for the foreign retailers to first invest in the back-end supply chain and infrastructure and only then would they be allowed to set up multi-brand retail outlets in the country. The idea behind this is that the firms must create jobs for rural India before they move into multi-brand retailing. Moreover, since 50 per cent of the investment must be made in the back-end infrastructure, the supply chain will be improved; it will help the farmers to sell their agricultural commodities at better prices immediately resulting in reduced post-harvest losses. In most of the cases they are not even expected to maintain warehouses to store their produce which can further bring their cost down.

FDI can be a powerful means to push competition in the retail industry. Indian consumers can now buy foreign brands in their own country because of the policy of single-brand retail. This can help them save a lot of money which they used to spend shopping abroad. The policy of allowing 100 per cent FDI in single brand retail can benefit both the foreign retailer and the Indian partner—foreign players will get a huge local market, while Indian companies can access their best management practices, designs and technology. It is therefore obvious that we should not only permit, but encourage FDI in retail trade. The Ministry of Commerce and Industry has also taken initiatives to break the various myths attached to FDI in retail as is depicted below:

The real story behind FDI myths

Myth	Reality
Kiranas and retailers will lose	Retailers will benefit from existing policy of sourcing their requirements from wholesale cash & carry stores at a discount. In countries such as China, Thailand, Indonesia, Brazil, Singapore, Argentina & Chile where there are no caps for FDI and where there are no conditions, small retail stores have flourished, leading to more employment.
The retail sector will be controlled by foreign stores	The FDI-backed stores can only operate in cities and every state has the freedom to allow or disallow FDI-backed retail investment.
FDI in multi brand retail may result in job losses	Contrary to this mistaken belief, FDI in multi brand retail will generate new employment opportunities, resulting in 1 crore new jobs.
Farmers will be exploited and will lose their fields and crops to foreign investors	On the contrary, farmers will receive better remuneration for their produce & will benefit from additional job opportunities resulting in overall improvement in their quality of life.

Another revolutionary leap for Indian economy

Ministry of Commerce and Industry
Government of India

In light of the above discussion, it can be safely concluded that allowing healthy FDI in the retail sector would definitely give a boost to the country's GDP and overall economic development. It will also help integrate the Indian retail market with the global retail market. With FDI in the retail sector, it is expected that better paying employment opportunities will be generated, which will be better that what the unorganized sector (*kirana* and other small time retailing shops) have failed to provide. It can be said that the advantages of allowing FDI in the retail sector are much more than the disadvantages attached to it. It will definitely lead to major increase in the levels of employment and will also result in the enormous development of the country's GDP.

LET US SUM UP

- In spite of the recent developments in retailing and its immense contribution to the economy, retailing continues to be the least evolved industry and that the growth of organized retail in India has been much slower as compared to rest of the world.
- Small-scale retailing can be divided into two types—one, where retailers move from one place to another called mobile or itinerant retailing, second, where retailers operate from a small fixed premise called fixed shop retailing
- Large-scale retailing is done by large organisations managed generally by big joint-stock companies. It is involved in selling of goods by large retailers in small quantities to ultimate consumers.
- Departmental Stores are large retailing institutions that carry a very wide assortment of product lines under one roof, such as clothing, home furnishings and household goods.
- Multiple shops or chain stores are defined as two or more outlets that are commonly owned and controlled, sell similar lines of products, have central buying, and operate in different localities of a particular area and/or in different parts of the country.
- Mail and telephone order retailing includes any ordering by mail or telephone from an advertisement or from a direct-mail appeal and delivery of products by means of parcel post. It involves selling through post for the retailers and shopping by post for the consumers.
- Consumer's cooperative stores are retail firms owned by its customers and managed by them with non-profit objectives. Their aim is to ensure the smooth supply of goods to their members at subsidised rates by eliminating the middleman.
- A Hire Purchase Trading House is a form of trade in which credit is granted to the buyers on the security of a lien on the goods sold. The purchaser enters into an agreement with the seller for paying the price of the goods purchased on instalments basis.
- In December 2011, the Indian government removed the 51 per cent cap on FDI into single-brand retail outlets and opened the market fully to foreign investors by permitting 100 per cent foreign investments in this area.
- Easing foreign direct investment was an important part of India's economic reforms, because it was believed that it would lead to an increase in the total volume of investment in the economy and enhance production technology.
- It can be safely concluded that allowing healthy FDI in the retail sector would definitely give a boost to the country's GDP and overall economic development. It will generate better paying employment opportunities for people and will protect the interest of farmers.

QUESTIONS TO CHECK YOUR PROGRESS

Short Answer Questions

1. List out the various types of small-scale retailers.
2. Explain the difference between mobile retailers and fixed shop retailers.
3. Where did the concept of departmental store have its origin?
4. Name the first departmental store in the world.
5. What are multiple chain stores?
6. Name the first chain store in the world and in India.
7. Explain three differences that exist between departmental stores and chain stores.
8. List out the benefits of consumers cooperative stores.
9. Differentiate between hire purchase houses and instalment selling.
10. What has been the major reason for the slow growth of mail order houses in India?

Long Answers Questions

1. In the light of the recent developments, explain the significance of retailing in India.
2. Explain the various types of small scale retailers with an example.
3. "Putting all your eggs in one basket", has been the major criticism in case of the departmental stores. Do you agree with the statement? Support it with example.
4. Lack of management skills has been the major reason for the failure of consumers' cooperative stores in India. Can you suggest certain steps to ensure the revival of such a good concept?
5. Keeping the large geographical diversity in India in mind, the multiple chain stores can be a great success. Give reasons in support of your answer.
6. Differentiate between hire purchase trading houses and instalment selling. Which one you consider is best and why?
7. The topic of FDI in retail in India is debatable. Give your views in support or against the movement with examples.
8. Suggest certain ways and means with the help of which the objections to FDI in retail can be overcome by the government.

CHAPTER 11

Rural Marketing

Learning Outcomes

After studying this chapter, you will be able to:

- Understand the concept of rural marketing
- Identify the reasons for the growth of rural marketing
- Compare the myths about rural marketing
- Illustrate the growth pattern in rural India
- Discuss the unique characteristics of rural marketing
- Define the marketing mix for rural marketing

Rural markets in India have emerged in a big way in the recent past. With 69 per cent of India's population living in rural areas, they present a significant market opportunity. Moreover, there are tremendous changes taking place, which makes them profitable markets of the future. Marketers should know how to penetrate these markets. According to an estimate given by the Tata Strategic Management Group Team (TSMG) (2013), close to a third of both Fast Moving Consumer Good's (FMCG) and durable sales is contributed by rural markets. Recent data shows that rural consumption has grown faster than urban in the last 2 years.

According to the TSMG Team (2013), rural penetration of key durables has seen a significant upward trend. TV penetration has moved from around 31 per cent in 2007 to 39.8 per cent in 2010 and motorcycles/scooter penetration from 9.5 per cent to 13.9 per cent in the same period. Region-wise trends in TV indicate that south India has led this growth with more than a 20 per cent increase in penetration, followed by north and west with around 5 per cent increase in each. Because of all these reasons Rural Marketing is coming up in a big way.

Rural Marketing is the process of developing, pricing, promoting and distributing rural-specific goods and services, leading to exchanges between urban and rural markets, which satisfy consumer demand. Some of the important reasons responsible for the growth in Rural Marketing are listed in the following section.

11.1 REASONS FOR THE GROWTH OF RURAL MARKETING

Some of the important reasons for the growing interest of marketers in Rural Marketing are as under:

11.1.1 Increasing Competition in Urban Markets

Competition in urban markets is getting tougher day by day and most of the markets are even reaching their saturation point. While on the other hand, rural markets today offer growth opportunities to firms caught in inter-firm rivalry in urban and metro markets. Companies like Hindustan Unilever, Brooke Bond, Colgate-Palmolive, etc., have successfully penetrated these markets.

11.1.2 Socio Economic Changes in Rural India

The socio-economic sphere in rural India has undergone tremendous changes. This scenario is not what it was 10 years back, and this is due to various developments which have taken place in the social and economic sphere. To name a few:

Increase in Productivity

In rural areas as the yield per hectare in farming has gone up due to technology and modern farming methods.

Increase Productivity has resulted in More Income

In the hands of the farmers resulting in more purchasing power.

Hope for Better Standard of Living

Hope for better standard of living is being accelerated with companies and banks adopting villages for integrated rural development programmes. Companies like Tata steel, Tata motors, ITC, etc., have initiated programmes which encompass education, health, modern farming practices, land development initiatives and creative marketing of agricultural produce, industrial and craft items, thus facilitating integrated rural development.

The Social Changes

The social changes have been fuelled by the reach of television and radio in these areas. Due to satellite connectivity, around 95 per cent of the entire nation has an accessibility to radio connectivity and around 85 per cent of the nation's population has accessibility to television connectivity.

Impact of the Media

The growing reach of the electronic media has created a huge change in the lifestyles of rural consumers because of TV programmes like daily soaps and other serials. People in rural parts are spending more on lifestyle products these days.

Access to Internet

Access to internet is also increasing in rural areas resulting in more and more of cybercafes being present there. Because of this, people in these areas have access to information about the outside world and are able to sell their agricultural produce at better rates in organised markets.

All the socio-economic changes, largely fuelled by technology, government policies, corporate strategies and satellite communication mean more demand for consumer goods.

11.1.3 Information Technology Reaches Rural India

The project 'e-choupal', launched by ITC in Madhya Pradesh, called for setting of an Internet kiosk for giving information on crop prices, soil conditions, weather forecast and other information which could help the soya farmers of the state. Such a revolution has changed the face of rural India and the growth of Internet facilities is taking place at a fast pace.

11.1.4 Income Generation Through Self-Help Groups

Project 'Sakti', launched by Hindustan Unilever Ltd., utilised self help groups (SHGs) for developing the rural women entrepreneur's direct-to-home sales force. The task of the members is to educate the rural consumers on health and hygiene benefits of Hindustan Unilever brands and nurture customer relationships.

11.1.5 Educational Profile

The educational profile of the rural consumer has also undergone substantial changes because over the years the literacy rates have gone up. People in rural areas have access to various educational facilities, schools and colleges, therefore the level of overall awareness and education is going up.

The changing preferences of consumers in rural markets are nicely depicted in the Table 11.1.

Table 11.1 The Changing Preferences of Consumers in Rural Markets

Needs	Old products	New products
Brushing teeth	Neem sticks, charcol, rocksalt, husk	Tooth paste, tooth powder
Washing utensils	Ash, brick powder, coconut powder, etc.	Washing powder, soaps and liquids
Transport	Bullock cart, horses, donkeys	Tractors, mopeds, scooters, motorcycles
Hair wash	Shekakai power, retha, besan	Shampoos and hair care soaps
Irrigation	Wells, Canals, Water lifters, wind mills	Bore wells, motors, power generators, pump sets

11.2 MYTHS ABOUT THE RURAL MARKETING

There are certain myths prevalent about the rural consumers, hence, it will be better for us to understand and have certain clarity on these myths.

11.2.1 Myth Number One—All Villages are Equally Populated

This is certainly a myth because according to the 2011 census, only 0.3 per cent of Indian villages have a population of under 5000 persons and around 61.3 per cent of the Class I towns have a population of above 1,00,000 persons. The detailed composition of all the town classes is given in Table 11.2, which makes it quite clear that all the villages are not equally populated.

11.2.2 Myth Number Two—Rural Consumers are a Homogenous Lot

This certainly is a myth because it will be genuinely wrong to treat all people living in villages alike. There are people with different educational and income backgrounds. They differ as far as their likes and dislikes are concerned. As a result, there is a demand for a variety of goods to meet the different needs of different people.

11.2.3 Myth Number Three—Being Illiterate, Rural Consumer is Not Able to Discriminate between Products and Brands

This is not true as people in rural areas also have access to information through radio, television and the Internet. They also know about the various brands existing in various product categories and can differentiate between them on the basis of their characteristics.

11.2.4 Myth Number Four—Only Low-Priced Products will Sell in Rural India

This certainly is not true because in rural India, even though a majority of the people are price conscious, we do have people who are quality conscious. People in rural areas also ask for a variety of consumer goods and are ready to pay a price for the value delivered.

The information provided in the box is an eye opener and supports all the issues discussed above. It clearly highlights the fact that a lot can be done about Rural Marketing if the marketer tries to tap these markets in a rational manner.

Growth Patterns in Rural India

An analysis of rural India indicates that companies cannot look at it as one homogenous market. Varied growth patterns suggest the need to have a tailored micro-market approach in order to address districts even within the same state. There are differences across different product and service categories as well. More than 90 per cent of districts in rural India have experienced positive growth over a three-year period. But, there has been significant variation observed in the growth pattern, with select districts contributing a disproportionate share to this growth. Based on their growth trend in the 2007 to 2010 period, we can classify rural India into four groups:

Diamonds—Districts which have demonstrated a consistently high growth from FY2007 to FY2010.

Resilient—Districts which have experienced moderate-high growth each year between FY2007 to FY2010.

Emerging—Districts which have shown low growth/decline in FY2007–2008, but have picked up steam from FY2008 onwards, showing growth rates of 12 per cent per annum.

Laggards—Districts which are growing at a low rate of less than 5 per cent per annum since 2008.

There are 79 Diamond districts in India, which have seen a growth of 35 per cent per annum at an aggregate level. These districts have contributed close to 28 per cent of India's rural growth and 15 per cent of rural demand. For instance, rural Bilaspur (Chhattisgarh) has seen its aggregate demand doubling in three years from 2007 to 2010, making it a Diamond district. There are 119 Resilient districts, together contributing to 31 per cent of rural growth, and 22 per cent of rural demand. These two groups of 198 districts, with only 35 per cent of the rural population, allowed players to address close to 60 per cent of the rural growth between 2007 and 2010.

The next 173 Emerging districts generate 31 per cent of the demand, but contributed only to 20 per cent of rural growth. These districts demonstrated low growth in FY2008 but picked up speed in subsequent years. There are 201 laggard districts which comprise a third of the rural population, contribute around 30 per cent of demand, but capture just 20 per cent of rural growth.

Category Trends

The aggregated growth in all durable and automotive categories follows overarching trends, with the 198 districts accounting for 60 per cent of durables growth in rural markets. Rural areas of Thiruvananthapuram, for example, have seen around 20 per cent annual growth in durables. For instance, more than 90 per cent of the growth in demand in the TV category is accounted for by the Diamond and Resilient districts put together.

In the two-wheelers category, 70 per cent of rural growth is actually being derived from these 198 districts alone, again an indication of their dominance. Mobile handsets are seen to follow a more ubiquitous growth pattern. For instance, these 198 districts contribute to only 55 per cent of the category growth, and even the laggards contribute to 30 per cent of the growth.

Thus, it can be safely concluded that the Diamond and Resilient districts require significant attention in terms of marketing and sales activities. Marketers are expected to reap higher returns on investment in these areas. Emerging districts need to be closely monitored to track triggers, including commodity price growth or industrial developments. Though the Laggards exhibit slower growth, players cannot ignore their aggregate demand. These markets need cost-effective marketing activities by minimising resources. Such insights indicate that instead of looking at rural markets as one group, focussed distribution and marketing initiatives by players in selected districts would enable them to profitably garner a disproportionate share of growth in rural India.

Source: Tata Strategic Management Group Team, "Growth markets in rural India," Brand Equity, The Economic Times, February 4th, 2013.

Questions for Discussion

1. From the above discussion, what has been your observation about the growth trends in India's rural markets?
2. Suggest suitable marketing strategies for Diamond, Resilient, Emerging districts and Laggards in rural markets.

11.3 UNIQUE CHARACTERISTICS OF RURAL MARKETING

Rural marketing is different than the urban marketing. Various unique characteristics of rural marketing are listed as under:

11.3.1 It Offers a Vast Market for Consumer Goods

Rural India offers a vast market for consumer goods, specially the convenience and shopping goods.

11.3.2 Access to Markets

One of the major constraints in the way of effective Rural Marketing is the limited access to various rural markets, as a majority of them are not even connected by metallic roads. Therefore, reaching them and ensuring the transportation of goods to these places creates a big problem for the marketers.

11.3.3 Value Driven Consumers

Consumers in rural areas are more value conscious as compared to the urban consumers. They are highly price sensitive and seek value, and prefer spending a smaller amount on consumer goods.

That is the reason companies which are planning to turn towards rural areas are trying to come up with smaller packages for rural India.

11.3.4 Value for Money

They do not buy cheap products but buy products and brands which promise to deliver higher value.

11.3.5 Reference Groups

The reference groups for rural consumers are primary health workers, doctors, teachers and the panchayat members. Village baniyas, mahajan or the old chachi of the village play an important role that of an influencer in the rural customer's decision-making in comparison to the various models or celebrities coming in advertisements in urban areas.

11.3.6 Media Habits

People in rural areas are very fond of music and folklore. The rural theatre called 'tamasha' or 'nautanki' are very popular ways through which messages can be conveyed to them. Print media does not have much of an impact in rural India.

Here we would like to cite an example of a success story of Maruti Udyog that has been successful in selling their cars in rural India.

Coke's Rural Marketing Strategy

India has a rural geographical area of 32,87,263 sq. km and a population of over 1.21 billion people. About 68 percent of India's population lives in rural areas and accounts for around 40 percent of Indian economy. In order to tap this potential market, the multinational giant, Coca Cola India drafted a rural marketing strategy based on 3 A's: (1) affordability, (2) acceptability, (3) availability. In order to make their drink affordable for the average rural worker in India, they launched a 200 ml bottle costing ₹5 only. The criteria of acceptability was met with the tag line—Thanda Matlab Coca Cola—and was targeted at rural and semi urban consumers. The series of Amir Khan ads were a great success and an important aspect focusing on rural audience. Besides TV ads, CCI also focused on 47,000 hatts (weekly markets) and 25,000 melas (fairs) held annually in the various parts of the country. Large wall painting and hoardings were also put up at various locations. In order to ensure the availability of their drink in 6,27,000 villages spread over 32,87,263 sq. km, the company decided to do away with their centralised distribution system and appointed large distributor hubs in selected villages, from where it got distributed to smaller villages through rickshaws. All these efforts paid well to this MNC and their share of rural market has grown for last so many years. Thus, it highlights clearly that if an organisation sets their right distribution and promotion mix, than they need not restrict themselves to India's urban middle class only.

Source: https://www.slideshare.net/passionatetowin/cokes-rural-marketing-strategies

Questions for Discussion

1. Explain the lessons to be learnt by marketers from Coca Cola's going rural policy.
2. "The marketing mix has to be designed differently for rural products". Do you agree with the statement? Explain in the light of the above-mentioned facts.

11.4 ROADBLOCKS OF RURAL MARKETS

Despite all the reasons cited above for the growth of rural markets and their unique features, it has been observed that going rural is not an easy task for the marketers as there are number of roadblocks which come in their way. Some of them have been listed as under:

Low Per Capita Income

Though over the years the situation in rural areas has improved, but still the per capita income in rural markets is increasing at a very slow rate. As agriculture is the main source of income of people in the rural India, their purchasing power depends on their agricultural produce. The year they have a good crop, they are able to make good money, and have huge purchasing power, as against those years when there are crop failures, people do not have the income to even sustain themselves.

Standard of Living

Because of the reason mentioned in the previous point, a majority of the people living in rural areas fall below the poverty line, therefore their purchasing power is not very high. Marketers have to design different marketing strategies to target their goods towards such low income group people.

Low Literacy Rate

The literacy rates are lower in rural areas as compared to the urban areas, thus, the marketers have to design different communication strategies to target the message to them. Print, as a media, is not very successful for rural markets and the marketers have to rely more on television and radio.

Transportation and Warehousing

Transportation and warehousing are the biggest challenges in rural markets. Most of the villages in India are not connected by proper roads, and do not have proper warehousing and storage facilities. Therefore, it becomes a big problem for marketers to carry the goods and services to such far-off rural areas and sell them off to the consumers.

Ineffective Distribution Channels

The distribution channels in rural areas are not very well organised, and at majority of places efficient intermediaries are also not available. This makes it difficult for marketers to ensure the availability of goods to the rural consumers.

Differences in Language and Culture

India is a country of different cultures and languages. These cultural differences make it difficult for marketers to design their goods for people in rural areas, and different languages create communication problems for the marketers.

Lack of Communication System

Communication networks, such as telephones, telegraphs and Internet connectivity are very weak for most of the rural areas. This makes it difficult for marketers to ensure speedy and effective communication with regards to goods and services to far-flung areas.

Presence of Spurious Brands

Rural consumers are highly price sensitive consumers. They generally prefer to buy low-priced products. Because of this reason, a lot of spurious brands or look-alikes are available, providing a low cost option to the rural customer.

11.5 MARKETING MIX FOR THE RURAL MARKETS

Keeping all the roadblocks discussed above in consideration, working out the marketing mix for the rural markets is going to be different for marketers than what it is for the urban markets. The marketers will need to adapt their marketing mix to suit the rural conditions. Some of the important policy considerations in all the 4Ps of the marketing mix are listed as under:

Figure 11.1 Marketing mix strategies for rural markets.

11.5.1 Product Decisions

Products for the rural markets will have to be simpler, easy to use, or easily maintainable. The product literature should be simple and well illustrated for the rural customer. Besides, it should be dispensable in single units. Identity in rural markets is often created through the visual logo of a product, the colour of the product, or the taste of the product. The marketers generally have three strategic options to follow as depicted in Figure11.2 given as under:

Figure 11.2 Product strategies for rural markets.

Extension

This refers to the strategy of extending the product from urban to rural markets without any specific modification.

Adaptation

Implies customising the product to suit the rural buyers' demography, income levels and seasonality.

Innovation

It involves inventing a new product keeping the rural consumer's specific requirements into account. Keeping in view the rural life style, the manufacturer and the marketers can design new products for them. The rural environment is different than the urban environment because of differences in culture, language, values and perceptions. Thus, rural products need to be designed keeping these environmental factors into account. Nokia's 1100 mobile phone model is a very good example of a customized model for rural markets. It was designed to protect it against rough usage; it was dust resistant and had a small torch light in view of the frequent power cuts in rural India. It was the first to introduce messaging in Hindi language, and was economical in order to cater to the semi-urban or rural consumers.

Small Unit Packaging

Given the low per capita income and value driven buying behaviour of rural consumers, small unit packages stand a good chance of acceptance in rural market. They allow consumers to spend a small amount at one time, buy only what they need, experiment with new products, and conserve cash at the same time. Various companies, especially those manufacturing FMCG products, have launched smaller packs of their products for example, small sachets of shampoos, pickles, biscuits, Vicks cough drops in single tablets, toothpaste, etc. Small packaging stands a good chance of acceptance in rural markets. The advantage is that the price is low and the rural consumer can easily afford it. For example, Hindustan Unilever is amongst the first MNCs to realise the potential of India's rural market, and have launched a variant of its largest selling soap brand, Lifebuoy at ₹ 2 for 50 gram.

Refill Packs/Reusable Packaging

Making use of reusable containers can add value to the products as rural consumers can efficiently reuse the plastic bottles. Similarly, the packaging of edible oil, tea, coffee, ghee, etc., in refill packs can make it available to the consumers at economical prices. Such measures can make a significant impact in the rural market.

11.5.2 Pricing Decisions

As explained earlier, rural consumers are highly price sensitive and value driven, therefore smaller units or pack size should be made available to them at a lower unit price, for example, ₹ 2, 3, 4 packs of Glucose biscuits, ₹ 1 shampoo sachets, Vicks 5 gram tin, etc.

11.5.3 Promotion Decisions

Promoting goods in rural India is different than promoting it for the urban consumers. A different promotional mix is going to be used in Rural Marketing. Use of advertising will be there, but the type of advertising is going to be different. Some of the common promotional strategies being used in rural markets can be listed as under:

Bold, Catchy and Colourful Advertisements

Advertisements should be bold, catchy and colourful. Use of illustrations and pictures should be made more in comparison to words and difficult expressions. A visual copy has a much greater appeal than just the audio and the print. Big advertisements on the walls of villages play a very important role.

Give Local Touch to Advertisements

For better identification of products amongst the rural consumers, some of the companies are even trying to give a local touch to their advertising campaign by using local expressions and language in their advertisements, for example, Coca-Cola targeted the whole Indian rural market with the positioning of their soft drink as *Thanda Matlab Coca-Cola* advertisements, because most of the villagers when wanting a soft drink refer to it as *Thanda*. Therefore, Coca-cola used that word to ensure synonymity.

Simplicity and Clarity

All promotional messages targeted at rural audience need to be simple and clear, which can be easily understood. Use of big bold pictures in bright colours is generally made in the advertisements. Rational appeals are used more often in comparison to other appeals in rural advertisements. Promotional message should highlight only the functional values of the product and explain how those values can make the consumer's life even better, and solve most of their problems.

Narrative Story Style

Promotional messages can be delivered in the form of an entertaining story, preferably told in the regional language, containing a message that depicts how the brand can deliver better value to their family and society.

Choice of Brand Ambassador

The selection of brand ambassadors for rural markets has to be done carefully as those celebrities whose charm works in urban areas might not find any followers in the rural areas. Use of local famous personalities should be made in the advertisements. Those celebrities from the movies, which have a local mass appeal, can also be brought into the local advertisements, for example, Govinda in Mirinda's advertisement has boosted the sales of the drink in rural markets.

Choice of Media

Radio is a more popular media in comparison to television because of its connectivity. Use of mobile vans with loudspeakers is one of the commonly used media in various rural areas.

Sponsoring Local Events

Rural sports like, *kabaddi*, kho-kho and bullock-cart race, rural fairs and haats have a special place in the life of rural consumers. Therefore, sponsoring such events can turn out to be a very big promotional incentive for marketers.

Use of Personal Selling

Use of personal selling for promotion is also made in rural India, but salesmen have to be simple and subtle, should be able to connect to the rural people, and should be able to communicate using rural expressions. Use of local men and women as salespeople will work out to be better in rural India in comparison to sending the trained salespeople from urban areas to rural markets.

Use of Sales Promotion Incentives

Use of sales promotion incentives such as free gifts and discounts can also help in accelerating the sales in rural areas.

From all the above discussion, it can be safely concluded that lots of changes are required to be made in the promotional mix to adapt it successfully to the rural markets.

11.5.4 Distribution Decisions

Distributing goods to rural markets is one of the biggest challenges for marketers in Rural Marketing as most of the places are not even connected by roads. Moreover, the number of villages in India is large and they vary in their size of population. Therefore, companies or distributors need to carefully examine the market potential of different villages, and serve them accordingly. For segmentation purposes, the composition of various classes of towns can be followed as given by Census figures of 2011, depicted in Table 11.2.

Table 11.2 Composition of Classes of Towns

Town class	Population	No. of towns	% of total towns	% of population	Decadal growth (2001–2012)
Class–I	1 Lakh and above	423	8.2	61.5	24
Class–II	50,000–99,999	498	9.6	12.3	15
Class–III	20,000–49,999	1,386	26.9	15.0	16
Class–IV	10,000–19,999	1,560	30.2	8.1	7
Class–V	05,000–09,999	1,057	20.5	2.8	8
Class–VI	Less than 5,000	237	4.6	0.3	–22
Total		**5,161**	**100.0**	**100.0**	

*10 Lakh + : 27; 5–10 Lakh: 42; 1–5 Lakh: 354

Source: Census 2011

Some of the marketers follow the strategy of introducing mobile distribution vans which go from place to place to sell the products. Selling through weekly rural markets or haats, melas and mandis is another big option available to the marketers. Most of the firms try to link the village grocers with the nearest wholesale distributors to ensure a regular and smooth supply of goods to them.

Finally, it should be clear to all the marketers that the future lies in going rural, therefore they should be prepared to initiate all the measures to successfully implement Rural Marketing strategies.

LET US SUM UP

- Rural markets are tomorrow's markets and marketers should know how to penetrate these markets.
- Rural markets today offer growth opportunities to firms caught in inter-firm rivalry in urban and metro markets.
- Due to various socio-economic changes, largely fuelled by technology, government policies, corporate strategies and satellite communication, has resulted in more demand for consumer goods.
- Growth of Internet facilities at a fast pace is a revolution that has changed the face of rural India.
- People in rural areas have access to various educational facilities, schools and colleges, therefore the level of overall awareness and education has gone up.
- Rural people ask for a variety of consumer goods and are ready to pay a price for the value delivered.
- Rural India offers a vast market for consumer goods, especially the convenience and shopping goods.
- One of the major constraints in the way of effective Rural Marketing is the limited accesses to various rural markets, as a majority of them are not even connected by metallic roads.
- Rural consumers are highly price sensitive and value seekers, and prefer spending a small amount on consumer goods.
- The reference groups for rural consumers are primary health workers, doctors, teachers and the panchayat members.
- People in rural areas are very fond of music and folklore. The rural theatre called 'tamasha' or 'nautanki' are very popular ways through which messages can be conveyed to them.
- Products for the rural markets will have to be simpler, easy to use, or easily maintainable. The product literature should be simple and well illustrated for the rural customer.
- Some of the companies follow the strategy of introducing mobile distribution vans which go from place to place to sell the products. Selling through weekly rural markets or haats, melas and mandis is another big option available to the marketers.

QUESTIONS TO CHECK YOUR PROGRESS

Short Answer Questions

1. Define Rural Marketing.
2. List out the three major reasons as to why marketers should go rural.
3. Rural consumers are a homogenous lot. Why this is called a myth?
4. What are the changes required to be made in the packaging of the goods to make them suitable to rural conditions?
5. How can marketers handle the price sensitiveness of the rural consumers?
6. How is the choice of celebrities in rural advertisements different than urban advertisements?
7. Name the three distributional strategies used to deliver the goods to consumers in rural markets.

Long Answer Questions

1. "The importance of Rural Marketing is increasing in view of its potential". Comment upon the statement giving various reasons for going rural.
2. "India consists of rural and urban markets". Briefly explain how they are different from each other from a marketer's point-of-view.
3. "Going rural is the need of the hour". Keeping this statement into account, suggest the various roadblocks which the marketers have to overcome in order to successfully launch their product in rural markets.
4. The marketing mix needs to be redesigned for going rural. Suggest the various marketing strategies followed while redesigning the 4 P's.
5. How can you support the statement that rural consumers are highly value driven? Explain with the help of various examples from the current marketing scenario.
6. Explain the various changes which are required to be made in the promotional strategy of a company for successfully promoting a product in rural markets.
7. Going rural is not that easy for marketers. What are the various roadblocks which come in their way?
8. Briefly explain the various myths attached to Rural Marketing with examples.

CHAPTER 12

Green Marketing

Learning Outcomes

After studying this chapter, you will be able to:

- Define the concept and objectives of green marketing
- Explain the principles of green marketing
- Report the procedure to design the green marketing mix
- Identify the green marketing initiatives
- Describe the challenges of green marketing
- Discuss the strategies of green marketing

Green Marketing, also known as *Ecological Marketing* or *Sustainable Marketing* has caught the frenzy of the corporate world over the last few years. The concept which has been in discussion and commercial execution since the 1980s has today captured a significant mind share of the corporate pundits and the consumers at large as they express a strong willingness to favour environmentally conscious products and companies. Moreover, with the growth of the societal marketing orientation and a growing consciousness amongst the marketers for fulfilling their social responsibilities towards consumers and society at large, the concept of Green Marketing has picked up well.

However, one of the biggest challenges facing Green Marketing initiatives has been a lack of clarity as to what is green and how green is green, indeed. In the absence of any structured framework or standards, organisations and consumers are making their own assumption and understanding of green attributes of their products, services and initiatives at large. Green Marketing is emerging as a rescue measure to ensure sustainable development all around. The desire to go green today incorporates the entire set of activities including product design, manufacturing practices, product packaging, including advertising and product promotion initiatives.

Although no consumer product has a zero impact on the environment, but in business terms the concept of 'green product' and 'environmental product' is used commonly to describe those products that strive to protect or enhance the natural environment by introducing such initiatives with the help of which they can conserve energy or resources, and reduce or eliminate the use of toxic agents and pollutants.

The American Marketing Association (AMA) (1995) has defined the concept of Green Marketing as:

> *The marketing of products that are presumed to be environmentally safe. It incorporates several activities such as product modification, changes to production processes and packaging, advertising strategies and also increases awareness on compliance marketing amongst industries.*

Dainora Grundey and Rodica Milena Zaharia in their book titled *Ecological Marketing*, defined *Green Marketing* as—

> *Consisting of all activities designed to generate and facilitate any exchanges intended to satisfy human needs or wants, such that the satisfaction of these needs and wants occurs, with minimal harmful impact on the natural environment.*

Thus, Green Marketing includes changes in the production as well as promotional activities aimed at making the product more environmental friendly. This change should be supported by the changing corporate policies and practices protecting the quality of environment, and reflecting their level of concern for the community.

12.1 OBJECTIVES FOR GREEN MARKETING

There have been various reasons as to why companies are increasingly going for Green Marketing initiatives. Some of the important ones are listed as under:

- **Corporate social responsibility:** Most of the companies go for Green Marketing initiatives as part of their Corporate Social Responsibility (CSR).
- **Moral obligation:** They believe that it is their moral obligation to be socially responsible.

- **Growing consumer awareness:** Another important reason for going green is the growing awareness amongst the consumers and an increasing demand for eco-friendly products.
- **Competitors' environmental activities:** These activities pressurise them to change their marketing activities.
- **Government regulations:** At times companies are forced to become more environmentally responsible because of various government regulations.

12.2 PRINCIPLES FOR GREEN MARKETING

There are four basic principles which distinguish Green Marketing initiatives from non-green ones, as mentioned below:

- Green marketers will not produce or distribute products yielding environmentally high impact side effects.
- Green marketers will seek to enhance rather than harm the viability of the environment in designing, producing and distributing products.
- Green marketers will take a proactive rather than a reactive stance towards legal requirements, seeking to exceed rather than simply to comply with legally mandated environmental requirements.
- Producers will have to share the social costs of whatever environmental spill-overs are created by their manufacturing and marketing of products for sale and use.

12.3 DESIGNING THE GREEN MARKETING MIX STRATEGY

The Green Marketing mix requires designing all the 4Ps differently than the normal marketing mix. Guidelines for designing an effective marketing mix for green products have been nicely depicted in Table12.1.

Table 12.1 Guidelines for Designing Effective Marketing Mix for Green Products

Green Product Design	Green products should be designed keeping in mind the following guidelines: • Products should be organic in nature and made from recycled material. • Products can be recycled or reused. • Products should meet or exceed environmentally responsible criteria and should be thoroughly tested. • Packaging is a major component of domestic waste; therefore packaging reduction initiatives can reduce the environmental impact of a product while also resulting in cost saving to the companies. • Even if packaging has to be done, use of recyclable and biodegradable materials should be made.

<table>
<tr><td>Green Product Pricing</td><td>Set realistic prices keeping the following guidelines:<ul><li>Keep prices as low as possible as concern about the overpricing of green product has made consumers skeptical about certain green claims and has reduced the consumption of such products.</li><li>Even if the prices of green products are high, they need to be justified on the grounds of offering additional value such as improved performance, varied functions, better designing, visual appeal, or taste.</li><li>Environmental benefits alone may not be a justification for higher prices. It is essential to communicate the potential hidden savings in green products which the consumers can avail in the long run, such as longer product life, low consumption of power, etc.</li><li>Environmentally responsible products may prove to be comparatively less expensive when their overall operational costs are taken into consideration. For example, battery operated or electronic cars prove to be more fuel-efficient vehicles in the long run.</li></ul></td></tr>
<tr><td>Green Product Promotion</td><td>Green marketers should reinforce their environmental credibility and should promote it aggressively with the help of the following guidelines:<ul><li>Never overstate environmental claims or establish unrealistic expectations amongst consumers. Always communicate in simple words through sources that people trust.</li><li>Larger corporations may run major green advertising and public relations campaigns to promote their commitment to environmental improvement.</li><li>Use of Internet, through e-mail, Web sites, search engines, blogs, product ratings sites, and other digital platforms should be made to tap consumers and diffuse credible 'word-of-mouth' about various green products.</li></ul></td></tr>
<tr><td>Green Product Distribution</td><td>Distribution is a key issue in attracting the right customers for green products and behaving in an environmentally responsible way. It can be carried out effectively with the help of following guidelines:<ul><li>It has been found that customers will not go out of their way to buy green products; therefore wherever possible, these products should be made available to them easily.</li><li>Their easy availability and comfort in purchase can increase the demand for green products and can also reduce the environmental pollution as consumers do not have to drive their vehicles long distances for such products.</li><li>Managements should carefully plan for the physical distribution activities so that they can minimize the negative impact of their logistics operations on the environment. One such example is reducing the number of miles driven by keeping more regional inventory, or by using fuel-efficient vehicles for distribution activities.</li></ul></td></tr>
</table>

Thus, from the points mentioned in the above table, it is quite obvious that marketers have to make conscious efforts to design green products, price them appropriately, promote them aggressively and make them widely available to people to ensure their increased demand. The aspects of Green Marketing mix are shown in Figure 12.1. The various principles and strategies which should be followed by marketers for effectively initiating Green Marketing practices are explained in the preceding paragraphs.

Figure 12.1 Green marketing mix.

12.4 GREEN MARKETING INITIATIVES

The 'Go Green' initiative is an organisation wide initiative to build awareness and consciousness for our environment amongst people, processes and customers. Most of such initiatives have been undertaken by the industry in India as they are strongly influenced by the concept of the 3R's —Recycle, Reuse and Refuse. Examples include various banks which have introduced banking through Internet so that consumers can carry out various banking transactions from their home or place of work, and they do not have to travel to their bank branches. Banks are also providing other environmental friendly services, such as paperless banking, no deposit slips, no withdrawal forms, no cheques, no money transactions and all transaction done through shopping and ATM cards.

In their pursuit of ensuring a healthy environment and sustainable development, various consumer and industrial goods' companies are also initiating green efforts. One such example is the Tata Group of Companies. They have reflected their commitment to the eco-system by introducing various environmental friendly changes in their production processes and marketing techniques. Tata Motors is setting up an eco-friendly showroom using natural material for its flooring and energy efficient lights. The Taj Group of Hotels is in the process of creating eco-rooms which have energy efficient minibars, organic bed linen, and napkins made up of recycled papers. The rooms will have CFLs and LEDs. Developing Indica EV, an electronic car that would run on polymer lithium ion batteries, was another initiative towards Green Marketing.

Another good example is that of ITC, a company which has strengthened its commitment to green technologies by introducing techniques in their business with the help of which they can take into consideration the international standards on environment, health and safety. Various other initiatives have also been launched by them, such as Rainwater Harvesting, Solid Waste Recycling, e-Choupal and Sustainable Community Development initiatives for women, etc.

IDEA Cellular, one of the mobile companies in India, is trying to paint India green with its national level campaign of 'Use Mobile, Save Paper'. Nokia, another mobile operator has announced various Green Marketing initiatives in India. Their company is trying to take back used mobiles and chargers from customers for the purpose of recycling them by installing recycled bins at various locations and educating people on the necessity of reducing e-waste through recycling.

The list of companies initiating green efforts is long and the change is quite visible. But Green Marketing cannot be ensured simply by the efforts on the part of the corporate sector because much of their efforts have gone waste or unacknowledged due to the indifferent attitude of the consumer's towards their products and services.

12.5 GREEN MARKETING CHALLENGES

Although there is definitely a trend amongst the consumers to purchase green products and their willingness to pay a premium for them, the idea of going green appeals to only the deepest green niche of consumers. The vast majority of consumers, especially in a country like India look for their personal incentives in the purchase of the products. They are ready to purchase the green products only if these products offer a desirable benefit, such as efficiency and cost-effectiveness, health and safety, brand value, convenience, ease-of-use or improved product performance. Therefore, despite making an environmentally friendly product, marketers will not be able to generate a sizable response because of certain challenges, as depicted in Figure 12.2.

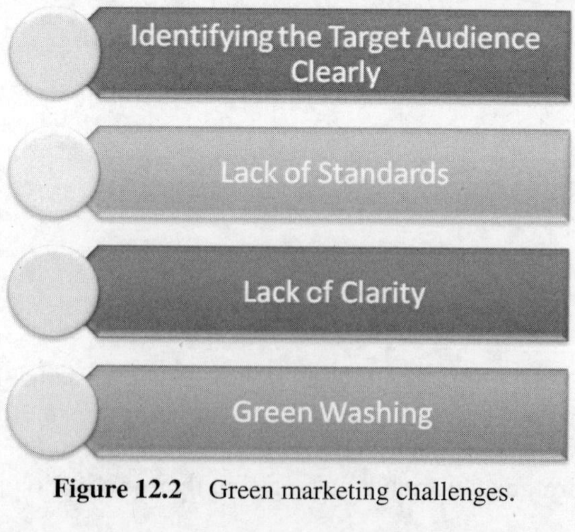

Figure 12.2 Green marketing challenges.

12.5.1 Identifying the Target Audience Clearly

The first and the most important challenge is to have a clear picture of their target audience, and design a focussed strategy which should provide them with benefits that motivate the consumers besides ensuring what is good for the environment.

12.5.2 Lack of Standards

Another Green Marketing challenge is the lack of standards or public consensus about what constitutes 'green'. In essence, there is no definition of 'how good is good enough' when it comes to a product or a company making Green Marketing claims. Hence, this lack of clarity adds to the confusion on the part of the business houses and consumers.

12.5.3 Lack of Clarity

As explained in the previous point this lack of clarity adds to the companies' reluctance to promote their green attributes as they are themselves not clear about them and consumers are also sceptical about such green claims.

12.5.4 Green Washing

At times it has been noticed that marketers take advantage of this confusion and purposely make false or exaggerated claims about the greenness of their products. Critics refer to this practice as '*green washing*'. They give false impressions to the consumers about the greenness of the products, take advantage of their innocence by promoting not-so-green products and increasing their profits. The primary objective of green washing is to provide consumers with the feeling that the organisation is taking the necessary steps to responsibly manage its ecological footprints, while in reality what they may be doing is not very environmentally beneficial.

Despite these challenges, Green Marketing concepts are becoming popular as more and more people and corporate houses are realising their social responsibility towards the environment.

12.6 GREEN MARKETING STRATEGIES

It has been observed during the analysis of past research and marketing strategies of various companies that Green Marketing efforts can be successful in generating the desirable response from the consumers if the producers deliver them value, knowledge and credibility. Some of the important strategies followed by successful companies have been listed below to guide the marketers to come up with effective Green Marketing initiatives.

12.6.1 Deliver Value to Consumers

The marketing of successfully established green products should ensure that their green benefits should be meaningful to the customer, such as energy savings and resource efficiency translating into cost savings. As exemplified by the Philips CFL bulbs, which are efficient as well as economical in comparison to the traditional bulbs.

12.6.2 Health and Safety

We must keep in mind that the primary reason as to why the consumers buy greener products is not to 'save the planet' but to protect their own health. Therefore, the product categories most closely aligned with health and safety issues are growing at a fast pace and are able to build a huge clientele. Health messages can apply to a wide variety of product categories. For example, market positioning of organic foods as flavourful and healthy alternatives to factory-farm foods has convinced consumers to pay a premium price for them.

12.6.3 Performance

The conventional wisdom is that green products don't work as well as non-green ones. It is therefore often quoted that 'they cost twice as much to remove half the grime'. Today, however, many green products are designed to perform better than conventional ones and can command a price premium. For example, in addition to energy efficiency, front-loading washers clean better and are more gentle on clothes compared to conventional top-loading machines.

12.6.4 Style, Status and Symbolism

It is very important that green products should be positioned as stylish, and should command a status symbol so that the consumers feel like buying and using them.

12.6.5 Convenience

Many energy efficient products offer inherent convenience benefits that can be highlighted for competitive advantage. For example, Philip's CFL bulbs need infrequent replacement and come with a one year warranty. Such benefits should be highlighted through the marketing communications.

12.6.6 Imparting Consumer Knowledge

Various marketing programmes try to impart knowledge to consumers regarding benefits of green products. The connection between environmental benefits and consumer values need to be told to the consumers. That is why many of the companies marketing green products employ compelling, educational, and marketing messages and slogans that connect green product attributes with desired consumer values. This has played an important role in their success. In a country like India where the majority of the people are uneducated and uninformed, it becomes very important for the marketers to educate the consumers to recognise green products as 'solutions' for their personal needs and the environment.

12.6.7 Green Advertising

It can make the green ideas and products more popular amongst masses. It draws attention to the fact that an aggressive promotion of the environmental products, benefiting and delivering desired personal value to the consumers, can broaden their acceptance of green products. Some of the examples of the successful green advertising campaigns are listed as under:

- The IDEA Mobile service provider tries to promote a social or an environmentally healthy message in every advertisements, such 'Walk while you Talk', 'Don't cut Trees', 'Save Paper, Use Mobile', etc.
- The advertisement for Aircel, another mobile service provider, has joined hands with the 'Save Tiger Campaign' and is trying to spread awareness amongst masses on this environmental issue.
- The advertisements for Surf Excel, where the advertisers are trying to prove the fact that their detergent consumes less water and each bucket of water saved is poured back into the pond, promoted the idea of water conservation.

12.6.8 Power of Word-of-Mouth and the Internet

It has been observed that consumers are getting skeptical about commercial messages. Word-of-mouth is perceived to be very credible as consumers are turning to the collective wisdom and experience of their friends and peers about products. It is in the interest of the marketers to use the Internet, and advertise through e-mail, Web sites, search engines, blogs, product ratings sites and other digital platforms which have opened up significant opportunities for tapping consumers' social and communication networks to diffuse credible 'word-of-mouth' about green products. When it comes to reaching out to consumers, social media applications are helping them reach out to customers faster. The digital platform is being used aggressively because it is greener than its alternatives and it is easier to influence the 'Facebook generation' with this. But the problem with this media is that it is still in its infancy and can reach out only to the e-literate population of India.

12.6.9 Authenticity of Product Claims

Authenticity is the foundation of effective Green Marketing. Green products must meet consumer expectations by delivering them promised consumer value and environmental benefits. Green claims should be specific and meaningful and should be communicated honestly.

12.6.10 Consistency and Commitment

Besides being authentic, claims of Green Marketing should be dependable and must stick to the sustainability initiatives and practices that have been made public. Dedication to these practices will illustrate to the consumers, the public and key stakeholders about the genuineness of the company, organisation or individual.

12.6.11 Third Party Endorsements and Eco-Certifications

Marketers need to be very cautious while making green claims. Third parties, government agencies, independent laboratories, non-profit advocacy organisations, or private consultants should provide green product endorsements or seals of approval to add to the believability of such green claims.

12.6.12 Transparency

Marketers must stick to the green initiatives honestly and make an effort to highlight the progress being made in this direction. They should also clearly list out the obstacles that still lie ahead. They should be real about the challenges they are facing in taking on their company's environmental, financial and social responsibility goals.

Finally, to conclude, it can be said that Green Marketing can be successful in the future only by implementing an integrated approach by all the interested parties—producers, consumers, and the government. Each of them is expected to contribute their bit to ensure the success of Green Marketing efforts in our country.

LET US SUM UP

- AMA defines Green Marketing as the marketing of products that are presumed to be environmentally safe. It incorporates several activities such as product modification, changes to production processes, packaging, and advertising strategies.
- Marketers have to make conscious efforts to design green products, price them appropriately, promote them aggressively and make them widely available to people to ensure their increased demand.
- In their pursuit of ensuring a healthy environment and sustainable development, various companies in the field of consumer and industrial products, electronics and information technology, and banking sectors are initiating green efforts.
- The primary objective of green washing is to provide consumers with the feeling that the organisation is taking the necessary steps to responsibly manage its ecological footprints. In reality, what the company may be doing is environmentally not very beneficial.
- Green advertising can make the green ideas and products more popular amongst masses.
- The Internet, through e-mail, Web sites, search engines, blogs, product ratings sites, podcasts, and other digital platforms has opened significant opportunities for tapping consumers social and communication networks to diffuse credible 'word-of-mouth' about green products.
- Marketers need to be very cautious while making green claims. Third parties, government agencies, independent laboratories, non-profit advocacy organisations or private consultants should provide green product endorsements or seals of approval to add to the believability of such green claims.

QUESTIONS TO CHECK YOUR PROGRESS

Short Answer Questions

1. Define Green Marketing as given by the American Marketing Association.
2. List out three important reasons for the 'Go Green' movement.

3. Explain the concept of 3R's.
4. What is green washing?
5. Name certain green initiatives being incorporated these days.
6. List out three important principles of going green.
7. How is efficiency and effectiveness important for green products?
8. What is Green advertising? Give two examples of Green advertisements.
9. "Third party endorsements are essential for adding authenticity to green claims". Comment.
10. Explain the government's role in the success of green products.

Long Answer Questions

1. "Going green has become a topic of discussion at various international platforms". Explain the various reasons as to why this has become such an important issue.
2. Explain the concept of Green Marketing and suggest certain strategies with the help of which it can be implemented effectively.
3. What are the basic objectives of going green? Why is it becoming so important these days?
4. "Going green is the strategy of tomorrow". Explain the statement in the light of various initiatives taken by the marketers.
5. How is designing the marketing mix for green products different than non-green products? Explain with the help of certain examples.
6. Site some of the examples where companies have taken the initiative to go green.
7. "It's a big challenge in front of the marketers to initiate Green Marketing strategies". Do you agree with the statement? Explain in the light of various challenges being faced by them.
8. The various social networking sites are playing a very important role in promoting the green initiatives. How can marketers effectively utilise Internet as a medium to promote green ideas?
9. Explain the significance of an integrated approach to handling the Green Marketing initiatives.
10. Give suitable examples from the current scenario of the organisations who have been successfully implementing Green Marketing initiatives.
11. Suggest certain steps to add to the popularity of green initiatives by marketers, consumers, and the government.

CHAPTER 13

Marketing of Services

Learning Outcomes

After studying this chapter, you will be able to:

- Understand the concept, nature and characteristics of marketing of services
- Compare between product and service
- Define the marketing mix for services
- Describe the future of service marketing in India

Till now we were talking about the marketing of physical products, which are tangible in nature. But these days' markets are flooded with numerous services which need to be marketed differently than that of the physical products. Service sector is contributing a lot towards the economic growth and development of our nation. Services are essential as they provide the basic infrastructure. No other sector can grow and no goods can be produced unless and until there is a strong service sector to backup the manufacturing sector. Services of various kinds are provided to people by the government, not-for-profit organisations and business organisations. Governments offer various types of services to ensure the smooth running of the economy, such as legal services, employment services, banks and financial institutions, hospitals, military services, airlines, transportation services, telecommunication services, police and fire departments, postal services, and educational services. Various private not-for-profit organisations also offer services; examples include museums, charitable organisations, temples and churches, schools and colleges, hospitals, and various other foundations. A large number of business organisations are also offering a variety of services to the consumers, for example, airlines, banks, telecommunications, hotels, insurance companies, entertainment companies, travel and tourism, real estate firms, schools and colleges, consulting firms, medical and law practices, etc.

Basically, *services* are intangible, inseparable, variable and perishable products. They are delivered by the service provider directly to the recipient. The quality of the service depends on the service provider. It might vary from person to person. As a result, services normally require more quality control, supplier credibility and adaptability.

According to Philip Kotler (1999)—

> *"A service is an act of performance that one party can offer to another that is essentially intangible and does not result in the ownership of anything. Its production may or may not be tied to a physical product.*

According to the American Marketing Association (1995)—

> *Services are activities, benefits, or satisfactions which are offered for sale or provided in connection with the sale of goods.*

According to William J Stanton (1994)—

> *Services are separately identifiable, intangible activities which provide want satisfaction when marketed to consumers and/or industrial users and which are not necessarily tied to the sale of a product or another service.*

From all the definitions given above, certain unique characteristics of services have emerged, some of the important ones are discussed as under.

13.1 NATURE AND CHARACTERISTICS OF SERVICES

There are various unique characteristics of services. Some of them are nicely depicted in Figure 13.1 as under:

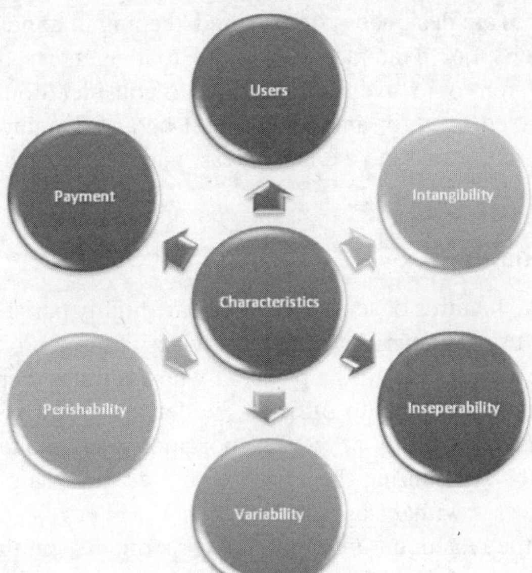

Figure 13.1 Unique characteristics of services.

13.1.1 Service Intangibility

As services are highly intangible, a consumer cannot touch them, see them, taste them or smell them before buying. It is because of this reason that a consumer who is buying a service can never visualise well in advance as to what is going to be the final outcome, whether he or she will be happy and satisfied with the quality of the service or not. For example, if a patient goes for surgery to a hospital he is never sure of the fact that whether he will be cured fully by the doctors or not. Whenever someone buys a tour package from a travel and tour agency one is never sure of the fact that whether they will be able to get the desired level of satisfaction or not. Thus, there always remains a level of uncertainty about the quality of services. Consumers can only draw conclusions about the quality from the place, people, price, equipment and communications that they can see. Therefore it is expected from the marketers to make the services tangible in whatever ways possible and send the right kind of signals about their quality to the consumers.

13.1.2 Service Inseparability

Another important characteristic of service is that services are attached to the service providers. They cannot be separated from their providers, whether the providers are people or machines. Generally, services are sold first and then are produced and consumed at the same time. While the service provider is providing the service the customer is always present and the provider-customer interaction becomes the essential part of Service Marketing. The efficiency with which the service is going to be delivered depends to a large extent on the degree of satisfaction delivered by the service provider to the customer.

13.1.3 Service Variability

Services vary in nature. Their quality and level of satisfaction delivered varies from one situation to another. Generally, services are designed or redesigned keeping in mind the specific requirements provided by the customers. For example, travel and tour agencies design tour packages for different people with different objectives or motives into consideration. For one person it might be a comfortable and relaxed stay, for another it might be an adventurous trip, the third person might be looking for natural beauty and exclusiveness, while the fourth person might be looking for an economical package.

13.1.4 Service Perishability

This is one of the exclusive features of services, as they are highly perishable in nature and cannot be stored for later sale or use. The perishability of services is not a problem in cases where their demand meets the supply, it only becomes a problem when at times there is huge demand for the services and the marketers are not able to fulfil all the demands, and at other times there is ideal capacity. It has been noticed frequently in the transportation and hospitality sector that all modes of transports are heavily booked during the office hours, while during the day buses and trains remain empty. Same is the case with restaurants that there is a huge rush in the evening hours while in the afternoon most of the restaurant are empty. This is one reason that these days restaurants have started offering 'happy hours' schemes to attract customers in their slack hours. Thus, service firms have to design strategies for ensuring a better match between the demand and supply.

13.1.5 Service Payment

Services are paid for in the form of fees or charges. The client may pay to the service provider in different forms, such as commission, fees, rent, premiums, salary, brokerage, etc. Charges depend on the quality of the service delivered, the time and place at which it is delivered, the staff and the equipment involved, the priority or the urgency of the situation, etc.

13.1.6 Service Users

The users of a service may be called *clients* (for management consultant), *patients* (for doctors), *owner/master* (for domestic servant), customers (for salesmen), or simply *users*. Users may be an individual, an institute or a group.

13.2 DIFFERENCE BETWEEN PHYSICAL PRODUCT AND SERVICE

Marketing of physical products can be differentiated from services on the basis of various parameters. Some of the important ones are listed in Figure 13.2 as under:

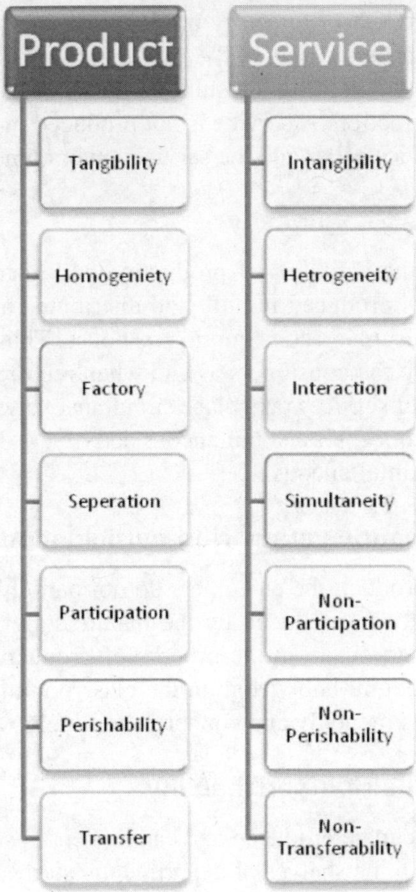

Figure 13.2 Difference between physical product and service.

13.2.1 Tangibility versus Intangibility

Products or physical products have a definite configuration, and specific characteristic features which can be easily seen, touched, smelt, and tasted, while on the other hand, service, though a product, does not have physical configuration. They cannot be seen, touched, smelt, and tasted.

13.2.2 Homogeneity versus Heterogeneity

Products are generally homogenous in nature. They can be standardised, where a product can be a perfect substitute for another. In contrast, services are highly heterogeneous, as most of the time the quality of the service provided by the service provider varies from person to person. For example, the same doctor treating two or more patients, where one gets treated properly while the other patient is not able to recover fully. Similarly, there are many teachers, lawyers, barbers, bankers, hairdressers and tailors who cannot give identical service in terms of quality, satisfaction or benefits.

13.2.3 Factory Production versus Interaction Production

A physical product is an end result of a factory production where different inputs are converted into output with the help of various processes. A motor car, a mobile phone, camera, computer, or television—all these products are the end result of a factory production. However, services are possible with buyer-seller interaction. A service is not produced in a factory or a technical unit; it is rendered only when the service seller and the service buyer come together.

13.2.4 Separation versus Simultaneity

In case of physical products the activities of production and distribution are separate from the act of consumption. Goods are produced in bulk and distributed all across various geographical boundaries. They await the consumer's consumption response. They can be kept in warehouses for months and can be delivered to the consumers as and when required. In contrast, the production, distribution and consumption of services take place simultaneously. A teacher delivering a lecture and the students grasping the concept is a simultaneous activity. A doctor treating a patient and the patient getting cured again is simultaneous.

13.2.5 Customer Participation versus Non-participation

In manufacturing a physical product, the customers do not participate in the production process. They can only consume the goods produced by the manufacturers. On the contrary, in case of services, the customer must participate in the process of production to consume a service. For example, if a student has to acquire knowledge in the classroom, he/she has to be present in the classroom physically as well as mentally and cooperate willingly with their teacher.

13.2.6 Perishability versus Non-perishability

Most of the physical products can be produced and can be kept in stock till the time they are sold. At times many goods pile up on the shelves of departmental stores for months together and await the consumer's response. As against this, services are highly perishable. Most of them cannot be stored and referred to in the future. Their benefit can be attained only simultaneously by the recipient. In case of services there has to be a perfect match between the demand and supply, only then will the customer be happy and satisfied. Supply can never exceed demand, and even if it does, an excess cannot be stored.

13.2.7 Transferability and Non-transferability of Ownership

Whenever physical products are purchased by the buyer's the title to the goods moves from the seller to the buyer. Thus, the ownership of the goods also gets transferred from the seller to the buyer. However, this is not the case with services. In case of services, the ownership of service is not transferable. That is, if a customer is buying the service he cannot own the entire reservoir of service of the service provider; For example, reserving a seat in a bus is not like owning the entire bus.

13.3 MARKETING MIX FOR SERVICES 7P's

We have learnt to design the marketing mix for goods, where we talked about the 4P's—product, price, place and promotion. In the same way the marketing mix for services is designed. As we all know that the basic nature of a physical product is different than that of a service. Products can be tangible, can be stored, can be transported to various places, and can be sold at a later date with the help of various wholesalers and retailers. While it has already been discussed that the services are intangible, inseparable, perishable, and variable in nature, their marketing mix has to be designed differently keeping these differences into account. When we talk about the marketing mix for services, there are seven P's instead of the four already discussed. Three more P's, such as people, physical evidence and process are added to the list. The marketing mix for services is nicely depicted in Figure 13.3.

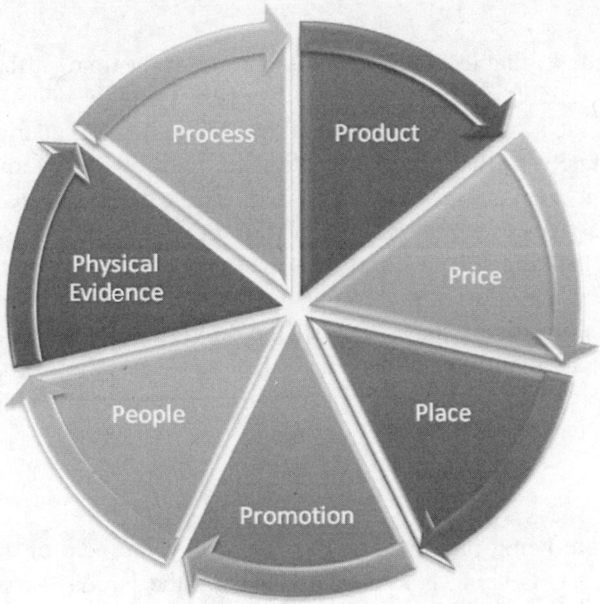

Figure 13.3 Marketing mix for services.

13.3.1 Product

While designing a product a manufacturer tries to provide lots of features and value added services to the customers to give them maximum satisfaction. In the same way, while delivering the services to the customers the service provider has to identify their target customers and deliver them the expected service quality. Because there is too much of competition in the service sector as well, the service providers are constantly looking for better ways and means to deliver better services to customers than their competitors. Top service companies set high service quality standards. They watch service performance closely and try to provide 100 per cent performance efficiency to their customers so that they are able to win them over from the competitors. As discussed already, services are variable in nature so organisations try to design services keeping their customers' needs and wants into consideration and give them maximum satisfaction.

13.3.2 Price

Prices can be highly variable in the service sector. It generally depends on the quality, timeliness, urgency, promptness and efficiency with which the service is delivered by the service provider. As there is tremendous price competition in the markets, organisations at times develop differentiated offers for their customers. Price is generally set in terms of the various features and additional services provided by the service provider. For example, a hotel might charge different prices from different customers for different types of rooms provided. A customer will have to pay a higher price for a deluxe room than a customer who is going for a standard room. The hotel will automatically charge a higher price for a customer who wants a pickup and drop service than a customer who does not want any such additional services. Airlines differentiate their offers for frequent flyers by offering them various award programmes and special services.

13.3.3 Place

Services are to be made available to the customers at the right time, at the right place, with the help of the right and reliable delivery systems. Marketers should develop a superior physical environment in which the service provider should be able to design superior quality services and deliver them appropriately to the customers. With the help of the Internet and various online services the delivery mechanisms have improved a lot. These days marketers are trying to provide certain value-added services to attract customers from the competitors', examples include many banks offering online banking services, railways and airlines offering online booking facility in order to help customers avoid driving, parking, waiting in lines and other hassles. But in case of certain services, the customers have to visit the service provider to take the advantage of their services, such as a patient has to visit the doctor and a hospital for the medical treatment. Therefore, the marketers should try to ensure a cordial environment at such places to deliver value added services to their customers.

13.3.4 Promotion

Services of all kinds are being promoted aggressively with the help of various possible media options. Lots of emphasis is being placed on advertising the various services such as banking, insurance, education, travel and tourism, health and hospitality, and telecommunications. Personal selling plays a very important role in the promotion of various services as most of the services are to be delivered to the customers personally by the service provider. Publicity adds to the credibility and prestige of the organisation rendering efficient services to their customers. Thus, a right mix of all the promotional tools is essential to promote services aggressively in today's competitive scenario.

13.3.5 People

They play a very important role in delivering the services efficiently to the customers. In order to deliver the best services to the customers and that too better than the competitors, it is very essential for organisations to empower their front-line service employees and give them authority, responsibility and incentives. It is expected of these employees to recognise customers' needs and wants, care about them, and serve them better. For instance, in the hospitality sector, the growth and development of various hotels depends to a large extent on the efficiency with which their customers are being handled by their hotel staff. Proper training is imparted to the staff, various interpersonal communication skills are taught to them, and they are constantly motivated to serve the customer well. Customers generally form an opinion about an organisation by the efficiency and commitment with which their employees serve them, therefore having a strong and committed workforce is essential for service organisations. In other words, organisations have to hire staff who care about people.

13.3.6 Process

In order to efficiently deliver the services to customers it is equally important for the organisations to ensure an efficient processing mechanism. Some of the organisations are able to serve the customers well, such as Domino's is able to deliver Pizza within 30 minutes only with the help of an efficient production and delivery process. With the help of technology, it is possible for the organisations to have efficient processing of services. This will ensure a consistent service and loyal clientele.

13.3.7 Physical Evidence (Physical Environment)

Even though physical environment plays a very important role in case of marketing of goods, its significance increases tremendously especially in case of services, because in most of the cases customers physically visit the service provider. For them the ambience of the place makes a lot of difference. For example, if someone is going for a treatment to a hospital the efficiency with which the administration of the hospital is taken care of and the hygiene standards maintained in the hospital play a significant role in delivering them better health services. While visiting a restaurant it is not only the menu options available which matter, rather the ambience of the restaurant makes a lot of difference.

Therefore, to conclude, it can be said that the service providers have to keep in mind all the 7P's in order to design their service mix and deliver efficient services to their customers.

13.4 FUTURE OF SERVICE MARKETING IN INDIA

The future of Service Marketing in India is very bright as the number and nature of services is growing tremendously. The disposable income of people is increasing at a faster rate as a result of which their purchasing power is increasing and they are asking for more and more of services. They are looking for a better lifestyle and an improved standard of living for themselves. Their wants are increasing at a rapid pace due to competition and status consciousness. Banks and other financial institutions are even coming forward to grant credit facilities on liberal terms and conditions to facilitate consumption. Thus, as a result of an increase in the marginal propensity to consume, there is a growing demand for all types of services whether it is in the field of health and hygiene, education, travel and tourism, telecommunications, or the financial sector.

Service sector is even required to support the industrial sector. None of the physical products can be produced unless and until there is a strong service sector around to provide the basic infrastructural facilities. Therefore, it can be safely concluded that in the times to come there is going to be a growing demand for services, and if the marketer wants to make the most of this situation, they should provide quality services to the consumers. A constant effort should be made by them to provide more and more of innovative, creative and value added services with the help of better technological setup.

LET US SUM UP

- Service sector is contributing a lot towards the economic growth and development of our nation.
- Services are intangible, inseparable, variable, and perishable products that are delivered by the service provider directly to the recipient.
- Services are highly intangible as a consumer cannot touch them, see them, taste them or smell them before buying.
- Services are attached to the service providers. They cannot be separated from their providers.
- Services are highly perishable in nature and cannot be stored for later sale or use.
- Products are generally homogenous in nature while services are highly heterogeneous, as most of the time the quality of the service provided by the service provider varies from person to person.
- Most of the physical products can be produced and kept in stocks till the time they are sold. As against this, services are highly perishable. Most of them cannot be stored and referred to in future. Their benefit can be attained only simultaneously by the recipient.
- When we talk about the marketing mix for services, there are seven P's instead of the four already discussed; three more P's, such as people, physical evidence, and process are added to list.
- There is going to be a growing demand for services in the future and if the marketers want to make the most of this situation, they should provide quality services to the consumers.

QUESTIONS TO CHECK YOUR PROGRESS

Short Answer Questions

1. Explain the concept of Service Marketing.
2. List some of the important services offered by the government.
3. Name a few important services offered by business houses.
4. Is the marketing mix for services the same as for goods?

5. Name the various P's of Service Marketing mix.
6. Define the concept of Inseparability.
7. Why are services perishable in nature?

Long Answer Questions

1. "Service sector is booming". Explain the statement and discuss factors leading to the service boom in India.
2. Define the word 'service' and explain its characteristics.
3. List out the various unique features of services.
4. "Marketing of services is different than marketing of products". Do you agree with the statement? Explain with the help of suitable examples.
5. Explain the elements of marketing mix with reference to services.
6. What is Service Marketing mix? Explain the various P's involved in it.
7. What is the future of Service Marketing in India? Explain with the help of a suitable example.

CHAPTER 14

Customer Relationship Marketing

Learning Outcomes

After studying this chapter, you will be able to:

- ❖ Explain the concept and characteristics of customer relationship management (CRM)
- ❖ Identify the reasons for the growing importance of CRM
- ❖ Define the steps towards relationship marketing
- ❖ Discuss the procedure for retaining customers by reducing defection
- ❖ Express the procedure to manage the customer loyalty
- ❖ Illustrate the limitations of CRM

Marketers these days are seeking more than just a one-time exchange or transaction with their customers because they have clearly recognised the fact that it is more difficult to create a new customer than retaining an old one. Thus, the focus of market-driven companies is on developing and sustaining relationships with their customers. This has led to a new emphasis on *Relationship Marketing*, which involves creating, maintaining and enhancing long-term relationships with individual customers as well as other stakeholders for mutual benefit.

According to the American Marketing Association (1995)—

> *Relationship marketing is marketing which consciously aim to develop and manage long term and/or trusting relationship with customers, distributors, suppliers or other parties in the marketing environment.*

In Relationship Marketing, a detailed database comprising of customers' profile, their buying patterns, and their contact details are maintained. Moreover, each valuable customer is assigned a marketing executive to fulfil his/her needs and maintain a long term relationship. Relationship Marketing is also called *Customer Relationship Marketing* (CRM). Which refers to a technology enabled process for customer interaction and relationship building.

14.1 REASONS FOR THE GROWING IMPORTANCE OF CRM

The movement towards Relationship Marketing is due to several factors. Some of the important ones are discussed below:

14.1.1 Goodwill and Prestige

One of the most important reasons for ensuring Customer Relationship Management is an increase in the goodwill and prestige of the companies which are able to retain their customers. Their loyal and satisfied customers promote products by giving a positive feedback to all their friends, family and peers, by word-of-mouth and through various social networking sites. Such companies are not only able to retain their customers but also add more customers with the help of these satisfied customers.

14.1.2 Cost-Effective

Another important reason as to why marketers are emphasising on Relationship Marketing is that it is often more cost-effective to retain customers than to acquire new ones. Marketers are giving more attention to retaining the customers for lifetime because it has been observed that reducing customer defections by just five per cent can increase future profits by as much as 25 to 85 per cent.

14.1.3 Demanding Customers

Companies have now recognised that customers have become much more demanding and it is very difficult to retain them. They desire superior customer value, which includes quality products and services that are competitively priced, convenient to purchase, delivered on time and supported by excellent customer service. As a result, these days all good companies are trying their level best to provide all such value driven services to their customers.

14.1.4 Personalised Products

Customers want personalised products and services that are tailored to their specific needs and wants. With the help of new technology, marketers are making it possible to consider and personalise a wide array of products and services including computers, automobiles, clothing etc., and serve their customers well.

14.1.5 Advances in Information Technology

Advances in Information Technology, along with the flexible manufacturing systems and new marketing processes, has made it possible for marketers to initiate mass customisation, whereby a company can make a product or deliver a service in response to a particular customer's needs and wants in a cost effective manner.

14.2 CHARACTERISTICS OF CRM

The characteristics of Customer Relationship Marketing, shown in Figure 14.1, are described as under:

- **Customer concern:** Relationship Marketing is concerned for the welfare of their customer. This is where the marketer wants to meet customer expectations and produce satisfaction.
- **Customer services:** Relationship Marketing is a means to provide excellent services to the customers in order to retain them in the long run.
- **Customer trust:** Trust is the key of a relationship, and companies can retain the trust of their customers by providing them with good quality and reasonably priced products, fair promotional means, convenient location, and excellent after sales service.
- **Customer satisfaction:** Customer satisfaction is ensured by providing them value for money, or in other words a product which gives them more benefits at lesser cost.
- **Customer retention:** It is more important for the companies to retain their old customers as it has been mentioned above that it is more cost effective to retain customers than to acquire new ones. Consider the following data about customer retention as has been given by Thomas V. Bonoma (1985)—
  — Acquiring new customers can cost five times more than satisfying and retaining current ones as it requires a great deal of effort to induce satisfied customers to switch from their current suppliers.
  — The average company loses 10 per cent of its customers every year.
  — A 5 per cent reduction in the customer defection rate can increase profit by 25 per cent to 85 per cent, depending on the industry.
  — Profit rate tends to increase over the life of the retained customer due to increased purchases, referrals, price premiums, and reduced operating costs to service.

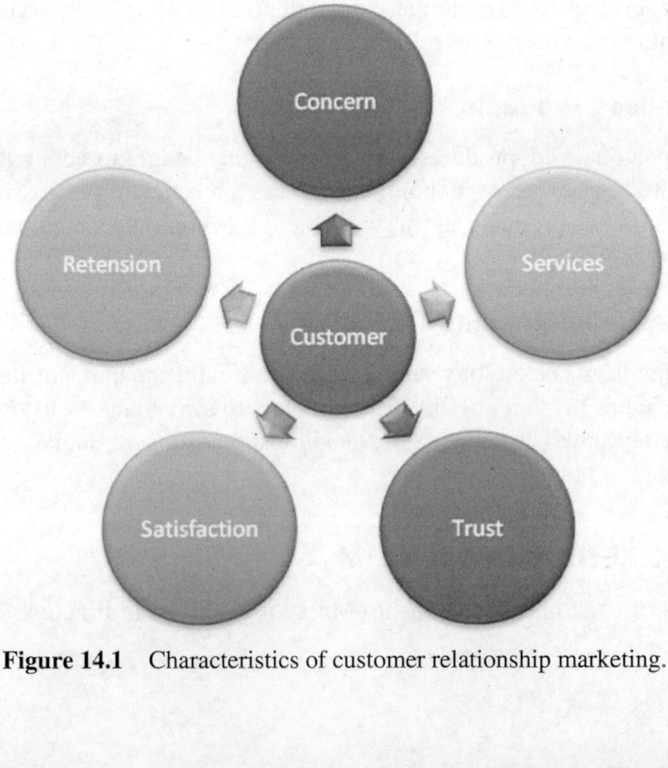

Figure 14.1 Characteristics of customer relationship marketing.

14.3 STEPS TOWARDS CRM

There are certain basic steps which are to be carried out in order to ensure effective Customer Relationship Marketing. Figure 14.2 clearly depicts these steps.

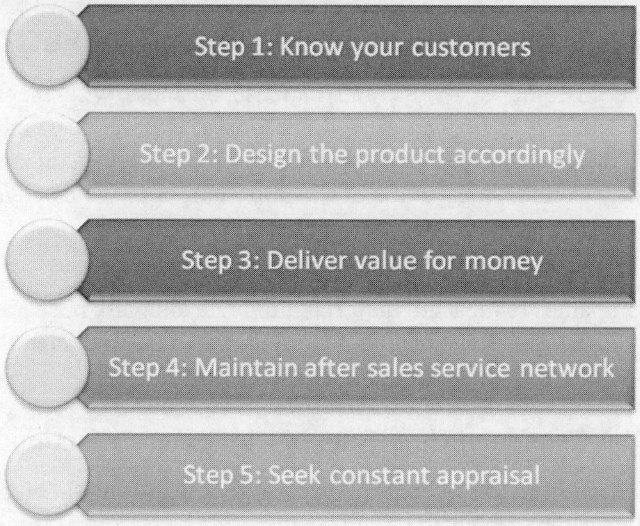

Figure 14.2 Steps towards customer relationship marketing.

14.3.1 Step One: Know Your Customer

It is very important for the marketers to first understand who their customers are. The demographic, geographic and psychographic profile of the customers must be clearly understood by the marketers so that the goods are designed according to their needs, wants and preferences.

14.3.2 Step Two: Design the Product Accordingly

After understanding the customer expectations with the help of improved technological setup, it is important for the companies to design the products as per the aspirations of the customers and ensure that the goods are made available to them at the right place with the right price.

14.3.3 Step Three: Deliver Value for Money

In order to retain customers for a long-term it is important that marketers should deliver value for money to the customers. They should be satisfied with the quality of the product, as well as the price at which it is being sold.

14.3.4 Step Four: Maintain after Sale Service Network

In today's competitive world if marketers want to retain their customers it is very important that they should provide them with an excellent after sales service network. Guarantee, warranty, repair and maintenance should be provided efficiently to the customers to hold their interest in the company's product.

14.3.5 Step Five: Seek Constant Appraisal from Customers

Seeking constant appraisal from customers through feedback and taking corrective actions is important for the companies to keep them satisfied and contended, and retain them for long.

14.4 RETAINING CUSTOMERS BY REDUCING DEFECTION RATE

In order to keep the customer's loyalty and increase business with them, it is important for companies to reduce the *defection rate*, or in other words, the rate at which the customers leave the organisation and join the competitor's organisation. In order to reduce the defection rate the companies must follow certain steps, some of the important ones are listed as under:

14.4.1 Define and Measure its Retention Rate

It is important for companies to measure their retention rate annually because it gives them an idea as to how many customers they have been able to retain. In case, the retention rate is low, it is an alarming situation which calls for further analysis.

14.4.2 Identify the Causes of High Rate of Customer Defection

It is important for the marketers to list out the various reasons for high defection rate and identify clearly the reasons that can be managed better. As there can be certain reasons regarding which not much can be done, for example, if some of the customers leave the region or go out of business. But a lot of marketing effort is required to retain those customers who are driven away by poor service, shoddy products, misleading claims, or high prices.

14.4.3 Compare the Lost Customers' Lifetime Value to the Costs of Reducing the Defection Rate

At times companies have to spend a huge amount to discourage defection and retain the customer's loyalty in the long run. Therefore, it becomes important for the marketers to make a simple calculation and compare the cost of retaining the customer with the lost profit and should spend that amount only if it is worth.

14.5 MANAGING THE CUSTOMER LOYALTY

Creating a strong and healthy connection with customers is the dream of any marketer and often the key to long-term marketing success. With the help of Customer Profitability Analysis marketers can learn to manage groups of customers that vary in loyalty, profitability and other factors. Customers' loyalty can be increased by providing them with additional value. Successful companies can improve that value by making use of the following strategies:

- **Hiring and Training Knowledgeable Employees:** Selecting and training employees towards product/service knowledge and friendliness/courtesy, increases the likelihood of the customers' complaints being handled effectively and satisfactorily. A dedicated team of employees always makes an effort to treat the customers well and provide them with an experience which they cherish. In order to motivate their employees, companies should follow the policy of giving awards to outstanding employees who have been able to keep their customers happy.

- **Increasing the Longevity of the Customer Relationship:** The better an organisation is likely to serve the customers, the more dedicated the consumers are going to be. Therefore, it is recommended to all the companies to take the long term interest of the customers into account and provide them with various value added services, besides providing them with the basic product. Sales from existing customers can be increased by giving them new offerings and opportunities.
- **Get Cross Departmental Participation:** Companies should ensure cross-departmental participation in planning and managing the customer satisfaction and retention process by creating superior products, services and experience for the target market.
- **Organise a Database of Information:** It is important for organisations to have a database of information on individual customer's preferences, contact information, purchase frequency, suggestions, and recommendations to serve them better in the long run.
- **Effective Feedback Mechanism:** Make it easy for customers to reach an authorized company staff and express their needs, perceptions and complaints so that they can be looked into by the concerned persons immediately.
- **Making Low Profit Customers More Profitable or Terminate Them:** To avoid the direct need for termination, marketers can encourage unprofitable customers to buy more or in larger quantities by offering them certain special benefits, features or services. But despite the efforts if the customers don't change their buying pattern, it is advisable to terminate such contacts, and divert the energy and resources towards more profitable customers.
- **Laying More Focus on High Profit Customers:** The most profitable customers can be treated in a special way. The organisation should perform various thoughtful gestures to communicate to them how valuable they are to the company. Certain gestures, such as conveying greetings on birthdays, New Year and Holi, Diwali gifts, or invitations to some special events can send them a strong positive signal.

14.6 LIMITATIONS OF CRM

Having discussed the importance of Customer Relationship Marketing, it is important for us to understand certain limitations or problems which come in the way of effective Customer Relationship Marketing. The following list of problems can prevent a firm from effectively using CRM:

When Situations are Not Worthwhile

The data base management might not be resorted to by companies when—

1. their product is a once-in-a-lifetime purchase (a grand piano);
2. customers show little loyalty to their brand (a new toothpaste);
3. the unit sale is very small (a small candy bar or chocolate);

4. the cost of gathering information is too high; and
5. there is no direct contact between the seller and the ultimate buyer.

Building and Maintaining a Customer Database Involves a Lot of Expenditure

It might not be economically feasible for an organisation to build and maintain a customer database which requires a huge investment in computer hardware, database software, analytical programs, communication links and skilled staff.

Lack of Customer Orientation in the Organisation

The indifferent attitude of employees, dealers and suppliers towards CRM might make it difficult for the organisation to be customer oriented and use the available information. Employees might find it easier to carry on the traditional marketing practices. Effective database marketing requires managing and training employees, as well as dealers and suppliers, but they might not be willing to undergo such trainings.

Not all Customers Want a Relationship with the Company

Some of them may resent knowing that the company has collected a lot of personal information and can put the information to misuse.

The CRM Practices Might Not be Practically Viable

As high volume customers often know their value to a company and can leverage it to extract premium service or price discounts, it may not be practically viable for the firm to serve them. These loyal customers may expect and demand more, and resent any attempt to charge full prices. They may not necessarily be the best ambassadors for the brand as well.

Thus, the benefits of Customer Relationship Marketing do not come without significant costs and risks, not only in collecting the customer data, but also in maintaining and revising it. A databank might yield more than its cost, but it has to be up-to-date, and contain information which is valid and acceptable to consumers.

To conclude, it can be said that Customer Relationship Management calls for a 360° approach, where all the departments of the company should work collectively and in a coordinated manner towards the goal of ensuring a satisfied, committed and loyal customer.

LET US SUM UP

- Relationship marketing involves creating, maintaining and enhancing long-term relationships with individual customers, as well as other stakeholders for mutual benefit.
- Relationship marketing is also called Customer Relationship Marketing (CRM), which refers to technology enabled process for customer interaction and relationship building.
- Marketers are emphasising on Relationship Marketing because it is often more cost-effective to retain customers than to acquire new ones.
- Customer Relationship Marketing is a means to provide excellent services to the customers in order to retain their trust and confidence in the long run.
- Acquiring new customers can cost five times more than satisfying and retaining current ones. The average company loses 10 per cent of its customers each year and a five per cent reduction in the customer defection rate can increase profits by 25 per cent to 85 per cent, depending on the industry.

- There are certain basic steps which are to be carried out in order to ensure Customer Relationship Management, such as know your customer, design the product accordingly, deliver value for money, render excellent after sales services, and seek constant appraisal from customers.
- Customers' loyalty can be increased by providing them with additional value with the help of a committed, trained and dedicated work force.
- The benefits of Customer Relationship Marketing do not come without significant costs and risks, not only in collecting the original customer data, but also in maintaining and minding them.

QUESTIONS TO CHECK YOUR PROGRESS

Short Answer Questions

1. Define the concept of CRM.
2. List out three important reasons for the growth of CRM.
3. How can customer's loyalty be retained by marketers?
4. Why it is that Customer Relationship Marketing is not very popular amongst marketers as well as consumers?
5. What is the role of employees in ensuring better CRM practices?

Long Answer Questions

1. Explain the concept of Customer Relationship Marketing. Why is it important for marketers to follow the CRM strategies these days?
2. In order to keep the customer's loyalty and increase their business it is important for companies to reduce their defection rate. Explain the various strategies with the help of which it can be reduced.
3. Explain the various stages involved in the implementation of the CRM.
4. Define the concept of customer loyalty and explain the various strategies used by marketers to retain their loyalty.
5. It is not very feasible to implement CRM in the Indian scenario. Can you list out the various reasons responsible for this?

CHAPTER 15

Managing Direct and Digital Marketing

Learning Outcomes

After studying this chapter, you will be able to:

- Understand the concept, features and importance of direct marketing
- Define the major channels of direct marketing
- Explain the concept of digital marketing
- Identify the key success factors in digital marketing
- Express the challenges involved in implementing online marketing
- Determine the guidelines for effective implementation of digital marketing
- Discuss the important decisions for digital marketing

With the availability of various media options and other technological developments it is possible for many more companies to sell their products and services directly to customers without bringing in the intermediaries. Even though the trend of direct marketing was there in the past as well but the growth in the opportunities in the recent past has been tremendous. Direct marketing has benefited both the consumers as well as the marketers as marketers are no longer at the mercy of the middleman to promote the sale of their goods or services and consumers are able to get goods at lesser prices because of the elimination of middleman's margin. Direct marketing has been made more feasible due to the wider options available to the marketers. The existing media-print and broadcast, catalogues, direct mail, and telephone, has been complemented by fax machines, e-mail, the Internet, and online services. Companies are increasingly using all these media options to make direct offers to existing customers and to identify new prospects. Direct marketing enables companies to target their offers directly to customers and to measure their results more accurately.

According to American Marketing Association (1995)—

> *Direct marketing involves the use of mail, telephone, fax, e-mail, or Internet to communicate directly with or solicit a direct response from specific customers and prospects.*

According to the Direct Marketing Association (1990)—

> *Direct marketing is an interactive marketing system that uses one or more advertising media to affect a measurable response and/or transaction at any location.*

In direct marketing, organisations communicate directly with target customers to generate a response or a transaction. It involves the use of a variety of activities, including database management, online marketing, telemarketing and direct selling through mail. One of the major tools of direct marketing is direct response advertising, whereby a product is promoted through an ad that encourages the customer to purchase directly from the manufacturer. The availability of credit cards and toll-free phone numbers has also facilitated the purchase of products from direct response ads. More recently, the rapid growth of the Internet is fuelling the growth of direct marketing, telemarketing is also being used. Some of the examples of the success of direct marketing are Reader's Digest magazine, Amway, Tupperware etc.

15.1 UNIQUE FEATURES OF DIRECT MARKETING

Some of the unique features of direct marketing are illustrated in Figure 15.1 and explained under:

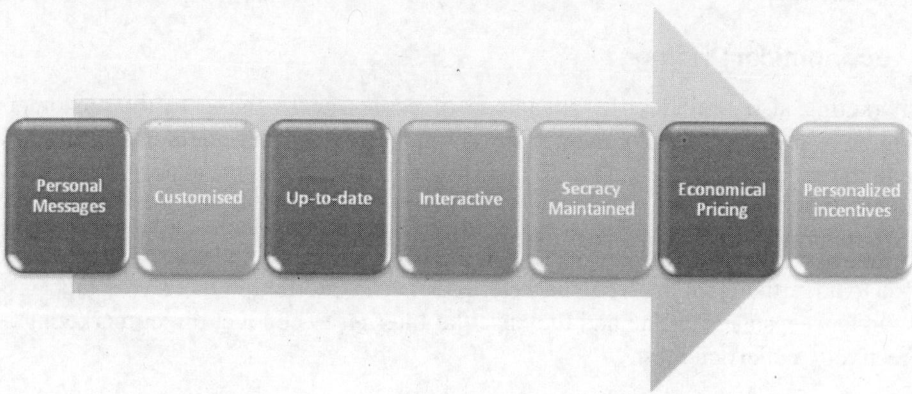

Figure 15.1 Unique features of direct marketing.

15.1.1 Personal Messages

The direct mail messages which are designed for a specific audience are addressed personally to the person concerned and have a bit of personnel touch to them as compared to all other promotional tools where a general expression is used.

15.1.2 Customised

Most of the direct marketing messages are customised keeping the target audience into account. They are delivered directly to the concerned person and a direct response is sought from them.

15.1.3 Up-to-Date-Direct

Up-to-date-direct marketing messages are designed frequently and are sent at short intervals, so as and when there is a change in the product, a new feature is added, or a new scheme is introduced it is brought to the notice of the target audience with revised messages.

15.1.4 Interactive and Instant Feedback

Direct marketing turns out to be a highly interactive medium, especially in telemarketing with the help of the toll-free number and Internet where customers log on to the websites, they can call or ask for additional information besides the one being delivered directly from the manufacturer. Customers can also provide their feedback immediately to the company.

15.1.5 Secrecy is Maintained

Direct marketing tools provide the manufacturers an exclusive advantage of keeping their advertising campaign secret from the competitors as they address their messages directly and personally to the target audience. In most of the cases the competitors does not gets to know about the promises being made by the manufacturer to the customers which gives the manufacturer a competitive advantage.

15.1.6 Economical Pricing

Direct marketing also provides the advantage of economical pricing to the customers as the manufacturer in this case can do away with the middleman so the middleman's commission is saved and the cost saving is passed on to the customers in the form of reduced prices.

15.1.7 Personalized Sales Promotion Incentives

In addition to advertising on the web, marketers offer sales promotion incentives such as coupons, contests, and sweepstakes online and they use the Internet to conduct direct marketing activities more effectively and efficiently.

15.2 BENEFITS OF DIRECT MARKETING

Direct marketing benefits both the customers and the marketers in many ways. Some of the important ones are listed as under:

- For customers shopping through direct marketing is a very **convenient and trouble-free experience.**
- **It saves time** and introduces customers to a larger selection of merchandise.
- **Consumers can do comparative shopping** by browsing through mail catalogues and online shopping services.

- **Direct marketing saves the botheration** of travelling long distances, traffic problems and parking hassles.
- **Marketers also benefit from direct marketing** as they can give a personal touch to their communication for their prospective customers.
- **Direct marketers can build a continuous relationship** with each customer and can get constant feedback from them.
- **Direct marketing can also give the advantage of reaching** prospects at the right time.
- **It permits the testing of alternative media** and messages in search of the most cost effective approach.
- **It can help marketers in measuring responses** to their campaigns to decide as to which one has been the most profitable.
- **Direct marketing also makes the direct marketer's offer** and strategy less visible to competitors.

15.3 MAJOR CHANNELS FOR DIRECT MARKETING

Direct marketers can use a number of channels for reaching prospects and customers. According to **Philip Kotler (1999)** some of the important ones are depicted in Figure 15.2 and mentioned as under:

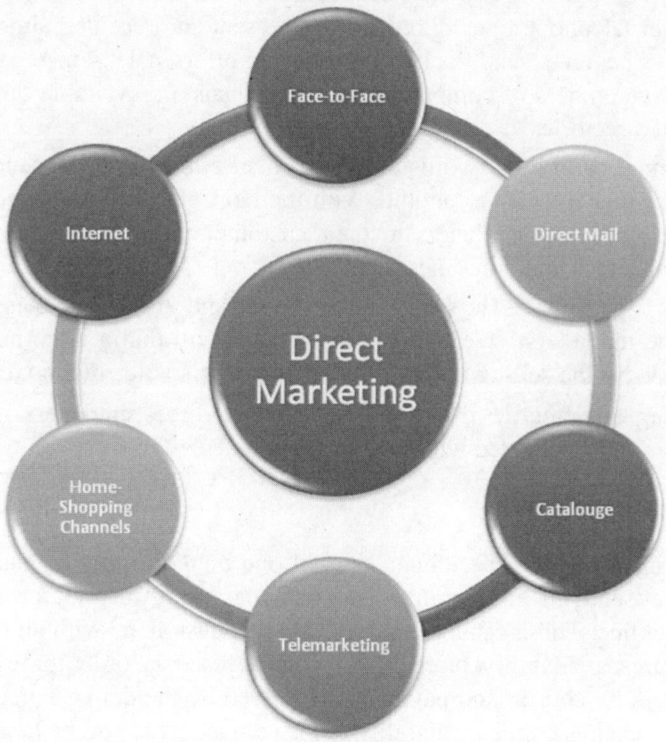

Figure 15.2 Major channels of direct marketing.

15.3.1 Face-to-Face Selling

This is the original and the oldest form of direct marketing. In this case the salesperson with products in hand would like to go and meet his customers personally. He will make the sales presentation, give the live demonstration of the product if possible, handle the various objections of the customers satisfactorily, and would like to finally sell the product to them. These days most of the companies hire professional salespeople for face-to-face selling. It is expected of them to locate prospects, develop them into customers, and grow the business. Some of the success stories of face-to-face selling are: Avon, Amway, and Tupperware.

15.3.2 Direct Mail

Direct mail marketing involves sending an offer, announcement, reminder, catalogue or other item to a person at a particular address through mail. Using highly selective mailing list, direct marketers send out millions of letters, flyers, fold outs, audiotapes, video tapes and CDs to prospective customers. It is a popular medium because through this the marketer can send personalised messages to the target audience. Although the cost per person works out to be quite high in direct mail as majority of the consumers treats this as junk and throws this in garbage bin. Moreover the success of direct mail depends to a very large extent on the efficiency of the postal and courier services. Until recently direct marketers used simply paper mail, but these days other forms of mail delivery are being used by them, such as:

1. **Fax mail:** Where marketers use fax machines to send a paper based message to their customers over telephone lines. Fax mail can be sent and received almost instantaneously. Marketers have begun to send fax mail announcing offers, sales, and events to prospects and customers. Fax numbers of companies and individuals are available through yellow pages and published directories.
2. **E-mail:** E-mail or in other words electronic mail allows users to send a message or file from one computer directly to another with the help of Internet connectivity. E-mails are being sent regularly by marketers to their customers announcing sales, discount offers, promotional schemes and other messages.
3. **Voice mail:** Voice mail is the system for receiving and storing oral messages at a telephone address. Some marketers have setup programs that will dial a large number of telephone numbers and leave the selling message in the recipient's voice mailboxes.

In constructing an effective direct mail campaign, direct marketers must decide on the objectives which are to be achieved with the target audience effectively.

15.3.3 Catalogue Marketing

Catalogue marketing occurs when companies mail one or more product catalogues to selected customers. They may send full-line merchandise catalogues usually in print form but also sometimes as CDs, videos or online. These catalogues try to provide customers with all the details about the products-their features, availability, price etc. Customers place the order through phone and goods are delivered to them by courier and payment is received by the delivery man. The success of a catalogue business depends on the availability of the contact details of the target audience and the efficiency with which the goods are delivered to the customers.

15.3.4 Telemarketing

Telemarketing describes the use of telephone operators to attract new customers, to contact existing customers, to ascertain satisfaction levels, or to take orders. Many customers routinely order goods and services by telephone. Some telemarketing systems are fully automated. Automatic dialling and recorded message players can dial numbers; play voice activated advertising message; and take orders from interested customers on an answering machine device or by forwarding the call to an operator.

Effective telemarketing depends on choosing the right person to make the telephone call, train them well, and provide them with performance incentives. Telemarketers should have pleasant voices and project enthusiasm. They should understand that the call should be made at the right time and they must understand as to how to end the conversation on a pleasant note.

15.3.5 At-Home Shopping Channels

Some television channels are dedicated to selling goods and services. Home shopping network, which broadcasts 24 hours a day, consists of the program's hosts offering bargain prices on such products as household appliances, jewellery, cloths, etc. All the details about the products are provided to the viewers along with the feedback from the customers who have already been using the product. Viewers call in their orders on a toll-free number and receive delivery within 48 hours.

15.3.6 Online Marketing

The most recent form of direct marketing is online marketing. It uses Internet technology to attain marketing objectives. It is one of the recent developments in the field of marketing. It has increased the horizon of the marketers and has provided them with a broader platform to operate. It can be defined as achieving marketing objectives through the use of electronic communications technology such as: Internet, e-mail, E-books, database, and mobile phone.

E-marketing or online marketing is taking the help of digital technologies which form online channels, such as, web-sites, e-mail, databases etc. to provide information to the consumers, handle their doubts and queries, procure orders, receive payments, and deliver goods through courier.

Online marketing consists primarily of the distributing, buying, selling, marketing, and servicing of products or services over electronic systems such as the Internet and other computer networks. Through online marketing, only information is exchanged or an order is placed. Actual delivery of physical products is made through different delivery systems (like post, Courier, and person) with appropriate mode of transportation. Goods are delivered to the consumers and the final payment is collected from them either through credit card or through cash on delivery.

From the discussion in the above paragraphs, certain unique features of online marketing have emerged. Some of the important ones are listed as under:

15.4 KEY SUCCESS FACTORS IN ONLINE MARKETING

Over the years online marketing has picked up tremendously in our country. According to 2012 CRISIL Report, Indian online retail industry will grow from ₹32 billion in 2012 to projected revenue of ₹100 billion in 2015. There will be over 180 million users in India with access to online retail by 2015. Counting on this potential growth, lots of ecommerce brands are trying to lure the

Indian consumer with their offerings ranging from fashion and lifestyle, to books and gadgets, and much more. Some of the popular online retail sites are Myntra, Ebay, Flipkart, Yebhi, Jabong, Babyoye, OLX, Quikr, 99 Acres etc. Indian e retail report 2012 has also provided us with certain interesting observations regarding the growing popularity of online shopping.

The Scope for Digital Marketing in India

The scope of digital marketing in 2020 and 2021 has seen drastic growth as India has the 2nd largest number of Internet users in the world. By 2023, the number of active Indian Internet users will grow to almost 666 million. Thus, this clearly indicates that a significant percentage of people are shifting online and it makes complete sense to start marketing online. In light of the COVID-19 pandemic, businesses are relying on digital marketing now more than ever. According to GlobalData, the growth of the Indian e-commerce market is pushing to ₹ 7 trillion by 2023 due to the lockdowns. With every consumer locked down in their homes, all traditional marketing efforts are out of the question. Businesses that didn't even have a social media page will now have to speed up their digital transformation and design a digital strategy to communicate with their audiences. The growth that we have witnessed on the Internet over the years especially since Covid, is here to stay. People are adapting to the new normal and in fact are now very comfortable with carrying out things online, be it for shopping, ordering food or medicines, or even carrying out banking transactions online! Hence, to cater to these new-formed demands of the consumers, digital marketing is extremely essential. In addition to this, an important aspect to consider is that the future generation will already be a part of the digital world and will be accustomed to everything being online. So to be able to deliver to these future consumers, companies must make digital marketing efforts starting today. All this clearly highlights on the growing importance of digital marketing.

Source: https://iide.co/blog/scope-of-digital-marketing/

Questions for Discussion

1. Do you believe in the growth of online marketing in India? Cite some of the reasons for the growth of online marketing from your perspective.
2. Give examples of few companies who have done well in the field of online marketing.

Several factors have contributed towards the success of any e-commerce venture. They may include:

15.4.1 Providing Better Service and Performance to Customers

Online marketing sites offer a responsive, user friendly purchasing experience, quite similar to personal selling.

15.4.2 Providing an Attractive Website

The tasteful use of colour, graphics, animation, photographs, fonts, and whitespace percentage may help in setting up attractive websites and catching the attention of the prospective buyers.

15.4.3 Providing Personal Attention

Personalised websites, purchase suggestions, and personalised special offers are an added attraction of the e-commerce.

15.4.4 Providing an Incentive for Customers to Buy

Through online marketing, marketers generally provide various sales promotions incentives, such as, coupons, special offers, and discounts, in order to give an extra incentive to them to purchase online.

15.4.5 Providing Value to Customers

Companies can provide value to customers by offering them products at competitive prices, as their online campaign is mostly hidden from the competitors.

15.4.6 Convenience in Shopping

Online marketing provides the consumers with a 24 × 7 access to the market. They can shop any time at their convenience. It also saves them from travelling long distances, traffic problems, and parking problems.

15.4.7 Effective Consumer Targeting

Targeting by behaviour, location, time, site, and site content is readily possible online. This tends to be more targeted compared to most off-line media.

15.4.8 Better Accountability

It is straightforward in online and easy to track response in comparison to the off-line which turns out to be expensive and error prone.

15.4.9 Detailed Information

The detailed information to support a decision can only be cost effectively delivered online.

15.4.10 Demonstration Effect

It is the best medium for demonstration and education as it is very convenient for the organisation to provide detailed information and demonstration of the product through their website.

15.4.11 Establishing Good Image

Online marketing can be used for establishing good image or improving bad image. By personal contact, it is possible to establish or improve brand image, and company's reputation.

15.4.12 More Interactive Experience

Online communications are always more interactive as they ensure two-way communication. They are considered closest to personal selling.

15.4.13 Personalised Communication

Online is the best medium to send personalised messages to the consumers as it is more straightforward. It even provides the opportunity of spreading word-of-mouth messages through various social networking sites.

In order to prove all the above points we would like to incorporate certain real life examples as given under.

Top Marketing Trends to Watch in 2022

Sooraj Balakrishnan (2021), Head of Marketing, Acer India conducted a research and stated the facts that after the months of wide-ranging customer response to COVID-19, marketers have gained some insights into the marketing trends that are working in this new normal. The ongoing pandemic has strongly affected the functioning of the businesses. More and more goods and services are being sold online. Months of wide-ranging customer responses to COVID-19 have given us some insights into the marketing trends that are working in this new normal and what can be expected in 2022. Some of the important ones are listed as under:

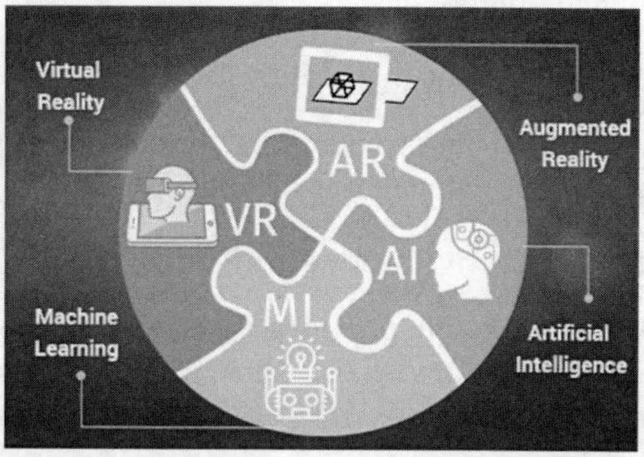

1. Conversational marketing: As trust and brand loyalty are becoming more connected, conversational marketing with the help of digital platforms is going to be an important factor in a successful marketing strategy. At every touch point consumers should be able to talk to the brand and get a response, which lives upto his fair expectation. So it becomes important for marketers to ensure that their business's contact intelligence is easy to find. Also, Chatbot—AI technology is continuing to lead the future of marketing as they cater to any number of consumers at one time. Having said this human touch is always more important than machines. Every customer-care department needs to have regular conversation and make customer feel part of the brand.

2. Machine-led Disruption: Artificial Intelligence and Machine Intelligence are the buzziest terms, used by every brand and marketers alike in today's world in managing their media planning and buying. These technologies help marketers in sending personalized messages to their target audience through focused media platforms.

3. Visual/Experiential: With Augmented Reality/Virtual Reality/Mixed Reality evolving rapidly in this new world order of experiences from home, it is important for marketers to take a serious look at these technologies for the promotion of their brands. They have to learn to use these technologies in creating the content, which is more relatable to their consumers besides advertising on different platforms.

4. Brand Transparency and Social Consciousness: In this digital world, transparency on social media is more important than ever before. Social media acts as a medium for brands to directly engage with their consumers, people are seeking out brands they can trust more frequently, so being transparent will help the brand to gain the trust of more users. By being transparent and socially conscious, a brand can deliver a message to consumers that they want to hear, and come across as honest.

5. Data privacy and respect: As for marketers, data is gold but; as for customers' privacy is the most valuable commodity in the online space. It is important for marketers to respect privacy and use customer data judiciously. It should never invade customer privacy or come across as intrusive or overburdening.

2022 will be the year to seize opportunities, lead from the front, learn from the crisis and be ready for the new customer behavioral trends emerging from this.

Source: https://brandequity.economictimes.indiatimes.com/be-blogs/marketing/4732

Questions for Discussion

1. What are your observations regarding the growth of online marketing in India?
2. What role does social media play in the growth of online marketing?

15.5 CHALLENGES IN IMPLEMENTING ONLINE MARKETING IN INDIA

Online marketing has been growing in India at a pace slower than what was expected of it due to various challenges. Some of the important ones are listed as under:

15.5.1 Failure to Understand the Basic Psyche of Indian Customers

Why they buy and how they buy—the reason why e-commerce is not able to pick up very well in Indian context is the basic psyche of Indian consumers. In India, most of the purchases are made after the physical examination of the product, "the touch and feel factor", plays a very important role in the final decision to purchase a product, which is missing to a great deal in case of online purchases. There is a social aspect of shopping as well, some people enjoy dressing up, going to market, talking to sales staff, to other shoppers, and to bargain, all this is not there in online buying.

15.5.2 Female Factor

Without indulging in any kind of gender bias, we would like to highlight another important aspect of buying behaviour in India. Here majority of the purchase decisions are made by the lady of the house, who is not e-literate in most of the cases, or does not have an access to online buying sites, or does not have the knowledge to purchase goods online.

15.5.3 Market Adoption and Demographics

In India markets are not yet ripe for the concept of purchasing something online. As the major part of our consumers is in the middle age-group, these people are not comfortable with the idea of online purchases. They do not trust most of the e-commerce sites and their payment systems.

15.5.4 Low Penetration Rate of Internet Access

In developing countries like India where majority of the poor households do not have an access to internet connectivity, it greatly reduces the potential for ecommerce.

15.5.5 High Cost of Acquiring Customer

The cost of acquiring customers and retaining those customers' is very high in India due to the low rate of customers coming directly to the site. Companies have to spend a huge amount on e-advertising and spreading awareness through various social networking sites.

15.5.6 Low Loyalty and Low Rate of Repeat Purchases on Net

Despite the fact that Indian market is very large and a major percentage of population is in the age group of 16–45, which constitutes a large segment of prospective consumer segment for the online sellers, but still the big brands have yet to be created on the net and cultivate high brand loyalty. Majority of the consumers on net are currently bargain hunters. They do not show much loyalty and generally do not turn up for repeat purchases. This has been one of the major reasons, which has stuck the popular sites like Snapdeal or Flipkart.

15.5.7 Cash on Delivery (COD)

Cash on delivery has been the major factor contributing towards the success of e-commerce in India as it has been able to counter the low credit card penetration and security issues on the internet. But COD is unsustainable in the long run as it pushes up the cost of transaction by ₹30–60 depending on the courier service thereby eroding the profitability. Another problem in this case is that of high returns as the consumers often change their mind by the time the goods arrive resulting in the returns which are generally 40–50 per cent of all the COD transactions.

15.5.8 High Capital Requirement

The capital requirement for setting up and maintaining any e-commerce venture is very high due to technological costs and lower initial margins contrary to the popular belief that it is economical to set up an e-commerce site. There is a huge investment involved in promoting the site, giving incentives to the customers to lure them to that site and retaining their interest for repeat purchases.

15.5.9 High Inventory Cost due to Poor Supply Chains

Most of the e-commerce companies generally complain that they have to invest a huge amount of money in maintaining sufficient inventory levels because of the unpredictability of the supply chains. This directly adds to their inventory costs and costs of running and maintaining their business.

15.5.10 Becoming the Victim of Organised Crime

Lots of customers are scared of buying goods online because they do not want to become the victims of organised crime as lots of frauds are taking place on the net.

15.5.11 Concerns about Security

Many people will not use credit cards over the Internet due to concerns about theft and fraud.

15.5.12 Lack of Instant Gratification with most E-Purchases

Much of a customer's reward for purchasing a product lies in the instant gratification of using and displaying that product. This reward does not exist when one's purchase does not arrive for days or weeks.

To summarise, I would like to insist on one thing that none of the issues mentioned above are insurmountable. These are simply the implementational problems which can be taken care of by careful planning and futuristic thinking. There is tremendous scope existing in this field and I am quite hopeful that in the years to come we will be able to overcome these hardships and make the most of the opportunities provided by e-commerce.

15.6 GUIDELINES FOR EFFECTIVE IMPLEMENTATION OF ONLINE MARKETING

In order to effectively use online marketing strategies marketers in India especially have to follow certain guidelines. Some of the important ones are listed as under and depicted in Figure 15.3.

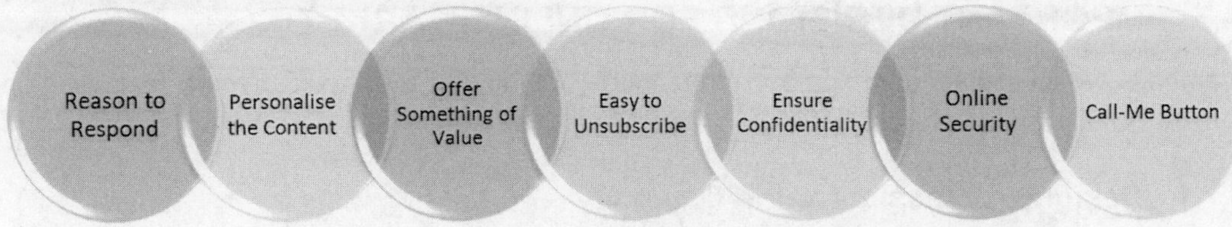

Figure 15.3 Effective implementation of online marketing.

15.6.1 Give the Customer a Reason to Respond

Companies should always offer surfer's powerful incentives for reading e-mail pitches and online ads.

15.6.2 Personalise the Content of Your E-Mail

It is always better to give a personal touch to the e-mails sent to the customers online as it helps in developing more affinity with the product.

15.6.3 Offer Something the Customer could not get via Direct Mail or Off-Line

The deal which is offered online should always be made more lucrative to the consumers in comparison to what is being offered off-line, so that there should be an incentive for them to buy online.

15.6.4 Advertise through Television and other Mediums

These days most of the online shopping sites are spending a huge amount on advertising through television and other popular mediums to catch the attention of the target audience and inform them about their unique features.

15.6.5 Ensure Confidentiality

Customers should always be given the feeling that the information provided by them will be kept confidential and will not to be misused by the firm.

15.6.6 Online Transactions should be Secure

It is always important to ensure the security of transactions online. Provisions regarding the security in the use of credit card online should always be executed properly.

15.6.7 Call-me-Button

Some sites include a call me button on which the customer can click and can get an answer to all their queries and questions. Customer service representatives can in principle respond quickly to these messages.

15.7 IMPORTANT DECISIONS FOR ONLINE MARKETING

A company which is planning to go for online marketing have to take such an important decisions, some of the important ones are listed as under:

15.7.1 Designing Website for the Company

The first and the foremost important work which a company has to perform for going online is to carefully design an attractive website. The website must include the necessary webpages that must be linked with the home page. Normally, websites include the details about the company name, address, registered office, phone numbers, fax and e-mail address, products and detailed features of each of the product, price list and related incentives, special achievements, and other relevant information. Website must be designed carefully in an attractive, convenient, and professional manner so that the consumers can have an easy access to the needed details.

15.7.2 Designing Web Address

When the website is ready, it must be given its name or address. It is known as URL-Universal Resource Locator. The address must be set carefully. It must not be too long or too short. It must also be meaningful and easy to remember. It should indicate the type of business the company is in and the name of the country or the place. In short, address must be short, attractive, meaningful and simple.

15.7.3 Presence in Search Engines and Directories

Once the Web is ready, it must be entered into search engines, and directories so that web visitors can find it easily and have access to the information regarding the company. There are many search engines like Google, Yahoo search, MSN search, etc. The address must be present in all the search engines. In the same way, many directories are available like business, art, medical, publication, employment, film, sports, government, education, science and technology, etc. website must be placed in suitable directories.

15.7.4 Advertising the Website

As we all know nothing sells unless and until a specific effort is made to sell. So in order to make the website known to all, it must be properly advertised. Attempts must be made to popularise the website. In some way, Web address must be communicated in advertising the product through different mediums.

15.7.5 Monitoring and Updating

Once the website is successfully launched on the Internet, it must be constantly monitored for updates. Expert staff can be maintained to handle the website. Regulating and updating website can meet the changing needs of the company as well as the market.

So we can conclude that online marketing is not free from its own set of problems. Keeping the current scenario into account it is comparatively very difficult for online marketers to ensure the success of their website and earn profits. But in the time to come with lots of changes expected in the consumers profile we can expect the online marketing to be doing very well.

LET US SUM UP

- Direct marketing is an interactive marketing system that uses one or more advertising media to affect a measurable response from the target audience.
- Consumers can do comparative shopping through direct marketing by browsing through mail catalogues and online shopping services. It saves their time and introduces them to a larger selection of merchandise.
- Marketers also benefit from direct marketing as they can personalise and customise their messages for their prospective customers. It can help them build a continuous relationship with each customer.
- Direct marketers can use a number of channels for reaching prospects and customers, such as, face-to-face selling, direct mail, catalogues, telemarketing, at-home shopping channels and online.
- Online marketing can be defined as achieving marketing objectives through the use of electronic communications technology such as: Internet, e-mail, E-books, database, and mobile phone.
- Through online marketing, only information is exchanged or an order is placed. Actual delivery of physical products is made through different delivery systems (like post, Courier, and person) with appropriate mode of transportation. Goods are delivered to the consumers and the final payment is collected from them either through credit card or through cash on delivery.
- Several factors have contributed towards the success of any e-commerce venture, such as, better service and performance to customers, providing personal attention, an incentive for customers to buy, and more value to them.
- Due to several reasons, the e-commerce business has grown at a slow pace, examples include, the problem of access to Web commerce, failure to understand customers, lack of instant gratification with most e-purchases, and the social aspect of shopping.
- In order to effectively use online marketing strategies marketers in India especially have to follow certain guidelines, some of the important ones are: give the customer a reason to respond, offer something the customer could not get via direct mail or off-line, ensure confidentiality, and security of online transactions.
- A company which is planning to go for online marketing have to take such an important decisions, as designing the website for the company and its Web address, ensuring the presence in search engines and directories, advertising the website and regulating and updating website in order to meet the changing needs of the company as well as the market.

QUESTIONS TO CHECK YOUR PROGRESS

Short Answer Questions

1. Define direct marketing as given by Direct Marketing Association.
2. List out three unique features of direct marketing.
3. Why is direct marketing important for customers?
4. Why is it significant for marketers?
5. What is teleshopping?
6. What is online marketing?
7. List out five main reasons for the growing importance of online marketing.
8. Name any specific problem being faced by online marketers in India.

9. Give two examples of products, which have been sold successfully through online marketing.
10. Name any two steps that are required to be taken to add to the popularity of online marketing in India.

Long Answer Questions

1. "Direct marketing provides goods to customers at cheaper rates because it is able to do away with middlemen," do you agree with the statement explain in the light of benefits of direct marketing to consumers.
2. "Direct marketing is equally advantageous to the marketers," list of the various reasons in support of your answer.
3. Explaining the concept of direct marketing. How is direct marketing different from marketing through middlemen?
4. What is the role of various channels in direct marketing? Explain with the help of suitable examples from the current scenario.
5. Examine the scope of online marketing in India.
6. What is Internet marketing? What is its significance for business organisations and consumers?
7. Examine the significance of e-commerce for business organisations, for consumers and the economy.
8. If a producer creates a really revolutionary new product and consumers can learn about it and purchase it at a website on the Internet, is any additional marketing effort really necessary? Explain your point of view.
9. What are some of the advantages and disadvantages of using Internet for shopping?
10. Discuss the benefits of direct marketing to customers and companies and the trends fuelling its rapid growth.
11. Online shopping through websites makes it possible for individual consumers to get direct information from hundreds of companies they would not otherwise know about. Will growth of online marketing services ultimately eliminate the need for retailers and wholesalers?
12. Online marketing offers great promises for the future. As you are the sales manager for a consumer product company selling ready-made garments make a case that would persuade your superiors that going online would be a good investment. Given the potential positive and negative outcomes.

CHAPTER 16

Consumerism

Learning Outcomes

After studying this chapter, you will be able to:

- ❖ Define the concept of consumerism and the reasons for the consumerism movement in India
- ❖ Determine the reasons for the failure of consumerism in India
- ❖ Discuss the measures available for consumer protection
- ❖ Identify the basic objectives of voluntary organisation
- ❖ Explain the laws for protecting consumers
- ❖ Understand the functioning of the Consumer Protection Act 1986

Business is not an end in itself but a means for human welfare. What is good for the public is good for the business but not vice versa. That is one of the reasons that most of the businesses have started focusing more on their profitability and neglecting their social responsibilities. Government of India is committed to a socialistic pattern of society which ensures growth and social justice to all. Moreover business people make use of public money so it becomes their responsibility to protect and promote the welfare of the public. The **Gandhian principle of trusteeship** has also stressed upon the inherent responsibilities of business to its customers and others. According to **Gandhiji**—

> *Customer is the most important visitor on our premises he is not a hindrance in our work, rather he is the purpose of it. We are not doing him a favour by serving him rather he is doing us a favour by letting us serve him.*

According to **Peter F. Drucker** (1990) one of the renowned management scholar—

> *There is only one valid definition of business purpose: to create a customer. It is the customer who determines what business is. The customer is the foundation of business and keeps it in existence and it is to satisfy the customer that society entrusts wealth producing resources to a business enterprise.*

Despite such noble thoughts being shared by such noble people, we all understand that consumer is one segment which is highly exploited by manufacturers and marketers for their selfish interests. It is mainly because of this reason that the consumerism movement has come up in a big way. Consumerism as a movement started in way back in sixties in most of the developed nations, but in our country the pace of consumerism has been very slow. This is mainly due to the fact that majority of consumers in our country are uneducated, uninformed, and indifferent. They are practically at the mercy of the marketers. Consumerism is a social movement against malpractices indulged by marketers. It is basically the movement to protect consumer rights and interests.

Need for consumerism has been felt mainly because of the fact that the consumer orientation even till date is not being practised by most of the business houses. These concepts are practically on paper, because in actual reality majority of the manufacturers are still practising the product orientation. The manufacturers prefer to produce products which can be conveniently made and try to sell them off to consumers by hook or by crook. So consumerism is not just to fight against traders to protect consumers' rights, but it is also important to educate consumers for their rights. It is aimed at increasing consumer awareness, enforcing government to exercise meaningful control over business activities, and to inspire independent social organisations to participate actively in this regard. Even though the spread of consumerism has been slow a shift is taking place from **Caveat Emptor** the philosophy of let the buyer beware to **Caveat Vendor** where the focus is on let the seller be aware.

The term consumerism has been defined by different people as under:

Richard H. Buskirk and James Bushkirk have defined consumerism as—

> *An organised effort of consumers seeking redress, restitution and remedy for dissatisfaction they have accumulated in the acquisition of their standard of living.*

Philip Kotler's (1999) perspective on consumerism is that—

> *It is not limited to organised efforts only but, is a social movement seeking to augment the rights and powers of buyers in relation to sellers.*

So from both the definitions it is quite evident that consumerism is a movement, it is a conscious effort which is to be made by the government, social organisations, and various consumer bodies to protect the interest of consumers. This not only includes protecting the consumers from exploitation but also recommends educating them and making them more aware about their rights. The former president of USA **Mr. John F. Kennedy** talked about the four basic rights of consumers—the right to safety, right to be informed, the right to choose and the right to be heard. Our Constitution has also SIX fundamental rights to the consumers, as depicted in Figure 16.1, such as, right to education, right to choose, right to be informed, right to safety, right to be heard, and right to redress. From all this it can be concluded that it is very important to ensure the safety of consumers' rights and their proper implementation. "Jago Grahak Jago" and many more such movements are some small initiatives which have been taken in this direction.

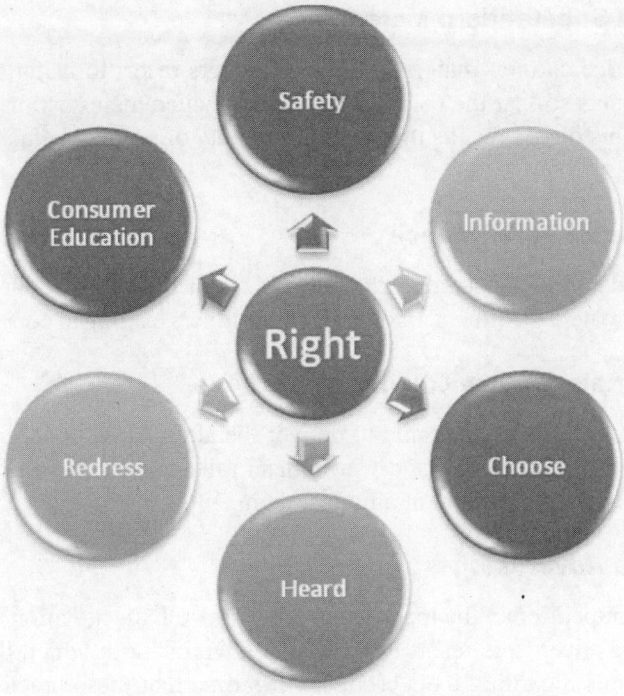

Figure 16.1 Fundamental rights of consumers.

16.1 REASONS FOR CONSUMERISM MOVEMENT

The various reasons because of which the need for a movement called consumerism has been felt are listed as under:

16.1.1 Illiteracy

Majority of consumers in India are uneducated and uninformed about various product choices. Most of them are not aware about products, their ingredients, price, and related services. If they are not protected, they can be easily cheated.

16.1.2 Poverty and Lack of Information

Provide the traders an easy platform to mislead the consumers. It has been one of the most important reasons for consumers being exploited by marketers in India as a sizeable percentage of India's population still resides under the poverty line.

16.1.3 Rising Prices

With growing rate of inflation over the last several years, prices of most of the products have been constantly increasing putting tremendous burden on the lower and middle income group of consumers. There has been constant resentment on the part of such consumer segment resulting in the emergence of consumerism movements.

16.1.4 Supply of Substandard Materials

In order to ensure price cutting, majority of the marketers resort to using substandard materials for making the products so that they should be able to reduce their cost of production and make profits there in. All this finally results in an inferior quality of product being made available to the consumers.

16.1.5 Poor Product Performance

Most of the time products do not stand by the features claimed by them. Poor product performance generally results in greater resentment amongst the consumers leading to consumerism movements.

16.1.6 Inappropriate Service Quality

So many times the marketers are not able to deliver the after sales services promised by them or they are not able to fulfil guarantees and warranties to the consumers which is again one of the important reasons leading to resentment amongst them.

16.1.7 Deceptive Advertising

Due to intensified competition in the markets, in order to catch the attention of the target audience most of the times the advertisers resort to deceptive advertising in which they make misleading and exaggerated claims regarding their products. It's time that these practices of marketers and advertisers should also be checked.

16.1.8 Inappropriate Packaging

Also plays a very important role in misleading and misguiding the consumers. Marketers intentionally use inflated packages for their products to give a wrong impression to the consumers. For example in case of, Kellogg's cornflakes the package is made to look so big and grand while the actual content inside does not justify the size of the package.

16.1.9 Faulty Measurement of Weights

At times the weight mentioned on the package is also not appropriate. For example the weight mentioned is 1 kg while in actual the content is 900 g.

16.1.10 Artificial Scarcity

Marketers at times create an artificial scarcity of the commodity in the market in order to inflate their prices. This is highly unethical and needs to be curbed immediately.

16.1.11 Black Marketing

As mentioned earlier when an artificial scarcity of commodities is created it directly results in hoarding and black-marketing. All this results in increased prices to the consumers for essential commodities putting in that extra financial burden.

16.1.12 Adulteration

Indian markets are still dominated by traders therefore consumers are more likely to be cheated by them for adulteration.

16.1.13 Global Markets

Now, Indian markets have become global markets. Because of liberalisation, privatisation, and globalisation there has been lots of disinvestments, privatisation policies of the government, and attacks of multinational companies on Indian markets. So this borderless trade throughout the globe has confused consumers resulting in an important role being played by consumerism to awaken the consumers for their rights and to help them fight against undesirable marketing practices indulged by Indian and foreign marketers.

16.1.14 Confusion in Markets

With tremendous growth in science and technology, especially in information technology, and excessive market promotional activities, consumers are generally found lost. They seemed confused. Consumerism can serve as a guide to assist them to protect their interests by helping them make suitable buying decisions.

Increased product awareness for consumers has to be widely practised as a remedy to all these problems.

Certain examples asking for consumerism movement

1. Toothpaste tubes are filled with air at the other end.
2. On a package of biscuits, one finds more packaging material than the quantity of biscuits.
3. 1 litre of milk contains 40 per cent of water and packed and labelled as pure milk.
4. One kg of sugar packet weighs only 970 g whereas labelled as net weight one kg.
5. Actual rate of LPG cylinder is always found lower than what it should be.

16.2 PROBLEMS LEADING TO FAILURE OF CONSUMERISM

Though consumerism has a vital role to play in a developing economy like ours to ensure consumer awakening against any kind of unfair trade practices and educating them for their rights, its pace has been very slow. Needless to state that consumerism has not been very successful in India. At present, our consumers are still cheated; substandard and duplicate products are constantly over flooded in the market; erotic, senseless, and misleading advertisements are still exhibited openly through mass media; non-profit voluntary social organisations have not been found very effective; and partial failure of government machinery to implement the laws formulated to protect consumers. There are legal provisions, but not effectively and adequately implemented. Due to an inadequate role of consumerism, it can be said that consumerism is in its initial stages in India. Failure of consumerism can be attributed to following reasons:

- **Inactive, lethargic**, and submissive nature of Indian consumers.

- **Poverty, illiteracy,** lack of reliable information, and inadequate supply of certain essential products.
- **Lack of social sensitisation** amongst buyers and sellers.
- **Lack of willingness** to fulfil social responsibility or social obligation on the part of the business people.
- **Inadequate role** of voluntary organisations.
- **Lengthy, tedious, and less reliable** legal procedures. Utter delays in the court verdict or judgement.
- **Senseless, excessive, and short-sighted** liberalisation and privatisation policies and practices of government.
- **Poor and inefficient role** of public sectors.
- **Failure of the government** to implement the laws and legal provisions successfully.

16.3 MEASURES FOR CONSUMER PROTECTION

Consumer can be protected mainly by three ways as projected in Figure 16.2:

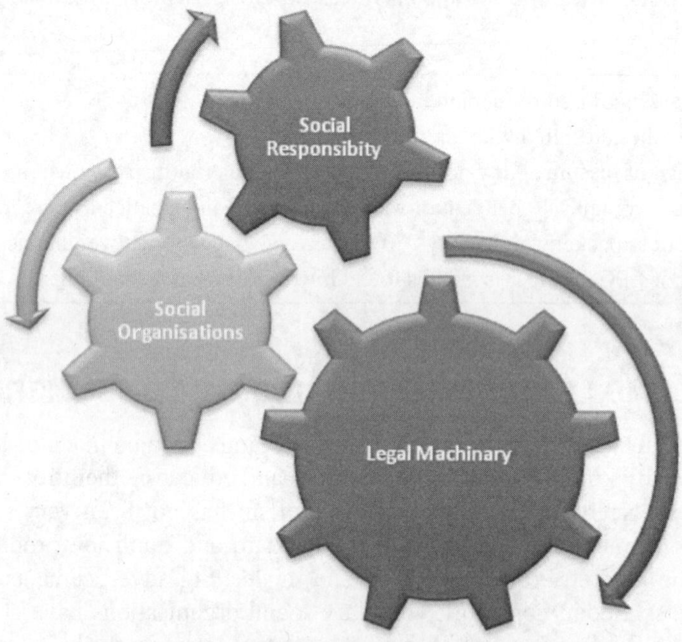

Figure 16.2 Measures for consumer protection.

1. When marketers consciously decide to **fulfil their social responsibility** towards consumer and do not resort to unethical practices.
2. When control over the undesirable activities of the markets is exercised with the help of various **voluntary organisations**, such as, the consumerism movement.

3. When **government exercises statuary control** over the illegal activities of the marketers with the help of an effective legal machinery.

The consciousness of business people does work in Indian scenario but we still have many marketers who do not fulfil their social responsibilities and profit turns out to be their major motive. In pursuit of making profits, they at times resort to such activities which call for the consumerism movement. Consumer movements picked up in India in the year 1965, when housewives of Bombay gave shape to a voluntary organisation called "**AWARE**" association of women against rising expenses. It was set up for consumer education, protection and representation. Some other voluntary organisations which are working for the constant protection of consumers are:

- Indian Federation of consumer organisations
- National consumer protection council
- Non government organisations (NGOs) etc.

Most of these voluntary organisations are working with certain basic objectives, such as:

16.3.1 Basic Objectives of Voluntary Organisations

- **Spreading education** and making people aware of their rights.
- **Ensuring an alert** and informed consumer.
- **Keeping an indirect check** over the activities of marketers and advertisers.
- **Making the better quality products** made available to consumers at reasonable prices.
- **Self-regulation** on the part of the marketers.
- **Arranging for centre and state governments support** to various consumer protection movements.
- **Legalisation of consumer** protection.
- **Ensuring a strict legal framework** which can ensure speedy redressal of grievances.

Even though these social organisations are trying to contribute towards consumerism movement in India, their efforts are not sufficient to keep a check on the un-ethical practices being followed by corrupt marketers and advertisers. It is because of this reason that our Constitution has provided us with strong legal machinery. There are lots of laws and acts passed from time to time to protect the interests of consumers. Most of these laws have been amended from time to time to meet changing situations. Some of the important ones are listed as under:

16.4 SEVERAL LAWS FOR CONSUMER PROTECTION

(a) The Sale of Goods Act 1930 which provides some safeguards to buyers of goods in case goods do not fulfil the express or implied conditions and warranties.

(b) Drugs Control Act, 1940.

(c) The Industries (Development and Regulation) Act, 1951.

(d) The Prevention of Food Adulteration Act, 1954.

(e) The Essential Commodities Act 1955 whose objective is to control the interest of the general public, with the production, supply and distribution of trade and commerce in certain commodities declared essential.

(f) The Trade and Merchandise Marks act 1958 tries to seek the registration and better protection of trademarks and to prevent the use of fraudulent marks on merchandise.

(g) The Monopolies and Restrictive Trade Practices Act, 1969.

(h) The Patents Act, 1970.

(i) The Indian Contract Act 1982 which prescribes the conditions in which promises made by the parties to a contract (buyers and sellers) shall be legally binding on each other.

(j) The Standards of Weights and Measures Enforcement Act, 1985.

(k) The Consumer Protection Act, 1986

Despite all these, the status of consumers in India remains deplorable because of loopholes in many such laws.

16.5 THE CONSUMER PROTECTION ACT, 1986

Being the latest one in the legal machinery, the consumer protection act provides effective safeguards to consumers against defective goods, unsatisfactory services, unfair trade practices and other forms of exploitation. The act made provisions for establishment of proper machinery for the speedy settlement of consumer disputes and redressal of grievances. This act lays down a timeframe for disposal of cases. It provides for quick and inexpensive redress of grievances. Consumers do not have to hire lawyers they can make their own representations simply on a plain paper where no stamp duty is required or stamp paper is required. It covers all the six basic consumer rights already discussed. In the Act, three level redressal agencies work as judicial machineries to settle consumers' disputes, as depicted in Figure 16.3.

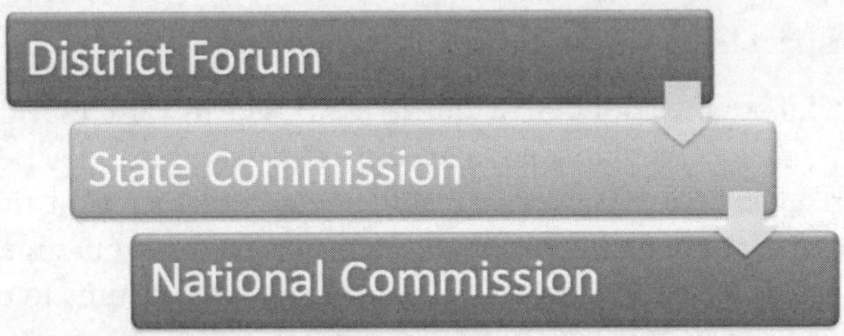

Figure 16.3 Three tier judicial machinery of CPA.

16.5.1 Judicial Machinery to Settle Consumer Disputes under CPA

(a) Consumer Dispute redressal Forum at the district level in each of the districts of every state (the District Forum).

(b) Consumer Dispute Redressal Commission at the state level in each state of the country (the State Commission).

(c) National Consumer Redressal Commission at the national level (the National Commission).

Level I—District Forum

Every State government has to establish by notification, under the Clause 10 to 15 of the Act a District Forum with prior approval of the Central government, in each district of the state. Important provisions are:

(i) The state government establishes district forum in each district. If government wishes, more than one district forum in each district can also be established.

(ii) The District Forum shall consist of person who is or has been qualified to be district judge nominated by state government. He is the president of such forum and two other members including a person who is eminent in education, trade and commerce, one of them shall be a lady.

(iii) The District Forum shall work as semi-judiciary machinery. It cannot issue the stay order.

(iv) Qualifications of other members should be: (as per the amendments 2002)

- Their age must not be less than 35 years.
- They must hold graduation degree from the recognised university.
- They must have required knowledge and at least 10 years experience to deal with matters related to economics, trade, commerce, law, accountancy, industry, and Public Administration.

Other provisions related to appointment of members in the district Forum:

- This act also specifies conditions under which one can be disqualified as a member. Appointment must be made as per the recommendations of committee appointed for the purpose (Clause 1A).
- One can continue as a member of the forum for five years or up to the age of 65 years whichever is earlier.
- Member can resign from the post by the handwritten application addressed to the state government.
- Members of the district forum are paid salary, honorarium, and other benefits as per the state government rules.

District Forum can entertain complaints against defects and deficiencies in goods and services whose value and compensation of the claim is less than ₹20 lakhs. The forum can order:

- To remove the defects.
- To replace the goods with new goods of similar description.
- To return the price to the complainant.
- To order the payment of compensation to the sufferer.

Level II—State Commission

Every State by a notification under Clause 16 of the Act with a prior approval of the Central government has to establish a state commission. As per 2002 amendments, following provisions have been made:

Each State Commission shall consist of

(i) A person who is or has been a judge of high court appointed by state government is the president of the commission.

(ii) Other members, not less than two and more than the limit specified, with qualifications, experience, and ability to deal with such matters like economics, law, commerce, etc., where one of them shall be a woman.

(iii) Qualifications of other members are:
- Their age must not be less than 35 years.
- They must hold graduation degree from the recognised university.
- They must be honest, intelligent and respectable having required knowledge and at least 10 years experience to deal with matters related to economics, trade, commerce, law, accountancy, industry, and Public Administration.

(iv) The State commission can entertain complaints where the value of the goods or services and compensation if any claimed exceeds ₹20 lakhs but does not exceed ₹1 crore and they can also entertain appeals against the orders of any District Forum within the state.

Level III—National commission

National consumer disputes redressal commission has been formed by a notification of the central government in August 1988.

National commission shall consist of:

(i) A person who is or has been a judge of the Supreme Court appointed by Central Government as the president of the commission.

(ii) Other members, not less than four with ability, experience, and knowledge to deal with problems relating to economics, law, commerce, accounting, industry, public affairs, etc., where one of them should be women.

(iii) The National commission can entertain complaints where value of the goods or services and compensation if any claimed exceeds ₹1 crore and they can also entertain appeals against the orders of any State commission.

16.6 SOME IMPORTANT PROVISIONS OF CPA

There are some important provisions related to consumer dispute redressal agencies. These are discussed as under:

16.6.1 Provisions for Complaints

The clause 12 specifies the manner in which complaint shall be made. As per Amendment 2002, one has to pay specified fees while registering the complaints with the district Forum. Within 21 days from the date of receipt of complaint, the Forum shall decide on whether to execute the complaint. Complainant is given a chance to put forward all the facts before the complaint is rejected.

16.6.2 What is a Complaint?

As per the act, 'complaint' means any allegation in writing made by a complainant that:

(i) an unfair trade practice or a restrictive trade practice has been adopted by any trader;

(ii) the goods bought by him or agreed to be bought by him suffer from one or more defects;

(iii) the service hired or availed of or agreed to be hired or availed of by him suffer from deficiency in any respect;

(iv) a trader has charged for the goods mentioned in the complaint a price in excess of the price fixed by or under any law for the time being in force or displayed on the goods or any package containing such goods with a view to gaining any relief provided under this act.

16.6.3 Who can Complain?

Under clause 2(B) of the act, a consumer, or one or more of the consumers when they hold common interest, or any voluntary consumer organisation registered under the Companies Act, 1956 or under any other law for the time being in force, or the Central government or any State government can make complaint. In case of consumer's death, the representative or the legal heir of the customer can also complain.

16.6.4 Jurisdiction of the Forums

Jurisdiction of each of the forum is determined by the value of goods or compensation contained in the complaints. A complaint with the value of compensation less than 20 lakhs to be dealt with the district Forum; in between 20 lakhs to 1 crore it shall be dealt with the State commission; and complaint involving more than 1 crore falls within the jurisdiction of the National commission.

16.6.5 Redressal of Dispute and Remedial Action by Forums

If any of the consumer dispute redressal agencies is satisfied with any of the allegations contained in the complaints, it shall issue an order to opposite party directing them to take one or more of the following actions such as:

- To remove the defects pointed out by appropriate laboratory from the goods.
- To replace goods with new goods of similar description, this shall be free from all defects.
- To return price to the complainants.
- To pay amounts to the consumers for any loss or injury suffered by the consumer due to the negligence of opposite party.

16.6.6 Provision of Appeal

Appeal against order of any District Forum can be made to the State Commission. Appeal against orders of State commission can be made with the National commission, and appeal against order of the National commission can be made with the Supreme Court. The time limit for appeal is 30 days from the judgement by any of the redressal agencies. However, for certain valid reasons, such time can be extended.

16.6.7 Legal Actions

If a trader person against whom a complaint is made fails or omits to comply with any order made by any of the redressal agencies, he shall be punishable with imprisonment for any term not exceeding three years or with a fine not exceeding ₹10,000 or with both.

So from the discussion taking place in the above-mentioned paragraphs we could gather the fact that the government and the legal machinery is trying to ensure a speedy redressal of the consumers' grievances. But the problem is that legislation alone cannot ensure protection and satisfaction of consumers. Whole hearted cooperation of consumers' association and business communities is also very important to effectively implement the various laws. Above all the most important fact is that consumer of today should act like a mature, informed, and conscious consumer and should be able to protect their own rights.

LET US SUM UP

- Government of India is committed to a socialistic pattern of society which ensures growth and social justice to all.
- Consumerism is a social movement against malpractices indulged by marketers. It is basically the movement to protect consumer rights and interests.
- Consumerism is not just to fight against traders to protect consumers' rights, but it is also important to educate consumers for their rights. It is aimed at increasing consumer awareness, enforcing government to exercise meaningful control over business activities, and to inspire independent social organisations to participate actively in this regard.
- It is very important to ensure the safety of consumers' rights and their proper implementation. "Jago Grahak Jago" and many more such movements are some small initiatives which have been taken in this direction.
- The various reasons because of which the need for a movement called consumerism has been felt are poverty and lack of information; rising prices; supply of substandard materials; deceptive advertising; creating artificial scarcity of the products, and black marketing etc.
- Consumerism has not been a great success in India mainly because of the indifferent attitude of the business people; in effective non-profit voluntary social organisations; and partial failure of government machinery to implement the laws formulated to protect consumers.
- There are lots of laws and acts passed from time to time to protect the interests of consumers. Most of these laws have been amended from time to time to meet changing situations.
- Being the latest one in the legal machinery, the consumer protection act provides effective safeguards to consumers against defective goods, unsatisfactory services, unfair trade practices and other forms of exploitation.
- It provides for quick and inexpensive redress of grievances. Consumers do not have to hire lawyers they can make their own representations simply on a plain paper where no stamp duty is required or stamp paper is required.
- In the Act, three level redressal agencies work as judicial machineries to settle consumers' disputes: District forum, State commission, and National commission.

- Legislation alone cannot ensure protection and satisfaction of consumers. Wholehearted cooperation of consumers' association and business communities is also very important to effectively implement the various laws.
- Above all the most important fact is that consumer of today should act like a mature, informed, and conscious consumer and should be able to protect their own rights.

QUESTIONS TO CHECK YOUR PROGRESS

Short Answer Questions

1. Explain the concept of consumerism.
2. List out five major reasons as to why the need for consumerism is felt.
3. Explain Coveat Emptor and Coveat Vendor.
4. What are the various fundamental rights of consumers?
5. Name the voluntary organisation which started consumer protection movement in Mumbai.
6. Name the act which gives protection to the brand name and the brand mark of the company.
7. List out five important acts regulating the practices of marketers.
8. List out the various levels of forums or agencies in consumer protection act.
9. Explain the two basic objectives with which the consumer protection act was formulated.
10. How feasible is self-regulation in consumerism?

Long Answer Questions

1. Define consumerism. Why do consumers need protection?
2. What are the underlying reasons for consumerism?
3. Are we going too far on consumerism? Explain.
4. Describe the need for consumer protection in India.
5. "Consumerism is a shame on marketing," comment upon the statement given by Peter F. Drucker.
6. Defend the statement, "consumerism is an opportunity rather than a threat."
7. Explain the remedies available to consumers in India against the supply of substandard and defective products.
8. Critically examine the consumer protection act, 1986.
9. Explain how the consumer protection act, 1986 seeks to regulate various marketing decisions in India.
10. Briefly explain as to how consumer interest is sought to be protected under the consumer protection act, 1986.
11. Briefly explain the machinery for the redressal of consumers grievances under the consumer protection act, 1986.

Glossary

Acculturation—The process by which people in one culture or subculture learn to understand and adapt to the norms, values, life styles and behaviours of people in another culture or sub-cultures. For example, acculturation is the process by which a recent immigrant learns the way of life of the new country.

Acquisition value—The users' perception of the relative worth of a product or service to them. Formally defined as the subjectively weighted difference between the maximum a buyer would be willing to pay for the product or service, less the actual price of the item.

Adopter categories—Persons or agencies that adopt an innovation are often classified into five groups according to the sequence of their adoption—innovators, early adopters, early majority, late majority and laggards. This is important when considering how long it may take for the general public to 'adopt' a product or service.

Advertising—The placement and purchase of announcements and persuasive messages in time or space, in any of the mass media by business firms, nonprofit organizations.

Agent—A channel institution which represents one or more suppliers for a fee.

Aggregation—A concept of market segmentation that assumes that most consumers are alike.

AIDA—A sequence of steps in various forms of promotion, notably personal selling and advertising, consisting of attracting attention, holding interest, arousing desire and generating buyer action.

Attitudes—Enduring systems of positive or negative evaluations, emotional feelings, and action tendencies with respect to an object. Consumer's overall liking or preference for an object (Assael).

Audience—The number and/or characteristics of the persons or households who are exposed to a particular type of advertising media or media vehicle.

Benefit segmentation—The process of grouping users into market segments on the basis of the desirable consequences sought from the product.

Brand—A name, term, design, symbol, or any other feature that identifies one seller's goods or services as distinct from those of other sellers. The legal term for brand is 'trademark'.

Broker—A channel institution which puts a specific buyer(s) and seller(s) in contact with one another in one or more commodity(ies) or service(s) with a view to achieve a sale or benefit.

Budget—The detailed financial component of the strategic plan that guides the allocation of resources and provides a mechanism for identifying deviations of actual from desired performance so that corrective action can be taken.

Channel conflict—A situation in which one channel member perceives another channel member to be acting in a way that prevents the first member from achieving its distribution objectives.

Channel control—The actions of a firm to regulate the behaviour of other companies in its distribution channel.

Channel of distribution—An organised network of agencies and institutions, which in a combination perform all the functions required to link producers with the end customers to accomplish the marketing task.

Channel power—The ability of a firm to influence or determine the behaviour of another channel member.

Chain store system—A group of retail stores of essentially the same type that are centrally owned and have some degree of centralized control of operation.

Competition—The rivalry among sellers trying to achieve such goals as increasing profits, market share and sales volume by varying the elements of the marketing mix—price, product, distribution and promotion.

Competitive strategy—The adoption of a specific target market and marketing mix stance in the market place.

Consumer—The ultimate user of goods, ideas or services.

Consumer behaviour—The behaviour of the consumer or decision maker in the market place of products and services.

Consumer characteristics—The demographic, lifestyle and personality characteristics of the consumer.

Consumer product—A product that is intended for purchase and use by household consumers for non-business purposes.

Consumer satisfaction—The degree to which a consumer's expectations are fulfilled or surpassed by a product.

Contractual vertical market system—An arrangement under which independent firms—producers, wholesalers, and retailers—operate under contracts specifying how they will operate in order to improve their distribution, efficiency and effectiveness.

Convenience product—A consumer good and/or service (such as soap, candy bar and shoe shine) that is bought frequently, often on impulse, with little time or effort spent on the buying process. A convenience product usually is low-priced and is widely available.

Convenience sample—A non-probability sample of individuals who just happen to be where the study is being conducted when it is being conducted.

Communication—The verbal or non-verbal transmission of information between someone wanting to express an idea and someone else expected or expecting to get that idea. The four elements are message, a source of the message, a communication channel and a receiver.

Copyright—A copyright offers the owner of the original work, that can be printed, recorded or 'fixed' in any manner, the sole right to reproduce and distribute the work, to display or perform it and to authorize other to do so, during the author's lifetime and for fifty years thereafter.

Core product—The central benefit or purpose for which a consumer buys a product or service. The core product varies from purchaser to purchaser.

Culture—The set of learned values, norms and behaviours that are shared by a society and are designed to increase the probability of the society's survival. These include shared superstitions, myths, folkways, mores and behaviour patterns that are rewarded or punished.

Customer—The actual or prospective purchaser of products or services.

Database—A compendium of information on current and prospective users that usually includes demographic data as well as use data, volume and content.

Demarketing—The process of reducing the demand for a product, or decreasing consumption.

Demographics—Objective characteristics of consumers such as age, income, education, sex or occupation (Assael).

Direct mail—One form of Direct Marketing in which firms mail to consumers—letters, brochures and even product samples, and ask them to purchase by mail or telephone.

Direct marketing—Marketing efforts, in total, directed toward a specific targeted group–direct selling, direct mail, catalog or cable for soliciting a response from the customer.

Distribution—The marketing and carrying of products to customers.

Distribution channel—An institution through which goods or services are marketed giving time and place utilities to users.

Economic environment—Part of the macro-environment encompassing wealth, income, productivity, inflation, credit, employment, etc., which affect the companie's markets and opportunities.

Environmental analysis—Gathering data regarding political, cultural, social, demographic, economic, legal, international and ecological forces, identifying trends affecting companies.

Environmental monitoring—Keeping track of changes in the environment.

Exchange—All activities associated with receiving something from someone by giving something voluntarily in return. This is the heart of the marketing process.

Exclusive distribution—A strategy in which a supplier agrees to sell its products only to a single wholesaling middleman or a retailer in a given market.

Expected price—The price at which customers consciously or unconsciously value the product.

Family—A group of at least two people in a household based on marriage, cohabitation, blood relationship or adoption.

Family life cycle—A sociological concept that describes changes in families across time, emphasizing the effects of marriage, divorce, births and deaths on families and changes in income.

Feature—The use of advertising, displays, or other activity, generally by a retailer, to call special attention to a product, generally for a limited period of time.

Focus group—A method of gathering quantitative data on the preferences and beliefs of consumers through group interaction and discussion, usually focused on a specific topic or product.

Goods—A product that has tangible form in contrast to services that are intangible.

Green marketing—Any marketing activity of a firm that is intended to create a positive impact or lessen the negative impact of a product on the environment in order to capitalise on consumers' concerns about environmental issues.

Image—The sum of beliefs, ideas and impressions that a person has of an object or agency.

Inflation—A condition where demand outstrips supply or costs escalate, affecting an upward change in prices.

Information system—A system for gathering, analysing and reporting data aimed at reducing uncertainty in business decision making.

Innovators—A group of venturesome consumers that are the first to adopt an innovation.

Intangibility—A characteristic of a service indicating that it has no physical attributes and, as a result, is impossible for consumers to taste, feel, see, hear, or smell before they buy it.

Macro-environment—The conditions facing a company including demographic, economic, natural, technological, political and cultural forces.

Market—The set of actual or potential users/customers (Kotler).

Market area—A geographical area containing the customers/users of a particular firm for specific goods or services.

Market demand—The total volume of a product or service bought/used by a specific group of customers/users in a specified market area during a specified period.

Market development—Expanding the total market served by—

1. entering new segments;
2. converting nonusers; and
3. increasing use by present users.

Market positioning—Positioning refers to the user's perceptions of the place a product or brand occupies in a market segment.

Market profile—A breakdown of a facility's market area according to income, demography, and life style (often.)

Market research—The systematic gathering, recording and analyzing of data with respect to a particular market, where market refers to a specific user group in a specific geographic area.

Market segmentation—The process of subdividing a market into distinct subsets of users that behave in the same way or have similar needs.

Market share—A proportion of the total sales/use in a market obtained by a given facility or chain.

Marketing—The process of planning and executing the conception, pricing, promotion, and distribution of ideas, goods and services to create exchanges that satisfy individual and organisational goals.

Marketing channel—A set of institutions necessary to transfer the title to goods and to move goods from the point of consumption.

Marketing mix—The mix of controllable variables that the firm uses to reach the desired use/sales level in a target market, including price, product, place and promotion—4P's.

Marketing opportunity—An attractive arena of relevant marketing action in which a particular organisation is likely to enjoy a superior and competitive advantage.

Marketing plan—A document composed of an analysis of the current marketing situation, opportunities and threats, analysis, marketing objectives, marketing strategy, action programmes, and projected income statement.

Maturity stage of product life cycle—Initial rapid growth is over and use/sales level off.

Media—Any paid for communication channel including television, radio, posters, etc.

Message—An informative communication about a product or service placed in a communication channel.

Micro-environment—The set of forces close to an organisation that have direct impact on its ability to serve its customers, including channel member organisations, competitors, user markets, publics and the capabilities of the organisation.

Objectives—The desired or needed result to be achieved by a specific time. An objective is more specific than a goal, and one objective can be broken down into a number of specific actions.

Perception—Perception is the cognitive impression that is formed of 'reality' which in turn influences the individual's actions and behaviour towards that object.

Penetration price—The charging of a low price in order to gain volume sales conducted under conditions of little product uniqueness and elastic demand patterns.

Physical distribution—The act and function of physically distributing goods and services, including the elements of transport, warehousing and order processing.

Physical distribution management—The development and operation of process resulting in the effective and efficient physical flow of products.

Place—In the channels of distribution, the physical facilities point of location.

Potential market—Set of users who profess some level of interest in a designed market offer (Kotler).

Price—The formal ratio that indicates the quantities of money goods or services needed to acquire a given quantity of goods or services.

Price floor—The minimum price which can be charged bounded by product cost.

Price competition—A strategy in which a firm regularly offers products priced lower than the competitors, usually accompanied by a minimum of services.

Price discrimination—A situation in which different customers pay different prices for the same product according to the value delivered to them.

Price elasticity of demand—The responsiveness of quantity demanded to price changes.

Price war—A form of price competition that begins when one firm decreases its price in an effort to increase its sales volume and the other firm retaliates by reducing prices on the competing products.

Primary data—Unpublished data from individuals or organisations.

Product—A bundle of attributes or features, functions, benefits and uses capable of exchange, usually in tangible or intangible forms.

Product abandonment—A decision and subsequent action by a firm to withdraw a product that has insufficient or declining sales and lacks profits.

Product adaptation—Modifying a product that sells successfully in one market so as to suit the unique needs or requirements of other markets.

Product life cycle—The four stages products go through from birth to death—introductory, growth, maturity and decline.

Product mix—The full set of products offered by an organisation.

Product positioning—The way users/consumers view competitive brands or types of products.

Product strategy—A set of decisions regarding alternatives to the target market and the marketing mix given a set of market conditions.

Promotion—The offer of an inducement to purchase, over and above the intrinsic value or price of a good service.

Promotion mix—The various communication techniques, such as advertising, personal selling, sales promotion, and public relations/product publicity available to the marketer to achieve specific goals.

Psychographic analysis—A technique that investigates how people live, what interests them, what they like—also called lifestlye analysis or AIO because it relies on a number of statements about a person's activities, interests and opinions.

Psychographic segmentation—Dividing markets into segments on the basis of consumer life styles.

Public relations—The form of communication management that seeks to make use of publicity and other non-paid forms of promotion and information to influence feelings, opinions or beliefs about the firm and its offerings.

Quantity discount—A reduction in price for volume purchases.

Questionnaire—A document that is used to guide what questions are to be asked respondents and in what order; sometimes lists the alternative responses that are acceptable.

Reach—The number of people or households exposed to a particular advertising media or media schedule during a specified time.

Reference group—A group that the individual tends to use as the anchor point for evaluating his/her own beliefs and attitudes.

Respondent—A person who is asked for information using either written or verbal questioning, typically employing a questionnaire to guide the questioning.

Retailer—A channel institution which acts as an intermediary between other channel institutions and the end user, and who usually breaks bulk, charging a margin for its services.

Roles—The behaviour that is expected of people in standard situations.

Rural population—The part of the total population not classified as urban.

Sales promotion—Demand stimulating devices designed to supplement advertising and facilitate personal selling.

Sample—The selection of a subset of elements from a larger group of objects.

Sample survey—A cross sectional study in which the sample is selected to be representative of the target population and in which the emphasis is on the generation of summary statistics such as averages and percentages.

Shopping good—Goods and products can be classified as convenience, shopping or specialty. A shopping good is one in which more time is spent selecting (browsing) than a quick convenience good.

Skimming price—The charging of a high price in order to gain maximum revenue conducted under conditions of product uniqueness and inelastic demand patterns.

Social class—A status hierarchy by which groups and individuals are classified on the basis of esteem and prestige.

Specialty good—A specialty good is one that users/consumers will spend more time searching for, travelling to and pay higher for.

Subculture—The segments within a culture that share distinguishing meanings, values, and patterns of behaviour that differ from those of the overall culture.

Stabilise prices—A status quo-oriented pricing goal in which a firm seeks to maintain its current situation by pricing its products in such a way as to avoid price competition.

Target market—The particular segment of a total population on which the retailer focuses its merchandising expertise to satisfy that sub-market in order to accomplish its profit objectives.

Target market identification—The process of using income, demographic, and life style characteristics of a market, and census information for small areas to identify the most favourable locations.

Technology—The purposeful application of scientific knowledge; an environmental force that consists of inventions and innovations from applied scientific and engineering research.

Telemarketing—A form of non-store retailing in which a sales person initiates contact with a shopper and also closes the sale over the telephone.

Transportation—A marketing function that adds time and place utility to the product by moving it from where it is made to where it is purchased and used.

Value—The power of any good to command other goods in peaceful and voluntary exchange.

Values—The beliefs about the important life goals that consumers are trying to achieve. The important enduring ideals or beliefs that guide behaviour within a culture or for a specific person.

Value pricing—A form of price competition in which a firm seeks to improve the ratio of products' benefits to its price and related costs.

Wants—The wishes, needs, cravings, demands or desires of human beings.

Wholesaler—A channel institution which purchases and sells in bulk from either the original suppliers and/or other channel intermediaries, charging a margin for its services.

Wholesaling middlemen—A firm engaged primarily in sales and all activities directly related to the sale of goods and services to businesses and other organisations for resale, used in producing other goods and services, or operating an organisation.

References

1. Assael, Henry. (1987). *Consumer Behaviour and Marketing Action.* Boston: Kent Publishing Co.
2. Balakrishnan, Ravi. (February 6th, 2013). Is the 'Right Here Right Now' campaign a game changer for Pepsi? *Brand Equity*, The Economic Times.
3. Balakrishnan, Ravi. (February 27th, 2013). Lifebuoy: How the brand's transformation win its fans. *Brand Equity,* The Economic Times.
4. Balakrishnan, Ravi. (February 13th, 2013). BlackBerry 10 arrives with a bang: Can it grab the No 3 slot in each market it's launched in? *Brand Equity*. The Economic Times.
5. Bapna, Amit. (February 13th, 2013). Growing importance of Internet. *Brand Equity*, The Economic Times.
6. Bapna, Amit. (February 13th, 2013). Aircel striving to establish a human connect with its new brand campaign. *Brand Equity,* The Economic Times.
7. Beck, E. (January 5th, 2006). *Earth-Friendly Materials Go Mainstream.* New York Times.
8. Belch, George, E. and Michael, A. Belch. (2003). *Advertising and Promotion*. Tata McGraw-Hill: New Delhi.
9. Bennett, Peter, D. ed. (1995). *Dictionary of Marketing Terms.* Chicago: American Marketing Association.
10. Berry, Leonard L. (1995). Relationship marketing of services: Growing interest, emerging perspectives. *Journal of the Academy of Marketing Sciences*, Vol. 23(4).
11. Bhambhani, Anu. (April 22nd 2011). G-Talk, the India Inc way. *The Economic Times.*
12. Bonoma, Thomas, V. (1985). *The Marketing Edge: Making Strategies Work.* New York: Free Press.
13. Chamikutty, Preethi. (Nanuary 16th, 2013). Will Parle-G be relevant to the next generation. *Brand Equity*, The Economic Times.
14. Davis, J. (1993). Strategies for environmental advertising. *Journal of Consumer Marketing,* Vol. 10(2).

15. Drucker, Peter, F. (November 20th, 1990). Marketing 101 for a fast-changing decade. *The Wall Street Journal.*

16. Fowler, G. (March 6th, 2002). Green sales pitch isn't moving many products. *Wall Street Journal.*

17. Frazier, Moore, H. and Bertrand, R. Canfield. (1977). *Public Relations: Principles, Cases, and Problems.* 7th Edition. Burr Ridge IL: Irwin.

18. Friedman, T.L. (March 27th, 2005). Geo-greening by example. *New York Times.*

19. Ginsberg, J.M. and P.N.Bloom. (2004). Choosing the right green marketing strategy. *MIT Sloan Management Journal*, Fall Issue.

20. Green, Paul, E. and Donald, S. Tull. (1978). *Research for Marketing Decision.* 4th Edition. Prentice-Hall: US.

21. Grubler, A. (2006). Doing more with less: Improving the environment through green engineering. *Environment,* March, Vol. 48(2).

22. Harish, B. (January 5th, 2009). Best marketing practice: Take-back campaign by Nokia. *Marketing Practice.*

23. Hawken, Lovins, and Lovins. (1999). A road map for natural capitalism. *Harvard Business Review*, May-June Issue.

24. Irani, Delshad. (January 16th, 2013). Surf excel's facebook driven campaign 'Fulfill a Wish'. *Brand Equity*, The Economic Times.

25. Irani, Delselshad, and Ravi, Balakrishnan. (February 6th, 2013). Marketing professionals: Lessons on the road. *Brand Equity*, The Economics Times.

26. Indian e Retail Report 2012. (March 19th, 2013). Online shopping saga. *Brand Wagen*, The Financial Express.

27. Kassinger, Ruth. (2002). *Build a Better Mousetrap: Make Classic Inventions, Discover Your Problem Solving Genius and Take the Inventor's Challenge.* Hoboken NJ: John Waley & Sons.

28. Kotler, Philip. (1999). *Marketing Management.* The Millennium Edition. Prentice-Hall of India Private Limited: New Delhi.

29. Kotler, Philip, and Kevin, Lane, Keller. (2012). *Marketing Management.* 14th Global Edition. Pearson Education Limited: England.

30. Lawernce, J. (January 29th, 1991). The green revolution: Case study. *Advertising Age.*

31. Leiber, R. (December 29th, 2005). The dirt on green housecleaners. *Wall Street Journal.*

32. Levitt, Theodore (1960). Marketing myopia. *Harvard Business Review*, July-August Issue.

33. Levitt, Theodore. (1969). *The Marketing Mode.* McGraw Hill: New York.

34. Makower, J. (2005). Green marketing: Lessons from the leaders. *Two Steps Forward,* September Issue.

35. McCarthy Jerome, E. (1996). *Basic Marketing: A Managerial Approach.* 12th Edition Homewood, II: Irwin.

36. McLaughlin, K. (August 2nd, 2005). Has chicken been drugged?. *Wall Street Journal.*

37. Medh, Kinjal. (December 31st, 2012). New informed consumer. *Brand Equity*, The Economic Times.
38. Monga, Priyanka. (April 15th, 2011). Live closer to nature. The *Hindustan Times*.
39. Ojha, Abhilasha. (February 24th, 2013). Things that make market in India different. *Brand Equity*, The Economic Times.
40. Ottman, J.A. et al. (2006). Avoiding green marketing myopia. *Environment*, Vol.48, June Issue.
41. Rapp, Stan, and Tom, Collins. (1990). *The Great Marketing Turnaround.* Prentice Hall: Upper Saddle River, NJ.
42. Ray, Tima. (March 28th, 2011). Riding the green wave. *The Times of India.*
43. Rosen, E. (2000). *The Anatomy of Buzz: How to Create Word-of-Mouth Marketing.* Doubleday: New York.
44. Shanklin, William, L. and John, K. Ryans. (1984). Organizing for high tech marketing. *Harvard Business Review*, November-December Issue.
45. Stanton, William, J., Michael J. Etzel and Bruce J. Walker. (1994). *Fundamentals of Marketing.* McGraw-Hill, Inc.: New York.
46. Tan, C. (August 4th, 2005). New incentives for being green. *Wall Street Journal*.
47. Tata Strategic Management Group Team. (February 4th, 2013). Growth markets in rural India. *Brand Equity*, The Economic Times.
48. Trout, Jack. (2000). The land of non-standard marketing. Published in *Differentiate or Die: Survival in Our Era of Killer Competition.*
49. Wells, William, D. and Geroge, Gubar. (1966). Life-cycle concepts in marketing research. *Journal of Marketing Research,* November Issue.
50. https://vishalbheeroo.wordpress.com/2013/09/22/make-lifebuoys-help-a-child-reach-5-campaign-a-reality/
51. https://thisisnotadvertising.files.wordpress.com/2012/02/coke_connect_land.jpg
52. http://mydigitalinsight.blogspot.com/2019/11/starbucks-three-main-benefits-for.html
53. https://digitalmarketinginstitute.com/blog/corporate-16-brands-doing-corporate-social-responsibility-successfully
54. https://brandequity.economictimes.indiatimes.com/be-blogs/marketing/4732
55. https://iide.co/blog/scope-of-digital-marketing/
56. https://www.slideshare.net/passionatetowin/cokes-rural-marketing-strategies
57. https://home.kpmg/in/en/home/insights/2020/12/understanding-impact-consumer-behavior-due-to-covid-19.html

Index